Duple

70 years of coachbuilding

Alan Townsin

Venture *publications*

ISBN 1 898432 46 5

Copyright Venture Publications Ltd 1998

Printed and bound in Wales

Cover Illustration

This splendid preserved Midland Red coach, dating from 1948 and based on the operator's
own C1-type chassis, is one of many surviving examples which show Duple craftsmanship.
Even though built to the customer's own specification, there are clear indications of the
characteristic Duple way in which its own excellent styling standards of those days
influenced the end result. It was photographed during a break in rural Staffordshire whilst
on a run from the BAMMOT Museum at Wythall.   *Photograph: John A Senior*

Title Page

Duple built bodies for three once well-known operating concerns which bore the name of this
publisher, so it seemed appropriate to select one for the title page of this volume. The
smallest of them, though the most consistent customer, was Venture Transport (Hendon)
Ltd, based only a small distance from the Duple factory of those days. Founded in 1927, it
was running a fleet of ten coaches in the mid-1930s, using a distinctive primrose and black
livery. This Leyland Lion LT5A model of 1934, BMG 335, had the rear entrance body style
much favoured by Duple customers that year.

Opposite

Duple were always very publicity concsious; the extent of the photographic collection that
has survived is considerable, in its full extent it must have been enormous. Before the
second war someone apparently meticulously photographed vehicles from almost every
order; sadly the photographer's name is not recorded. This early example is unusual in
showing five of an order for fifteen 28-seat coaches lined up in Edgware Road outside the
Duple premises in the spring of 1930. They were ready for delivery to Elliot Bros (Bournemouth)
Ltd, in those days proprietor of the network of Royal Blue express services linking London
to much of the south and west of England.

Advertisement on page 6

This gem, the earliest Duple advert traced so far and dating from November 1927, shows
an ADC 417-type single-decker, the style being broadly similar to examples by other
bodybuilders on this chassis. Duple was still quite new to bus or coachbuilding at this stage.
The Associated Daimler is thought to have been supplied to Slieve Bloom Motor Services
of Dublin, and if so must have been a very early export from the factory.

CONTENTS

Schoolboys like to have favourites, and I had decided by the age of 12 or so that Duple was mine among coach bodybuilders perhaps a little unfairly since at that age I didn't even know about some of its rivals. Yet, 60 years later, I still think that most Duple products of that era were wonderfully elegant. Even though I have not always been so happy with some of Duple's later designs, I remained impressed by the firm's shrewd grasp of its typical customers' needs through changing times.

The founder, Herbert White, assembled a very effective team, especially after the move from the original Hornsey premises to Hendon in 1926. In this, W. E. Brown, formerly of Strachan & Brown, played an important role. It was by no means coincidental that his arrival in 1928 (just as the firm had decided to concentrate on coach and bus production instead of the convertible car/vans that gave the firm its name) was followed by success and rapid growth. The White and Brown dynasty, extending to a second generation, was to continue for almost four highly successful decades.

Duple rapidly became the leader in its field despite difficult economic times. By the mid-1930s, Duple's position had become very strong, aided greatly by the volume production of standardised bodies for the Bedford coach chassis which dominated the up-to-26-seat market.

Yet the sheer variety of output, especially in the 1930s, seems astonishing when judged by today's standards. Duple was willing to build almost endless different designs, often singly or in very small numbers, in rapid succession to suit individual users' wishes. The firm was by no means alone in this latter approach, but I don't think any other could claim such variety.

Yet almost all these designs were well-proportioned, tidy, well made and neatly finished - despite the variety, it was usually easy to recognise them as Duple products from characteristic outlines or details.

I suspect that, one day, the best coach bodies of that era will be recognised in much the same way as furniture from the age of artist craftsmen before the onset of machine-made products. Indeed I contend that those who designed and built them were artists, having none of today's computer aids in the drawing office. The craftsmen trusted to interpret the designs, very often using hand tools, were responsible for much of the neat detailing.

The outbreak of war in 1939 soon forced a break with this approach. Although bus and coach production continued on a very small scale for a year or two, war work had priority. Then the manufacture of utility buses became a major activity from 1942, though even there Duple seemed to put more emphasis than most on retaining as acceptable appearance as possible. Yet durability was also often above average.

INTRODUCTION

After the war, the combined pressures of huge demand and the volume production techniques learned in wartime led to a more production-minded approach. There was greater emphasis on standardised design and soon, for example, the Bedford OB Vista coach almost became part of the landscape as almost every village coach operator seemed to acquire at least one. Yet several designs were still being offered for larger chassis, quite apart from 'bespoke' orders built to customer specification.

Another legacy of wartime was increased militancy on the part of trade unions and Duple began to suffer increasingly from strikes. An attempt to switch to metal-framed construction, in the belief that it would allow more efficient production as well as by-passing problems in the supply of good-quality timber, seems to have been frustrated largely by resulting labour problems despite the recruitment of the hitherto highly successful Colin Bailey from Leyland to take charge of the project.

In the end, this and the inter-related higher cost of labour in London was to cause Duple to move bus work away to the Midlands from 1952 and by 1970 the whole business, by then concentrating on coaches, had moved to Blackpool.

For a time, Duple regained much of its dynamism with a more successful switch to metal framing with the Dominant range which had a very successful ten-year run from its introduction in 1972. Even so, the firm never regained the lead in terms of numbers of coaches built, lost to Plaxton at the end of the 1960s.

The 1980s brought uncertainties of a new kind, and the collapse of the traditional lightweight coach business was a major blow to a firm whose prosperity had substantially depended on it for almost half a century. The take-over by Hestair in 1983 brought new possibilities and the consequent association with Dennis led to the development of the promising if hardly pretty Integral 425 coach but on the other hand alienated some dealers linked to other chassis builders. A management buy-out in November 1988 barely even brought breathing space. The decision to close the Blackpool factories and sell most of the remnants of the business to Plaxton came in July 1989, bringing to an end a 70-year story.

This book concentrates on Duple's main factories at Hendon and then Blackpool, with no more than brief mention of its activities in the Midlands, which will be described in more detail in a forthcoming volume on Willowbrook to be published by Venture. The broad extent of the Duple empire inevitably means that there is more to be told - for example the story of Burlingham before the take-over, another true centre of elegance in its halcyon days. In particular, I would welcome more information about the designers responsible for those elegant coaches that first caught my eye so long ago - maybe at some future date some of these aspects might justify a further volume.

Alan Townsin
Steventon, Hants, 1998

ACKNOWLEDGEMENTS

The seed leading to the compilation of this book dates back to nearly two decades ago when Martin Montano was working for Duple and showed John Senior and me a few of the albums of photographs he was building up as a personal venture to recreate the record of the firm's heritage, conveying the variety of body styles built over the years. Sadly, he did not live to complete that task but his work gave rise to the thought of what might be done.

There was a precedent, in the form of Eric Ogden's book on Duple published by TPC in 1976, based largely on such material as then available from company employees – let me at once acknowledge the quality of Eric's work, for while I have sought to avoid repetitiveness I found it a valuable source of information not given elsewhere.

However, as so often happens, the more I delved into the subject the wider the concept grew. Bob Smith very kindly lent me his Duple body number lists, painstakingly compiled largely from PSV Circle news sheets over many years. Then, through Maurice Doggett, co-author of the Venture histories of Eastern Coach Works, I was put in touch with David Gray, Honorary Publications Editor of the PSV Circle, who was able to let me have copies of complete entries relating to buses and coaches from official records for the late 1920s and early 1930s, as well as valuable notes on the several body numbering systems in use over the years. I must also acknowledge the benefit of being able to consult other PSV Circle publications. Others who helped with notes on various aspects of the story included John Gillham and Stewart Brown.

Special thanks are due to Geoff Atkins for providing a wide-ranging selection of photographs of Duple-bodied vehicles he has taken, some dating back to the early 1930s and in themselves covering a span of half a century.

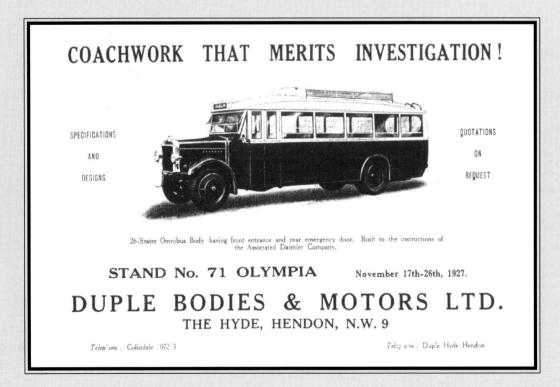

COACHWORK THAT MERITS INVESTIGATION!

SPECIFICATIONS AND DESIGNS

QUOTATIONS ON REQUEST

26-Seater Omnibus Body having front entrance and rear emergency door. Built to the instructions of the Associated Daimler Company.

STAND No. 71 OLYMPIA   November 17th-26th, 1927.

DUPLE BODIES & MOTORS LTD.
THE HYDE, HENDON, N.W. 9

Telephone: Colindale 1072/3   Telegrams: Duple Hyde Hendon

PHOTOCREDITS

Most of the illustrations in this book were originally issued for publicity purposes by the Duple concern. The prints used come largely from the Senior Transport Archive (STA), many of which were the subject of a project by John Senior and the late Martin Montano to produce a photographic archive record of Duple group products, particularly valuable and still on-going by John. A few others of Duple origin come from the author's collection.

Credit for other illustrations where known is as follows but a number of pictures, some of particular relevance to the story, have come into both the author's collection and the Senior Transport Archive over the years where the origin is unknown and apology is made for any resulting failure in acknowledgement

AEC/Author's collection	12(foot), 21(2nd top left), 29 (top two),32(foot), 43(foot), 45(2nd bottom), 83(foot).
AEC/STA	11, 19(top), 25(foot), 38(top right), 53(2nd top),56(foot), 81(foot), 100,116(botom two), 117(2nd row, right), 118(top).
J. M. Aldridge	99(top).
G. H. F. Atkins	27(foot), 29(bottom two), 35(foot),39(foot), 40(top left), 41(top), 45(top), 49(top two), 54(both), 61(top), 66(foot),70, 71(top two), 72(top) 76(all), 77(top),85(foot), 87, 93(foot), 101(top left), 102(both), 103(bottom left), 104(foot),105(foot), 106, 108, 114 (2nd top) 119 (top),121(top), 123(top), 134, 139(lower),146(top).
Author's colln	3, 14(centre & foot), 46(foot), 88(foot), 101(foot), 123(foot), 131(foot).
W. T. Cansick	132.
David Cole	159(both)
A. B. Cross	63(foot).
J. E. Cull	47(foot).
Daimler/BCVM	118.
Duple/M.J. Tozer collection	11(top).
M. Fowler	135(centre).
J. C. Gillham	63(2nd top).
Guy/BCVM	65(top right).
Leyland/BCVM	78(foot).

R. Marshall	66(top), 68(botm left),149.
R. Marshall collection	55(2nd top).
R. A. Mills	61(bottom right).
Omnibus Society	40(foot), 43(top), 45(2nd top), 46(top),50(3rd down), 67(top).
D. E. Parker	88(top).
S. L. Poole	64.
J. A. Senior	Cover, 67(foot)
Allen T. Smith	65(bottom left).
E. J. Smith	103(top).
STA	1, 2, 6, 8, 15(foot), 103(bottom right), 110(bottom left), 113 (top), 129(foot), 141, 148, 157(top), 159(upper).
STA/R. N. Hannay collection	47(top), 61(bottom left), 81(top), 89(foot),90, 94(foot), 95(top), 97(top & 2nd bottom left), 101(top right), 103(centre left).
STA/National Express	rear cover
A.A.Thomas	150(both)
Vauxhall Motors /Author's colln	99(foot).
Vauxhall Motors /STA	113(foot), 115, 116(top), 129(top), 133,136(top left).
Vauxhall Motors /L. J. Taylor collection	120(centre left).
David Wayman	142, 143(top), 146(foot), 154(both),155(lower), 156(foot), 158.
Tony Wilson	155(top)

FRONTISPIECE

Duple's move from London to Blackpool, following the takeover in 1960 of Burlingham based in that town, and completed in 1970, was part of a general exodus of bodybuilders from the capital; although not publicised at the time spiralling costs and trade union intransigence were the main reasons. Duple's new empire had already taken in Willowbrook, though later that firm was to become detached again. Eventually, in 1989, Plaxton acquired most of the remaining assets when Duple succumbed to an adverse turn of events, and bodybuilding in Blackpool ceased. This picture from more confident days show a Leyland Leopard with Commander III body for Grey Green in the late 1960s.

1 THE EARLY YEARS

Duple Bodies and Motors Ltd was founded in 1919 by Herbert R. White, being based initially at a small factory at Pembroke Road, High Street, Hornsey, in North London. The name was intended to convey the idea of bodywork that would enable a single vehicle to perform the dual or duplex function of a car or a goods vehicle suitable for whatever trade in which the owner was engaged. This was a concept Mr White had wanted to pursue since well before the Great War of 1914-18 which had just ended.

He was aged 42 at the time, having been born in Salisbury in 1877, and like many others of that era had graduated to motor vehicles from an earlier career largely associated with bicycles. He had been apprenticed to an ironmonger and although there had been a spell as a dairy farmer, by 1912 he and his brother Ernest were agents for the Rover Cycle Company. A failed business venture led to him being able to take over the assets, moved to the premises of a friend in Fareham, Hampshire, where he built the first application of the dual-function idea, a vehicle called the Bifort, a name also coined to convey alternative purposes, combined with the idea of strength. It used a Rover car chassis with a Fondu engine of Belgian origin and the interchangeable bodies were made by a firm called Hinxman. The prototype won a hill-climb competition in July 1914 and prospects looked encouraging, with a sale price of 195 guineas, but only eight vehicles had been produced when what was later called the First World War broke out on the 4th of the following month.

Herbert White had a varied career in the war, at first helping to make Mills bombs at Portsmouth, then acting as an ambulance driver in Serbia and Italy before being commissioned in the Italian army. Towards the end of that conflict, he was commissioned in the newly-formed Royal Air Force, involved with motor transport.

With the return of peace, his aim was to pick up the threads of the Bifort body principle, now patented. No bodybuilding concern was willing to put it into production, which led to the decision to form his own company. He brought his former batman, Arthur Watts, into the business to deal with the work force needed though, in turn, the latter's brother George, who joined the firm in 1920, was to concentrate on the organisation of the business, rising to become Managing Director in 1936.

Former military vehicles were available cheaply in large numbers at the end of the 1914-18 war, though often they were in poor condition. Mr White bought a number of Ford T models, had them shipped to London, the chassis renovated and fitted them with new dual-function bodies made in the Duple factory. The demand proved to be strong and soon bodywork of this type was being made in quite substantial numbers. In the early days, motoring had been the preserve of the well-to-do and even after the 1914-18 war, car ownership was still far from widespread. Yet the value of a van or lorry to even quite small businesses was

Small beginnings. The original premises in Pembroke Road, Hornsey, with Herbert White at the door.

fast becoming evident, and many ex-soldiers had become familiar with motor vehicles, widening the potential market.

The Duple body based on the Bifort principle had the merit of looking almost indistinguishable from a normal two-seat

The Duple name referred to the duplex nature of a car which, by replacing the top part of the body with a van top, could change function quickly. The Ford T was the basis of most early examples, as here.

A remarkable early venture into the line of business that was to occupy most of Duple's attention for over 60 years was this Lancia six-wheeled charabanc, one of the last products to emerge from the Hornsey premises before the move to Hendon in 1926. The idea of three-axle layout was itself quite new at the time and it seems likely that the chassis used a conversion developed by Barton Bros, later to become a major Duple customer.

touring car of the day, with rounded tail. Yet it was claimed that in three minutes the car could be transformed into a van. This was done by removing what amounted to the decking at the rear of the car and fitting a van top, so shaped at its lower edges to fit on the rounded rear outline of the car body sides, yet generally incorporating two full-height doors at the rear. The resulting van was thus built on the lower part of the car body, which had a suitably low floor level over the rear axle. It was designed to be readily removed by means of a light sling in the garage to suspend the van body top, the car being driven out and the normal rear deck panel being refitted.

Such a vehicle had strong appeal to the proprietors of small businesses, gaining the benefit of a useful van during the working week and a car for week-end or evening use. In those days of more rigid class distinctions, the fact that, in car form, the vehicle did not have the stigma of appearing to be a 'tradesman's' vehicle was a particular benefit, and the dual facility of car or van ownership was made available at no more than marginal cost.

Not unnaturally, business grew and in addition to a notable bulk order for 100 Ford T models with such bodywork for International Motors Ltd, there was increasing variety. A report in *Motor Traction* in August 1920 stated that as the greatest demand was for bodies to fit Ford chassis they were being built in the largest numbers, but it was stated that any other chassis could readily be equipped. At that stage the bodies were finished in green, lined in white, as standard. One user with separate businesses in different parts of London had two trade van tops, one lettered to suit each, the owner using the vehicle in car form, fitting the appropriate trade body on arrival at each location. The cost was said to be little more than that for a normal two-seat touring body, thanks to the use of quantity production methods, every part being jigged and standardised.

Body designs based on the same principle of rapid conversion to or from car use were not only built on other chassis types but in forms adapted to suit different needs. One was not unlike a modern pick-up for use by farmers for carrying milk churns, and there were van versions with side-opening counters allowing use as a mobile shop.

With this type of skill, general bodybuilding to customers' instructions was a natural progression, so that conventional complete delivery vans were produced and, in due course, the occasional car or charabanc body. Overall demand was growing and the Hornsey premises becoming inadequate.

Although very few purely passenger bodies seem to have been built in that period, one vehicle photographed emerging from the Hornsey premises must have highlighted the space problem. It was a Lancia six-wheeled 33-seat charabanc, probably not too far short of 30ft long, with body of the 'torpedo' style that had been widely favoured since shortly before the 1914-18 war and having side doors for each of the seven rows of seats. The chassis seems likely to have been a conversion using the trailing-axle suspension system patented by Barton Bros Ltd of Chilwell, Nottingham, for its own examples of this type known as 'Barton Gliders' though by 1927 similar Lancia-based six-wheel conversions using Barton's patented design were being offered on the open market by Alldays Commercial Motors Ltd, whose works were in Fulham, London S.W.6. The date of the photograph is not recorded but such conversions had been begun by Barton for its own use in 1925 and Duple's decision to leave the Hornsey factory was made that year. Barton Transport Ltd, the successor to Barton Bros, was later to become a major Duple customer for bus and coach bodywork.

At Duple the word 'convertible' meant car/van, not the superior kind of open car as generally understood later, and manufacture continued after the move to Hendon. This example was on a Morris chassis, probably an Oxford, of the 'Flatnose' type as introduced for 1927. The curve of the tail of the car version of the body can be seen inside the van. Note the shelves and opening sides.

The move to Hendon

Work was put in hand on a new factory at The Hyde, Hendon, based on a prominent site of 2½ acres, previously farmland, facing the Edgware Road, one of the main routes out of London to the north-west. The contractors made very slow progress on the initial buildings and Mr White decided to complete the work using Duple employees, allowing production there to begin in 1926. At first the output was much as before, the car/van concept still having a strong following, though the type of chassis used varied, with models such as the Morris Cowley coming into stronger favour.

In 1928, however, the results of a decision to enter the bus and coach market much more strongly became evident, and from that year Duple began to build such bodywork in substantial numbers. The business began to expand and the number of employees grew from the figure of 40 or so at that date, climbing to 800 in little more than a decade.

As was often the case in those days, quite a large share of the early business could be described as relatively local. Even so, London and its surroundings provided a large and expanding market for such vehicles, with numerous independent operators running them on hire or excursion work. The day trip to the seaside was an important source of business for them, the journey itself part of the appeal in those days when car ownership was still beyond the means of most people and often having a social element when a works or office party was involved.

Independent bus services were also numerous despite the dominance of the London General Omnibus Co Ltd as part of the Underground group which then ran most of the tube railway lines, and the development of coach services running into London from surrounding districts was growing. Duple bodywork was supplied to operators of all these types.

Even so, by no means all the new coach or bus business was with small or London-based operators. Elliott Bros (Bournemouth) Ltd, better known by its fleetname Royal Blue, already running a London-Bournemouth express service, began a London-Salisbury-Plymouth service in May 1928 and other routes to the West of England began a period of rapid expansion later in the year. It took delivery of a new fleet of 26 coaches on ADC 424 chassis between April and July of that year. Duple supplied bodywork on seventeen of these, the balance coming from another London-based concern, Hall Lewis. The initials ADC stood for Associated Daimler Company, a short-lived marriage of the AEC and Daimler concerns, the 424 model being of Daimler design and, being of bonneted layout, the completed vehicles had quite a strong resemblance to luxurious Daimler cars of that period – the sleeve-valve six-cylinder engine used being much as in the 25hp model of the day. The bodywork was of centre-gangway layout with comfortable seats and glass side windows but there was a folding roof, retaining the charabanc facility for fresh-air travel still much in favour at the time and indeed still occasionally to be found on Duple bodies for excursion and tour operators in the south of England into the early 1930s.

Quite a high proportion of early Duple bodies were on Gilford chassis, made by a concern which had begun in Holloway Road, London, by selling ex-military American-built Garford vehicles but progressed to making its own chassis, generally using engines of American origin. Its coach chassis soon proved popular, offering lively performance at modest prices, and in December 1927 production was transferred to High

The first major order to be received by Duple for coach bodies was for the Royal Blue fleet of Elliott Bros of Bournemouth, built in 1928. It comprised seventeen vehicles on ADC 424 chassis having much of the look of a large Daimler car of the period – very 'upmarket' at that date, when the official Royal cars were supplied by Daimler. The bodies were of a type then quite common, with glass side windows but having a folding canvas roof over most of the length; the elegant design and neat detailing was a credit to a firm still new to such work. The example shown was RU 6728, with Duple body number 1279, first licensed in July 1928.

Gilford was a popular make among independent operators in the late 1920s, not least because of the lively performance from their American-made Lycoming six-cylinder engines. This 166SD is thought to be one of a pair with Duple 26-seat bodies (numbers 1434-5) supplied to T Wilkinson, of Sedgefield, County Durham, where they entered service as UP 2636-7 in 1929. The place names on the glass louvres over the windows (Hartlepool, Stockton, Middlesbrough) were served by Wilkinson, and the livery layout and the style of the fleetname are as used by this operator even though the 'Overoads' name is not known to the author.

Wycombe. A body building subsidiary, Wycombe Motor Bodies Ltd, was registered that same month with the idea of making coach bodies on production-line methods but, even so, there was more work bodying Gilford chassis than it could cope with, the policy tending to be to provide Wycombe bodywork when customers took up Gilford's hire-purchase facilities. Hence Duple became a major supplier of bodywork on Gilford chassis for a time.

As was to continue in the sector of the market Duple mainly served, body supply was often handled in conjunction with dealers or manufacturers, the sale to the customer being on the basis of a complete vehicle, as opposed to the usual practice of larger operators of ordering chassis and then bodywork directly from the respective makers. On this basis, Duple bodywork, often on Gilford chassis, began to appear in the fleets of operators in areas as remote as Northumberland by the latter part of 1928.

Expansion

A major influence on Duple expansion in 1928 was the arrival on the scene of W. E. Brown, hitherto a partner in Strachan & Brown, which was one of the leading London-based bus bodybuilders of the day, having its works at Acton. It had built up a substantial business, including the supply of bodywork to AEC and ADC in many cases where customers had placed orders for complete vehicles, but including work for many other operators, amongst them municipalities and major companies. The departure of Mr Brown led to some difficulties for that firm (which had been run as a partnership) and its reconstruction, henceforth being known as Strachans, but it was never as

successful thereafter. On the other hand, Duple's growth in the following few years, a difficult period for most firms, was perhaps the most dramatic among British coach bodybuilders of the time. In due course, Mr Brown's two sons, Denis and Reginald, also joined their father on the sales side of the firm, the former becoming Technical Sales Manager in later years and remaining with the firm until closure of the Hendon premises in 1970 and the latter becoming Sales Director.

Known Duple bus or coach bodies recorded as built in 1928 comprised 25 on ADC chassis (6 on type 416, 17 on 424 and 2 on 426), 1 Bean, 1 Brockway, 4 Dennis G, 5 GMC, 19 Gilford (17 on 166SD and 2 166OT), 1 Graham, 1 Guy, 11 Laffly, 2 Leyland Lioness PLC, 4 Maudslay (2 ML3B and 2 ML4B), 4 McCurd, 3 Morris, 2 REO, 1 Talbot, I Thornycroft, 4 Tilling-Stevens, plus two cases of rebodying of Dennis and one of Saurer chassis. This accounts for 92 bus or coach bodies that first year of major involvement in this market, quite apart from continuing output of the van/car 'convertibles' as they were usually called within the works.

This list gives an indication of the variety of chassis makes covered at that early stage. The number of chassis of foreign origin or name at 20 represented a minority, yet one much greater proportionally than was to apply in later years as raised import duties increasingly discouraged imports. The eleven Laffly of French origin outnumbered all the other foreign names, with the GMC as the nearest rival, though it is likely these may have been assembled at the General Motors plant, also at The Hyde, Hendon and hence quite a near neighbour of Duple. It had been producing Chevrolet and GMC vehicles for the British market since 1923.

Duple soon began to develop characteristic features – the high-mounted oval fleetname sign and slim destination box built into the front of the roof are examples here. This 28-seat coach, body number 1418, was one of a pair on ADC 426 chassis placed in service in 1929 by G. W. Batten of East Ham – it was registered HM 9651. The 426 was an AEC-designed four-cylinder model 'facelifted' with the Daimler-like radiator. In December 1933 they passed to London Transport and were operated until 1935 although not given fleet numbers.

In the late 1920s, the Great Western Railway had the most extensive of the bus systems run by the four big railway companies, many routes linking remote areas with its train services. Among fourteen 20-seat bus bodies Duple built for the GWR in 1929, two were on Guy OND chassis, body number 1542 being seen here before delivery as the operator's No. 1651 (UU 975). Two 12-seat hotel bus bodies were also supplied, one of these also being a Guy OND. Thornycroft chassis were used for the remaining buses.

Among the early users of Duple bus bodywork, one of the most prestigious was the Great Western Railway, which at that time was expanding an already substantial bus fleet used mainly on feeder services to its railway network. In 1929 Duple built twelve 20-seat bus bodies on Thornycroft A2 chassis for the GWR, plus a 12-seat hotel bus on the similar but shorter A1 and further buses seating up to 20 on Guy OND chassis. A change of policy led to railway investment in other bus companies in place of direct bus operation and most of the A2 models were actually delivered to the Western National Omnibus Co Ltd, a subsidiary of the National Omnibus & Transport Co Ltd set up jointly with the GWR and which was to be a major Duple customer in later years.

By 1929, output was growing as the firm's name began to be recognised as a major producer, particularly of coach bodywork. Elliott Bros (Bournemouth) Ltd not only gave its entire orders to Duple for bodywork on a total of 62 new coaches for its Royal Blue fleet in 1929 and 1930 but, as the company was rapidly expanding from its original London and west country services, with routes to Bristol, Birmingham and Coventry as well as along the south coast to Margate, they became a prominent sight on many of the main roads of southern England. The main 1929 delivery consisted of 25 AEC Reliance and six Daimler CF6 models, though at the end of the year one each of the AEC Regal, Maudslay ML6, and

Daimler CF6 were supplied, followed by a Leyland Tiger TS2, though the main 1930 delivery was of eighteen AEC Regal and nine CF6. All had basically similar Duple bodies, generally seating 28.

Nearer home, fleets of Duple-bodied coaches were being built up by several operators in and around London, often running what would nowadays be called commuter coach services into the capital. One of these was the Ledbury Transport Co Ltd, which took its name not from the Herefordshire town but from its address, Ledbury Road, London W.11, although the operational headquarters were in Reading and rather unusually in such a case, the fleetname, Thackray's Way, related to the proprietor's name. It standardised on Gilford chassis with Duple bodywork in 1929-30, favouring the bonneted 166SD and then the 168SD models, of which over 30 were still in the fleet when it came under Thames Valley control in 1935. Similar vehicle policy was followed by the Skylark Motor Coach Co Ltd of Ledbury Mews, W.11, but in this case the fleet of fourteen Gilford 166SD new in 1928-9 and five 168SD of 1930, all with Duple 26-seat bodies, were taken over by Green Line in 1932.

However, perhaps the most prominent name associated with Duple-bodied vehicles in the London area at that time was Premier – both The Premier Line Ltd and the Premier Omnibus Co Ltd, based at the same address of Leysfield Road, London,

Over the years, Duple built many 'one-offs' but this one must have been among the strangest. It was built on another Guy OND in 1929 for L. M. Grundel of Harrow, who used the fleetname Loumax. As a London area operator, this proprietor had to conform to the requirements set by the Metropolitan Police, which at that date were not permitting the provision of glass windscreens. Hence this body, Duple number 1727, had an open cab reminiscent of pre-1914 designs, the impression of shortness being increased by the use of an open entrance doorway at the rear. Loumax was taken over by the LGOC in July 1932.

Elliott Bros took delivery of 25 AEC Reliance and six Daimler CF6 coaches, all with Duple bodywork, between March and June 1929. Seen here is Reliance RU 8819, with body number 1520, parked in Arundel.

W.12. Here the chosen chassis make was Leyland and in most cases the Titan TD1, not only for thirteen double-deckers with typical London-independent-style open-staircase bodies for Premier Omnibus but also for nineteen Premier Line single-deck buses and coaches, all dating from between late 1929 and 1930. In addition there were a further six single-deckers on Leyland Tiger TS3 chassis. All passed to London Transport in December 1933. The double-deck bodies were to a design almost identical to that being used on similar chassis by Christopher Dodson Ltd, then the best-known bodybuilder supplying double-deck bodywork to London independent operators. It is understood that this was done with Dodson's agreement and it seems quite likely that the latter firm may not have been able to meet the delivery dates required, Duple probably getting the work partly because of meeting Premier's single-deck needs, these latter bodies having characteristic Duple features.

There was immense variety both in the models and the types of body produced, with plenty of instances where only one example of a particular design would be built. A great reservoir of skill in both designing and building vehicle bodies of varying designs was to be found in the draughtsmen and skilled wood and sheet metal workers who produced them, often incorporating

A third of Duple's total bus and coach body output in 1929 was on Gilford chassis, by far the biggest on any one make. One of ten on the 166OT chassis was this 32-seat saloon with body number 1618, originally supplied to the Northallerton Omnibus Co, for whom it was registered VN 535. In 1930 it came back to London to join the fleet of J. S. Ray, who operated the service between Oxford Circus and Hertford on which it is seen. Green Line Coaches Ltd took the business and route over in February 1932 and it in turn became part of the newly-formed London Transport in July 1933, as conveyed here by a sticker visible on the lower side panel of what had become GF22, giving the country department address of Bell Street, Reigate.

Premier Line Ltd, based in London W.12, had a fleet of Leyland coaches of the style shown, many of them based on Titan TD1 chassis normally intended as a double-deck model though others, as here, were on the dimensionally similar Tiger TS3. Duple was Premier's main bodybuilder though GK 5717, belonged to a late 1930 batch bodied by London Lorries Ltd though to the usual, basically Duple, design favoured by Premier. Most of the fleet passed to London Transport in December 1933, but this was among five which went to the Aylesbury Omnibus Co and then ran for the Oxford fleet from 1933 to 1938.

Elliott Bros, after taking one coach on the new AEC Regal chassis exhibited at the 1929 Show, chose this model for eighteen more for the Royal blue fleet delivered in June-July 1930 – successive Regal types were to be prominent in Duple's output for two decades. The 28-seat body style had become slightly more curvaceous, with a hint of the outswept skirt to be adopted later, though the multiple moulding strips were unusual. The example seen here is body 1812, registered LJ 1512. It passed to Southern National ownership when Elliott Bros sold out in 1935, was rebodied by Duple in 1938 and remained in service until 1953.

features specified by the purchaser and yet almost always well proportioned and neatly finished.

Recorded output of bus and coach bodies in 1929 virtually doubled to 184, among which no less than 26 makes and at least 43 types were represented. There were 26 AEC (1 Regal and 25 Reliance), 1 AJS, 2 Albion PR28 (a significant delivery, to Red & White Services Ltd, later to become a very important customer), 1 BAT Cruiser, 1 Bean 30-cwt, 2 Brockway JBF, 1 Chevrolet LQ, 1 Crossley Eagle, 8 Daimler CF6, 6 De Dion Bouton. 10 Dennis (2 G, 5 F, 1 EV and 2 rebodied), 2 Dodge, 1 Federal, 66 Gilford (9 CP6, 35 166SD, 10 166OT, 3 168SD and 9 168OT), 6 GMC, 1 Graham, 6 Guy (1 B, 1 FBB, 1 C, 3 OND), 3 Lancia Pentaiota, 4 Leyland Titan TD1 double-deckers, 4 Maudslay (2 ML4, 2 ML6A), 2 Reo Pullman, 1 Saurer (rebodied), 2 SPA, 5 Star VB4, 21 Thornycroft (1 A1, 14 A2, 5 A6, 1 BC) and 1 Tilling-Stevens. The number of chassis

of foreign make (though in some cases assembled in Britain) had risen to 27, but the proportion of the total was less, at 14%, a trend that was to continue.

At that stage, Gilford was thus easily the most numerous chassis make, the 66 examples representing just over a third of the total output, followed by 26 AEC and then the 21 Thornycroft, these influenced by the Elliott Bros and GWR orders respectively, with Dennis also just in double figures. Leyland's representation that year was a modest four, although this was the first stage of the substantial Premier orders mentioned above. Surprising as it may seem in retrospect, it was outnumbered by six chassis from the French De Dion Bouton concern, one of the pioneer makers of motor vehicles, then still selling bus chassis in Britain, though becoming increasingly rare. Another rare make was the Italian SPA, by then a Fiat subsidiary, but Lancia, also from that country was at that date very well-known in Britain for

Some operators continued to favour the bonneted style of coach, and GF 6677 with body number 1861 was one of four 26-seat coaches on the Gilford 168SD chassis built later in 1930 for the Ledbury Transport Co Ltd which, unusually, used its founder's name, Thackray, as fleetname. There had been 23 earlier Duple-bodied Gilford coaches built for this fleet in 1929-30. The operating base moved to Reading and when the firm sold out to the Tilling & British Automobile Traction group in 1935, it was placed under the control of the Thames Valley Traction Co, in whose livery this vehicle is seen.

Although coach and, to a lesser extent, bus bodywork had become the main line of business, Duple was still taking on a wide variety of work. Goods bodywork was also being built, and this continued alongside the passenger vehicles, though normally on a more limited scale. This Dennis lorry for Davis & Davis of Folkestone, smartly painted in traditional style, dated from the latter part of 1930.

its passenger chassis, largely used as a basis for charabanc bodywork and about to fade from the British scene in that context.

By that date, imported chassis were becoming less common in Britain than had been so in the earlier 1920s, partly because of the import duty imposed on them, although some makers had established British assembly factories which reduced this effect.

The Hendon works run by the giant American combine General Motors has already been mentioned and it is noteworthy that in addition to the six GMC models of varied types bodied by Duple in 1929, there was one Chevrolet LQ 14-seat coach sold to Pownall of Brighton – this model was the basis from which the original Bedford models of 1931 were developed, founding a marque due to play a very important part in the Duple story.

Sizes varied from 14-seat buses up to double-deckers, quite apart from some continuing business in small vans and the occasional car or lorry, though coaches seating between about 20 and 32 passengers had become the type of product particularly associated with the name and of growing importance overall. At the 1929 Show, Duple-bodied exhibits included an example of the recently introduced AEC Regal for Royal Blue and the Crossley Eagle, the former the first of numerous Duple-bodied Regals but the latter to remain unique.

A distinctive feature of many Duple bodies in the period 1929-30 was the use of an elliptical-shaped illuminated fleetname panel mounted on brackets above the front end of the roof.

However, in some cases, most notably that of Premier Line, this position was used for a larger destination display. More usually on a Duple coach body of that time, the destination box was quite slim and built into the front edge of the roof, in those days projecting a little ahead of the windscreen, the beading above and below it being run in smooth curves so as to merge with the cantrail moulding over the side windows. The rear dome panels were usually well rounded, though not to an exaggerated degree, and a general look of well-proportioned tidiness was beginning to emerge as characteristic of the make.

A significant development announced in June 1930 was the introduction of an all-metal sliding roof which, in its original form, allowed most of the length of a coach body to be opened, using aluminium-covered panels which slid over each other in a telescopic fashion. One of that year's batch of Daimler CF6 coaches for Elliott Bros was used for a press trip, and had four such panels.

The author has a clear boyhood memory of travelling through the New Forest in one of these Royal Blue CF6 coaches in 1937 (by which date it was owned by Hants & Dorset) and finding that, with the roof open to its full length, seats near the rear became decidedly draughty when it was running at above 30mph or so. Even so, the metal sliding roof principle was much superior to the previous idea of a folding canvas roof, which tended to develop cracks due to the repeated folding, and the sliding roof became widely used on British coaches in the 1930s, though usually with only part of the vehicle length

Another example of Duple variety was this body on a Minerva chassis, an upmarket Belgian make using a sleeve-valve six-cylinder engine. At first impression, it might be thought to be a hearse, but the high waistline and central window in the rear panel suggesting a door of limited width at that position and hence either a superior form of hotel bus or even, bearing in mind the dark (though not black) paintwork and lack of signwriting, a vehicle for collecting country house guests from a railway station.

opening. Duple patented the idea but it was made available to other bodybuilders under an arrangement with Sunsaloon Bodies Ltd, of Castleford Road, Sparkhill, Birmingham, which took up the world patent and manufacturing rights.

The 1930 output showed a further increase on 1929, with a total of 250 passenger bodies, but with not quite so many chassis makes at eighteen, and about 35 models represented. There were 77 AEC (76 Regal and one of the equivalent bonneted Ranger), 1 Albion PMB 26, 1 BAT Cruiser, 2 Bean 30-cwt, 1 Brockway, 21 Daimler CF6, 15 Dennis (2 30-cwt, 7 GL, 1 F, 1 EV, and 3 Arrow plus 1 rebodied of unspecified type), 1 Federal, 2 Ford (1 AA and 1 six-wheel), 64 Gilford (2 CP6, 8 AS6, 26 168SD, 28 168OT), 3 GMC (2 T19 and a T60), 3 Guy (2 OND and 1 FC), 42 Leyland (9 Titan TD1 double-deck, 19 TD1 single-deck and 14 Tiger), 5 Maudslay (1 ML3, 2 ML4 and 2 ML6), 3 Morris (1 16-seat, 1 Viceroy and 1 Director) 6 REO (1 20-seat, 5 Pullman), 2 Saurer (rebodied), 1 Thornycroft BC.

Thus AEC was now in first place, although this was largely due to an order for 50 Regal coaches for the Green Line fleet,

all recorded as delivered in 1930 though many did not enter service until early 1931 as explained in the next chapter. Even so the Regal, in its succeeding forms, was to figure prominently among Duple's output in forthcoming peacetime years until the early 1950s. Gilford dropped to second place despite a total nearly as large as in 1929 and indeed its importance was about to decline. Leyland moved up to third place and was to grow further in numbers in later years even though this year's figure was largely related to the orders place by the Premier concern. Dennis had yet to rationalise its model range effectively and was behind Daimler that year, though the latter was another concern whose importance in the coach market was about to wane. Imported makes were in decline, amounting to eleven vehicles, under 5% of the total, excluding the two rebodied Saurer coaches. Van bodybuilding continued – a batch of 80 Morris 10-cwt vans for the General Post Office had been completed early in 1930.

Thus by the beginning of the 1930s, Duple was firmly established as a coach bodybuilder of growing importance, and one beginning to develop distinctive design features as well as a degree of influence on national trends.

The arrival in the autumn of 1930 of an order for 50 30-seat bodies on AEC Regal chassis for Green Line Coaches Ltd held immense prestige as well as being the largest for coaches Duple had received up to then. Green Line was closely linked to the London General Omnibus Co Ltd, whose Chiswick works might have been expected to build these bodies had there not been urgency for delivery, as explained in the next chapter. The Chiswick body design was of rather taller build than then generally fashionable and the illuminated fleetname sign was mounted below cantrail level without intruding into the driver's line of vision, though a little untidy-looking. Overall, however the appearance was quite striking, aided by the original simple but effective apple green livery with a black waistband and silver roof. As built, the chassis had the larger 7.4-litre petrol engine then newly available in this model and up to 60mph could be reached, although later the earlier 6.1-litre unit became standard for the type and an altered rear axle ratio cut the potential speed down, even though still quite lively and smooth-running. The vehicle shown, T219, was delivered with Duple body number 2127 in time to enter service in January 1931. It was converted for ambulance use during the war but returned to passenger service with bus seats in 1945, surviving to 1950 when it was transferred to London Transport's museum collection. It is seen here revisiting Duple's works after painstaking external restoration to original condition in 1961 under the supervision of the late John Scholes, curator of the British Transport Commission museum.

2 GROWTH IN THE EARLY 1930s

The depression triggered by the 1929 Wall Street crash took two or three years to have its full impact, on both sides of the Atlantic. Sales of buses and coaches tended to be affected as the nations's economy slowed down in the early 1930s, though the effect was patchy and sometimes other influences boosted the figures. The struggle to secure orders meant that competition became very fierce, a matter of survival of the fittest. Yet, conversely, the strong tended to become stronger and Duple, despite only recently becoming a significant player in the bus and coach bodybuilding business, was growing when many others were struggling to remain in business at all. Output in 1929-30 was of the order of 200 coach or bus bodies per year but rose thereafter during a period when many other concerns' production was dropping, at least for a time.

Another factor inducing change in the industry was the passing of the Road Traffic Act of 1930 and its introduction of a system of road service licensing. Although this came into effect from 1st April 1931, services in operation at 9th February were given a status of existing services which, even though giving no guarantee of the granting of a licence, did have the implication of a degree of 'grandfather's rights' which led to a rush to establish services.

Green Line Coaches Ltd, created in 1930 as the express service arm of the London General Omnibus Co Ltd and involved in the creation of a network of services linking surrounding areas with central London, was prominent in this regard. An additional delivery of 100 coaches was urgently needed to augment the existing fleet for this purpose. The chassis chosen was the AEC Regal, already the LGOC/Green Line standard two-axle single-decker with the classification letter T, this batch being T207-306. They were described internally as 'bus/coaches', the bodywork being designed by LGOC, which had built part of an earlier batch. This time construction was put entirely in the hands of outside bodybuilders, Duple supplying 50 while Ransomes, Sims & Jefferies of Ipswich and Weymann's of Addlestone each built 25, the fleet numbers being intermingled though Duple bodied the first

example, T207. As well as being the biggest single order for coach bodywork Duple had produced up to then, the prestige of supplying a branch of the country's largest bus and coach operator was considerable; all 50 entered service between December 1930 and February 1931.

On a longer-term basis, the nature of the industry tended to alter, as the road service licence system gave greater security to existing operators, this applying to bus and express coach services and also to excursions, leaving only private hire as subject to unchecked competition. This not only put the bigger operators into a position of being part of 'the establishment' but also protected the status of smaller firms holding such licences – although licences were not transferable, it became the convention that the buyer of a firm which decided to sell out would generally be granted equivalent licences. Although purchases of small firms by larger ones continued, those who wished to continue knew where they stood and were no longer subject to the threat of direct competition in the same way. This was certainly a factor in a clearly discernible trend towards the purchase of vehicles with higher standards of comfort, appearance and finish in which Duple was already among the class leaders among coach bodybuilders.

Duple had also built some small bus or coach bodies in the 14- and 20-seat classes among its varied range of products from the late 1920s, based on a variety of chassis such as Bean, Dennis GL, Gilford CP6, Guy OND and Star Flyer, to mention only a few. Some of these chassis makes continued to figure among Duple body output of this size range into the early 1930s. Gilford introduced the AS6 model in 1930 as a more modern-looking successor to the CP6. A high proportion of AS6 models had Duple bodywork and it has been said that customers were recommended by Gilford to approach Duple for bodywork as 'in-house' Wycombe bodywork was not offered for this chassis.

Up to 1931, Duple had built only small numbers of bodies on the mass-produced chassis, often of American origin, popular in the late 1920s but a new generation of models suitable for use

J. N. Zarpas & Co, of Lagos, Nigeria is thought to have been Duple's first export customer for bus bodywork, beginning with two small Dennis buses in 1930 and a repeat order for four in 1931, seen here at Duple's works. The chassis is recorded as being of the 30-cwt type, though differing from the version quite often used for passenger work in Britain by being of forward-control layout and having larger-section tyres.

Another notable early export order was for twelve 29-seat buses on AEC Ranger left-hand drive chassis, type 670, for service in Athens – they were the first of this type, with chassis numbers 670001 upwards and dated from the early summer of 1931. They had Duple body numbers 2291-2302 and were cellulose painted (then a recently-introduced process) in bright yellow – the type of film used at that time has made it appear darker in this view. The fixing strips for the panels had been left unpainted, catching the light.

as small buses was beginning to emerge, often made by firms which were large-scale car manufacturers on one side or the other of the Atlantic. Duple was to build bus or coach bodywork on most of these, though in widely varying numbers. Among them were such makes as Commer, an old-established firm based at Luton in Bedfordshire but by then effectively the commercial-vehicle branch of the Coventry-based Rootes group making Hillman and Humber cars; Dodge, part of the large Chrysler group mainly operating in the United States though producing goods and passenger models at Kew, on the south-western outskirts of London, and Morris-Commercial, the Birmingham-based mainly goods vehicle branch of the Morris car concern.

However the name soon to prove by far the most important of the makers in this class, not least in the Duple story, was Bedford, the marque name chosen for the new range of goods and passenger models built by Vauxhall Motors Ltd at Luton from 1931. Since 1925, Vauxhall had been owned by the huge General Motors Corporation based in America, of which the main commercial vehicle make, especially at the lighter end of the scale, was Chevrolet, although there was also a GMC marque less well-known in Britain than America. Assembly in Britain was carried out at the General Motors factory which had

been built at The Hyde, Hendon in 1923, sales of Chevrolet growing quite rapidly and using up-to-date production methods. It was thus well-established when Duple moved in 1926 from Hornsey to premises only a short distance away, though there seems to have been little commercial contact between the neighbouring concerns during that period, apart from a few cases of GMC chassis and the odd Chevrolet bodied by Duple as buses or coaches. Yet the GM plant's output grew rapidly, especially after the six-cylinder Chevrolet LQ model intended for 30-cwt loads was introduced for the 1929 season – it also became quite popular as a 14-seat bus.

It was decided to move the main British production of the Chevrolet LQ to Luton using parts made mainly within the Vauxhall factory, though to Chevrolet design, even though the chassis came back to Hendon for testing. The initial Bedford 2-ton model of April 1931 had a close resemblance in appearance and general design to the Chevrolet LQ, though introducing some distinctive Bedford mechanical features.

The association with Bedford

Two very similar Bedford passenger models, the 14-seat WHB and 20-seat WLB, were announced in August 1931. Duple built

The introduction of the new range of Bedford commercial vehicles by Vauxhall Motors in 1931 was to have a strong influence on the Duple story, although it took a little time before it gained momentum. This early WLB with 20-seat body is seen awaiting delivery to L. B. Atkins (Beacon Motor Services) of Crowborough, Sussex, a small operator with an express service to London and a local route. The initial standard Duple body design for the model could have either a hinged door, as here, or a folding one, alternative emergency exit positions and other minor variations but the basic outline was soon to become a familiar sight in most parts of Britain.

Duple built only small numbers of double-deckers in the early 1930s. This one was on one of a pair of Dennis HV-type chassis, almost the last of that model to be built, supplied to Shoeburyness Motor Services in the summer of 1931, registered EV 1725. There was an echo of the three-window layout at the front of the upper deck common to most double-deck bodies built for London independent operators, perhaps inherited from the Dodson-designed bodies built by Duple for Premier, though now on a basically sloping profile.

a 20-seat bus body, No.2367, on the second WLB, chassis number 108002, this being for Vauxhall Motors. In due course it received a Middlesex registration number, MV 8996, which may suggest involvement by the GM plant at Hendon, evidently still in control of commercial vehicle activities at Luton in the early days. A 20-seat coach, also for Vauxhall, occupied the next chassis and body numbers (though oddly this chassis seems to have returned to Duple for a second coach body, No.2895, in 1932, for Hawkins of Minehead). The third in this initial run of bodies for the WLB, No.2368, was another 20-seat coach on chassis 108013 for Wordsell Bros of Earith, near Huntingdon – it was registered EW 7227.

Duple was among the four bodybuilders listed for the WLB in Bedford publicity issued at the time of the 1931 Commercial Motor Show, offering a complete 20-seat bus for £545, of which the body cost £280. The others were Waveney, of Lowestoft; Grose, of Northampton; and Rainforth of Lincoln.

Of these firms only Duple had the capability for production in the substantial numbers needed to meet the demand which arose and Duple-bodied Bedford WLB models were soon entering service all over the country. The coach version also offered at first generally differed from the bus mainly in having more comfortable seating and sometimes an external-opening car-type hinged entrance door instead of the folding type usual on the bus version. Duple did also build some 14-seat bus and coach bodies on the WHB chassis beginning in late 1931, but in smaller numbers, the model proving much less popular and being dropped in 1933.

Thus the Bedford-Duple combination began to dominate the smaller classes of bus and coach in a manner that was to continue in gradually growing size ranges. Soon the coupling of the two names regularly rolled off the tongue of anyone in that sector in the industry, a situation that was to last for over half a century. In addition to vehicles built for carrying the public, Duple-bodied WLB buses were sufficiently cheap and readily available to be used for such purposes as publicity campaigns, carrying sales-people to make door-to-door calls as well as for

private transport – the Transport & General Workers' Union had one, for example.

Even so, Duple continued to build bodywork on other makes of small bus or coach chassis in the early 1930s, including Commer, Dodge, Morris-Commercial and Leyland, the last-mentioned having introduced its Cub model towards the end of 1931.

At the other end of the scale, Duple built the occasional double-deck body, including at least one on a Dennis HV, for Shoeburyness Motor Services. Another was built on a Dennis Lance chassis for display at the 1931 Show. Some lowbridge double-deckers, along with a batch of single-deck buses, all on Daimler fluid-flywheel chassis, were supplied to Luton Corporation in 1932. However this proved not to be a fruitful line of business for Duple at that stage and double-deckers vanished from the agenda for several years.

Another noteworthy venture was the manufacture of bodies for export, a field in which only a limited number of British bodybuilders, mainly large firms, engaged at that period. Among Duple's earliest customers for bus bodies was J. N. Zarpas & Co, of Lagos, Nigeria, which began taking deliveries of buses, initially on small Dennis chassis around 1930-31. Other early orders executed included twelve 8ft-wide single-deck bus bodies on AEC Ranger normal-control chassis built for operation in Athens in mid-1931. Other export destinations that year included India and Afghanistan, where a Duple-bodied Commer Invader was built for operation across the North West Frontier, something of a legend for roving bandit tribes. By contrast, and very remarkably, Duple was chosen as the bodybuilder for a Renault single-decker used to convey visitors to and from that firm's factory from the Paris motor show in 1932. France was always a very self-sufficient market, very rarely importing motor vehicles or bodywork.

There were far more concerns building bus and coach bodywork in Britain than in more recent times, the trade still tending to be run as a localised type of business to some degree, with many companies drawing most of their trade from operators based within the same or neighbouring counties – several seaside resorts had coach bodybuilders originally established

Among the most remarkable contracts ever secured was to build what amounted to an opposite-hand version of a typical home-market Duple product on a Renault chassis for that manufacturer to use for factory visits to and from the Paris Motor Show of 1932.

London Lorries had been a significant competitor to Duple in the period around 1929-31, the body on this 1931 AEC Regal being typical of its products, complete with characteristic waistband in a speckled finish. It was one of six for Queen Line, which ran a London-Baldock service, all being taken over by Green Line in April 1933 and numbered T352-7

For the 1931 Show, Duple bodied a Dennis Lance double-decker, sold to A. F. England, an independent operator based in Luton. This may have influenced Luton Corporation in its choice of bodywork for a fleet of nine Daimler buses delivered in February 1932. The four double-deckers were of lowbridge layout, unlike the Dennis (which also later came into the municipal fleet), and the first, No.7 (TM 9881) with body 2684, is seen here in a snowy scene before delivery. This was a CP6, with conventional poppet-valve petrol engine, the others being CH6 with sleeve-valve engines though all had fluid-flywheel transmission.

on the basis of local demand. Even so, Duple was among a small number of firms beginning to emerge as leaders on a national scale in their respective fields. The natural system of survival of the fittest was accelerated by the depression, and several quite well-known firms went out of business or merged.

Among them was London Lorries, a concern whose name seemed rather inappropriate when the products were coaches; its factory was in Kentish Town. It had also blossomed as a coach bodybuilder in the late 1920s and the beginning of the 1930s, not only supplying various independent operators largely in the London area but also major operators such as the Bristol Tramways & Carriage Co Ltd, for whom London Lorries had been a principal coach body supplier on that concern's own B-type chassis for a time around 1929, and Southdown Motor Services Ltd, on Leyland Tiger chassis. The business was acquired by Duple in 1932, but the latter's production facilties

at Hendon proved able to cope with any orders which might have been transferred.

By that date building coaches was widely accepted as at the core of Duple's business and operators wishing to keep in touch with the latest styles as well as competitors took a keen interest in what Duple was producing in that increasingly fashion-conscious line of business.

At the 1932 Scottish Show, two Duple-bodied coaches were on display, both for Blackpool-based operators, which was intriguing in itself, when there was a progressive and well-established coach bodybuilder in that town, H. V. Burlingham

Coach design was in a transitional stage through much of the 1930s. These two Leyland Tiger TS4 models for A. Christy of Bolton, though well up to contemporary ideas in general outline, retained the running board at the sides and rear which was a vestige of the side-door charabanc era. They were registered WH 3877-8, had bodies 2868-9, and dated from May 1932.

Ltd, later to play an important part in the Duple story. One was an AEC Regal, registered FV 3093, for Wood Bros (Blackpool) Ltd, which used the fleetname John Bull Coaches and the other a Leyland Tiger TS4 for W. C. Standerwick Ltd, either FV 2513 or 2514. Both these concerns were acquired by Ribble Motor Services Ltd, and when a competition was organised in which members of the public cast votes for their choice among sixteen coaches belonging to this group these two, the only vehicles with Duple bodywork entered, came first and second. Both were of rear-entrance layout with seats for 28 passengers and a rear toilet compartment. The styling differed somewhat, the John Bull coach having a half-canopy cab, a feature fairly rare at that date (though sometimes it had been used in the late 1920s where canvas-topped bodies were mounted on forward-control chassis) whereas the Standerwick vehicle had a normal full-width canopy but both had

a well-raked profile, emphasised by the use of hinged sections to extend the nearside panelling alongside of the bonnet to echo the windscreen line, an idea that was to recur on some later Duple designs.

A chassis type which became quite prominent as a basis for Duple bodywork in that period was the Dennis Lancet, taking a substantial share of the market for forward-control passenger chassis from its introduction in November 1931. This was largely related to its low cost, widely publicised as £595 in chassis form, though this seems to have been an introductory offer, for it had risen to £650 by the following spring. Even so, it was still considerably cheaper than the AEC Regal or the Leyland Tiger, then costing over £1,000. The latter models were widely recognised as the leading full-sized coach chassis of the day and many Duple bodies of the period were built on

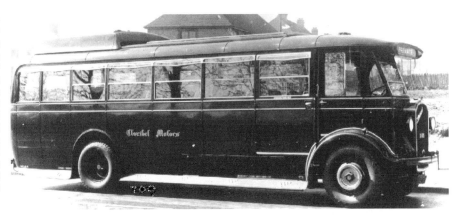

The Dennis Lancet, with its distinctive 'chunky' radiator, became a popular choice as a basis for coach bodywork among independent operators. This example dating from early 1933 for Claribel Motors (Ardwick) Ltd, a Manchester operator, had quite a simple style of body, with rear-end outline clearly related to that produced for the Bedford WLB, though with coach interior and sliding roof, offered on this model for a time. The engine of this model was derived from that in the Dennis E of the late 1920s but with a modest unladen weight of 5 tons 12 cwt, as here, performance was quite acceptable.

Gilford no longer figured so prominently in Duple's output as in 1929-30 but the 168OT was still finding customers in spring 1933, when this example, thought to be registered AGJ 569, was built for Brown's Coaches, probably the Streatham firm of that name. By then, the model's simple but lively six-cylinder side-valve engine was being built by Coventry-Climax, though to the original Lycoming design. The body style is noteworthy in the elimination of the 'peak' effect over the windscreen, then rare but later to become usual.

Auto Pilots Ltd was also a customer for a Duple-bodied Dennis Lancet in 1933, but of out-of-the-ordinary style. The concept of what was usually then called an observation coach had come from America, but British examples began to appear in the early 1930s. The operator ran a London-Folkestone express service and was taken over by East Kent about three years later, this vehicle, AKL 472, being among those added to the latter's fleet, although sold off subsequently.

examples of both, operators having found that they offered refined travel and reliable service justifying their cost. However the original Lancet (later to become known as the Lancet I) appealed particularly to independent operators, capturing much of the market hitherto covered by Gilford, by then beginning to decline, though Duple was still building the occasional body on 168OT chassis until 1933. Although the Lancet's 5.7-litre four-cylinder engine was neither as powerful or smooth as the Regal or Tiger models' larger units, or even the Gilford's engine, it provided adequate performance if overall weight was not too great and, with an early instance of flexible engine mounting, gave acceptable smoothness. Other makes on which Duple bodies were built in modest numbers in that period included Albion and Maudslay.

Duple was still building bodywork for goods vehicles and cars, if on a much smaller scale than coaches and buses. Like many firms in those days, it was quite willing to produce almost any type of bodywork on demand. Duple's flexibility and the skill displayed in producing bodies of specialised types, or with features to suit the customer's individual needs, often at short notice, seems quite remarkable by today's standards.

Duple's adaptability was used to take on a wide variety of work, valuable at a time of quite severe depression. These two furniture vans were built in 1933 on Maudslay ML3 chassis registered SF 3646 and 6045, originally single-deck buses dating from 1925 and 1926 respectively in the fleet of the Scottish Motor Traction Co Ltd. They had been taken in part exchange against new vehicles by AEC, and were sold to a Leeds concern, FTS.

Among the most interesting cars bodied by Duple was this Alvis Speed 20, dating from late 1932, registered YY 924. It was for Mr Lloyd Thompson of the Holdsworth concern, major suppliers of moquette, and had a larger boot than then usual and provision for removal of the rear seats to allow additional space for the carriage of luggage. It was painted black with green mudguards and wheels.

Glamorous in a different way was this Buick 8-50 four-seat tourer of 1933, with straight-eight 3.8-litre engine. At that date, Buick cars were being imported from Canada rather than the USA so as to get the benefit of reduced duty as Empire products but a traditional-style tourer was no longer standard.

Equally non-standard was this smaller sporting four-seat tourer on Vauxhall Light Six chassis, built a few months later. Vauxhall, like Buick, was a General Motors concern, and to some degree these cars were 'cousins', though here a British-style sporting flavour was the aim – note the fishtail exhaust.

A significant development of that period was the conversion of bonneted goods models to forward-control to give more body space, needing non-standard cabs and other work and Duple produced examples on Bedford and Dodge chassis. Such vehicles as special display vans or mobile shops could be counted as a throw-back to Duple's earlier days, as could cars with special features to suit the carriage of goods. The old convertible passenger/goods concept was even applied to at least one Bedford WLB 20-seater.

However, some Duple car bodies of that period were quite glamorous. There were sporting two-seater and drop-head models on the recently-introduced Vauxhall Light Six models, for example, offered as part of that model range, though built in much smaller numbers than the saloons. Particularly desirable was an Alvis Speed 20 on which a special coupé body was built towards the end of 1932 for the business use of Mr Lloyd

Thompson of J. Holdsworth & Co Ltd of Halifax, Here again, the boot space for luggage was unusually large and the rear seats were made readily removable to give extra space when needed. This firm was a major supplier of moquette to coachbuilding concerns, and in addition to Duple's experience in producing a vehicle well suited to visting Holdsworth's customers, it seems very probable that this deal had an element of barter about it.

Exports of British commercial vehicles to North America were never numerous, but a trade agreement resulted in the 15% tariff previously applied to British vehicles exported to Canada being withdrawn. AEC had already sold a number of its Ranger bonneted chassis to Canadian operators but in the spring of 1933, three further examples were exported to that market, this time complete with luxurious coach bodywork by Duple for long-distance operation. At that date the standard American long-distance coach was still of front-engined bonneted layout

AEC Ranger chassis had been exported to Canada from 1931, but these two for Canadian-American Coaches Ltd, seen before shipping in May 1933, broke new ground in being exported complete with Duple coach bodies built to a combination of British styling and features such as a sliding roof with transatlantic dimensions – they ran on a route connecting Detroit to Buffalo, two American cities, via a direct route running almost entirely through Canadian territory.

Two further AEC Ranger coaches for Canada had bodywork of a different design, with more rounded rear dome than on any home market Duple bodies, fewer but longer side windows and a single-panel windscreen – they were 32ft 6in long and 8ft wide. One was for Gray Lines but the other, shipped in December 1933, was for Royal Tourist Coaches. Also of interest in this picture is the 'convertible' van visible in front of the coach, with the car hood and rear deck panel assembly for use instead of the van top carried on the roof, ready for delivery. It appears to be of late 1920s design, probably a Morris, and may have been in for repair or repainting.

and thus the Ranger, especially with the 120bhp version of the AEC engine by then standard on all that company's six-cylinder petrol models, was directly comparable. Two vehicles were for Canadian-American Coaches Ltd, of Windsor, Ontario and one for Gray Coach Lines, a subsidiary of the Toronto Transportation Commission, this latter having a fluid flywheel and preselective gearbox, by then optional on AEC passenger chassis.

A further Ranger was shipped in December 1933 for display at the National Automobile Exhibition held in Toronto the following month, again with Duple body in the livery of Royal Tourist Coaches. Mr R. E. Brown, Duple's Sales Director, had made an extensive tour of Canada and the USA in August and September 1933 studying methods of both operators and manufacturers,

noting that the Rangers and other coaches were regularly run at 55-60mph for long distances. He expressed the view that there were good prospects for high-quality British products in Canada, though nothing more seems to have come of this particular initiative.

The Q coaches – unsuccessful but influential

A reason for this may have been interest on both sides of the Atlantic in alternative engine positions, though with different results. In Britain, the AEC Q side-engined bus and coach chassis introduced in 1932 captured the imagination of the industry, even if too advanced for its day to be built in large numbers. Although AEC did not build bodywork for its chassis,

The AEC Q side-engined model was not only remarkably advanced in its layout and design but set new standards in its appearance which were to have profound effect on the design of later vehicles on more orthodox chassis. Duple was chosen to build the first coach body on a Q-type chassis (the second of the single-deck type, number 762002), supplied to Elliott Bros for its Royal Blue fleet and seen here soon after entering service in August 1933. Although AEC did not have a bodybuilding department, designs were prepared and, especially in the era of G. J. Rackham as Chief Engineer, registered and then made available to bodybuilders. The basic outline of Q type single-deckers, including the curved profile at the front, had been defined by a styling model made before the first example, a bus, had been built by the LGOC in the spring of 1932. That did not have the sloping pillars for the side windows, and it may be that Duple designers played a part their development and other aspects of the design. However, this feature, and indeed the whole outline, were recorded in AEC drawings which were the basis of almost identical bodies built by other concerns.

This second Q coach body, slightly modified from the first and seating 36 passengers, was built by Duple on chassis 762003 for use as a demonstrator in time for the 1933 Show (other very similar bodies were built by Weymann and Harrington). This view shows the model's engine position, behind the offside front wheel – the layout required the passengers seated above the engine to face sideways. This vehicle was petrol-engined as built, but very soon was fitted with what was probably the first example of the AEC 7.7-litre oil (diesel) engine to go into a vehicle. It was registered as BME 130 and sold in 1934 to Waltham Belle.

Representative of 'conventional' bodywork being built in mid-1933 at about the same time as the first Q coaches is that on this Albion Valiant for Fallowfield & Knight Ltd, based in Hackney, London. This design was largely as established by the 1932 Show Standerwick coach – similar bodies were supplied to other operators on various chassis. The Valiant, introduced towards the end of 1932, had a 6-litre six-cylinder petrol engine and was Albion's answer to the success of the AEC Regal etc. Note the continued use of a roof-mounted name sign.

the firm's Chief Engineer, G. J. Rackham, took a keen interest in the design and appearance of the completed vehicles and registered body designs were produced by AEC for the new model. Prototype single- and double-deck buses were built before the end of 1932 and several further double-deckers were supplied to operators during 1933.

The first Q coach, which was chassis number 762002, the second single-deck example of the model to be built, was sent to Duple for bodying, being completed and supplied to Elliott Bros (Bournemouth) Ltd for use by its Royal Blue fleet, in August 1933 registered LJ 8001. The body, Duple No. 3666, conformed to the AEC design for the Q single-decker, with full-width front, looking very strange at that date in not having a radiator outline visible. It had a subtly curved profile which set a standard for subsequent design trends, and used sloping pillars throughout its length. This last-mentioned feature was also a novel idea at the time and required specially-made half-drop opening windows – a second broadly similar body ordered at the same time was built by Duple as a demonstrator. Another basically similar body was built for Elliott Bros in November 1933 and bodies based on the same AEC-design outline were also produced by Weymann and Harrington on other early Q single-decker chassis.

Quite apart from having quite a strong influence on the wider adoption of smoother outlines for both coaches and buses from the mid-1930s, this Q design was responsible for triggering the general adoption of sloping pillars on British coach designs. Duple incorporated this feature for some of its coach bodies on conventional chassis, beginning on a limited scale quite soon

after the first Q, and it was also adopted by other bodybuilders, gradually becoming quite widely accepted practice and remaining so until the early 1950s. Looking back from 60-odd years later, it seems quite a surprising convention, since it had no influence on the external shape and must have made manufacture more complex and expensive.

Yet during the period when the initial Q coaches were very much a talking point in the industry, other less dramatic design ideas were to be seen among Duple's production. Design was far from standardised, and it seemed as if almost any style the operator desired could be built and that individual draughtsmen were allowed to pursue their own ideas to some degree. On the whole, Duple designs usually had quite flowing lines, yet there were some using quite angular features, suggesting different minds at work.

The nature of bodybuilding in those days was such that individuality was given remarkably free rein, and in some ways certain of the leading bodybuilders, with Duple perhaps the leading British example, behaved almost in the manner of one of the styling studios of large car makers today, with the difference that the flow of individual ideas was allowed to appear in the products sold to customers, even if only a handful or even single examples of some variants were built, which meant that walking around a seaside coach park in those days could reveal a multitude of types and styles even among what was basically a similar model. The accompanying illustrations give some indication of this variety but any attempt to record all the variations on the various themes Duple produced in the 1930s would virtually fill the entire volume.

The idea of a four-bay rear-entrance coach had been used to good effect by Leyland on bodies for Ribble built on the first production batch of its new neater-looking Tiger TS6 model in spring 1933 but its body shops, perhaps preoccupied by problems with the early metal-framed bus bodies, did not follow this up. Duple saw the opportunity, offering such a body for the 1934 season, adding a 'different' touch by using tapered pillars – this example for Bradshaw of Plumstead may have been the first, though Christy of Bolton had two in February-March 1934. The neat appearance was to prove popular, examples being built for several well-known operators, notably a batch of five for Crosville, again on the TS6.

There was also a considerable amount of influence interacting between one bodybuilder or operator and another. For example, Leyland introduced quite an elegant coach body design for its Tiger TS6 chassis with modernised frontal appearance when that model was introduced in the Spring of 1933, supplying eighteen examples to Ribble Motor Services Ltd. It had four large side windows ahead of the entrance door, which was at the rear. Only quite limited numbers of the Leyland version were built but Duple also produced a four-bay design which had a general similarity, usually with rear entrance but which in most cases had pillars which tapered slightly, being thicker at the top. The detail work was neatly executed in a way becoming characteristic of Duple, and examples were built for quite a number of operators around 1934, often on Tiger TS6 chassis but also on AEC Regal and several other makes and models. Among the more interesting were twelve SOS ON models, with chassis built by the Birmingham & Midland Motor Omnibus Co Ltd, better known as MidlandRed, though

A simplified version of the four-bay design was also produced, using 'plain' pillars and waistband – side-by-side shaped fleetname and destination boxes were another recent option. This 1934 example was on a Gilford Hera chassis, a model introduced early in 1933 and effectively the successor to the 1680T, though having a Vulcan 7.4-litre petrol engine as standard – it was built only in modest numbers before the firm went out of business at the end of 1935. The coach shown was built for the Grey Pullman fleet of G. F. Burgoin of Haverhill, Suffolk.

The four-bay tapered-pillar coach body was fitted on several makes of chassis, possibly the most unusual being the SOS ON type. The Trent Motor Traction Co Ltd had a batch of twelve of this newly-introduced model, which had a 6-litre six-cylinder petrol engine, fitted with such bodies in 1934 – No. 689 (RC 1809) is seen in Nottingham in May of that year. The SOS was the marque name for chassis built by the Midland Red concern, usually fitted with bodywork also to that concern's standards. Trent was one of several associated companies using SOS vehicles but these vehicles marked a fresh policy in having other bodywork styles.

The sloping side-window pillars that had been a new feature of the bodies built for AEC Q chassis in the summer of 1933, began to appear in some bodies for other chassis the following spring. Among the first Duple examples was this Leyland Tiger TS6 with body number 4045 for J. Pearson & Sons of Liverpool. The wide window bays were reminiscent of the rear-entrance designs shown on the previous page, but here the entrance was at the front. The Pearson business, which traded as Happy Days Motorways, was taken over jointly by Crosville and Ribble in May 1935 and this coach, LV 6690, became Crosville K95.

they were for operation by the Trent Motor Traction Co Ltd.

These had vertical pillars, but rather similar bodies using sloping pillars were also built in quite large numbers by Duple in 1934-5, again on various types of chassis, mostly having front- or centre-entrance layout. Some had a stepped waistline, another feature fashionable for a time, and having some logic when, as was quite often the case for a time, the seats towards the rear of the coach were mounted on a floor which was about 3in higher than those at the front. The gangway was usually sloped gently upwards towards the rear to eliminate any need for a step along its length. For many years, Harrington, based at Hove, near Brighton, one of Duple's main rivals, produced many coaches of this pattern, winning prizes with a particularly harmonious version with half-canopy cab popular from 1934. At that stage, however, most Duple bodies had full-width canopies, the destination box and operator's name display panel apertures usually being shaped to blend harmoniously with the roof curvature.

As it turned out, only a dozen more AEC Q coaches were bodied by Duple after the initial pair. The model had only quite limited success, the main operator being London Transport, which took over the LGOC and Green Line as well as those other operators running regular services wholly within its area after it became responsible for operating such services from July 1933 – it did not favour Duple with any passenger vehicle orders (save under special circumstances in wartime, as described later), though some Bedford buses taken over from independent operators were rebodied as vans by Duple for its service fleet in 1935.

One of the problems with the Q as a basis for a coach with typical floor level of the period was the need for passengers seated over the engine compartment to face sideways, always unpopular on a coach. Duple did produce a revised design with a raised floor level which overcame this problem, one being supplied to Elliott Bros in 1934 and others being built for Skill's of Nottingham and Pearson's of Liverpool, though further orders for coaches on Q chassis favoured styles closer to the original outline. Overall, however, the industry was not yet ready for a general departure from the front engine position and demand fell away, Duple bodying only three Q-types in 1935 and a final one in 1936.

Although Duple was becoming increasingly regarded as a coach bodybuilder, bus bodies were produced in quite large numbers, running upwards from the standard Bedford WLB 20-seat version, this being mostly supplied to independent operators although Chester and Exeter were among municipal users. These were built on more of a production basis, this also applying to the similar bodies built on Dodge chassis.

The Dennis Ace, often called the 'flying pig' because of its snout-like projecting bonnet, was another contender in the 20-seat class from 1934, Duple building both bus and coach examples, an early user being Burnell's Motors of Weston-super-Mare, which had four with Duple bodywork.

Barton Transport Ltd, of Beeston, near Nottingham, began a long spell as a major Duple customer modestly with a couple of coaches on Leyland Lion LT5 chassis in 1933, followed by two more on the very different-looking LT5A model and one on an AEC Regal in 1934.

Export business continued to be developed, often on the basis of foreign travel by Duple directors – W. E. Brown toured

The standard 20-seat body produced mainly for Bedford WLB had not altered significantly since the initial design of late 1931. Dodge operated in Britain from a factory at Kew, using side-valve six-cylinder engines imported from its parent American company. Seen here is a demonstrator built in 1934 on the then new KB model and with body much as the WLB version. A minor change then new but applying to subsequent bus bodies for bonneted chassis was the oddly-shaped destination box, still projecting over the windscreen but now outward-sloping at the lower corners, which tended to look more dated than the previous simpler style.

A solution to the problem of the AEC Q's side engine position was to raise the floor level sufficiently to allow forward-facing seats to be used over the engine area at the same height as in most of the coach. The standard seating capacity was 37, as in the first example to be completed, with body 4038 for the Elliott Bros Royal Blue fleet, new in March 1934. Some of the grace and styling flair of the original version had been lost and it looked much stubbier. Three more similar bodies were built on Q chassis in 1934, for Pearson of Liverpool (this being a spacious 32-seater), Skill of Nottingham and Hull Bros (Lea Valley Coaches) of Cheshunt.

The other Duple bodies on AEC Q chassis were all of the lower-built layout. This one, with body 4076, for Bracewells (Colne) Ltd was of the style used, with minor variations, on six examples between late 1933 and mid-1935, the other customers being Royal Blue, Sutton of Clacton (2), Corona of Sudbury and Keith of Aylesbury. This one seated 35 and had the double display panels over the side windows used on the 1934-5 versions.

Barton Transport Ltd took two coaches on Leyland Lion LT5A chassis in the spring of 1934. Evidently someone in the Barton family had been impressed by the Q body design – not only were there the sloping pillars but also the two-tier side display panels, the lower one tapered and carrying wording on the Nottingham-Skegness express service. There were even the four brackets on the roof for the radio aerial – both Bracewells and Barton were early users of coach radio. The well-rounded rear dome was typical of Duple coaches of this period although the destination display was a Barton feature.

the Mediterranean in the winter of 1933-4, sending encouraging reports came back from Athens, Syria and Egypt. An unusual order came from the Ramleh Electric Railway in the last-mentioned country, for a 31-seat two-compartment bus body on an American-built GMC chassis shipped via New York to Duple's works and then shipped again after bodying to Alexandria at the beginning of 1934. The year 1933 had proved a record one for export business with substantial business from East Africa in addition to that already recorded. This proved significant on a long-term basis – Kenya Bus Services Ltd of

This GMC chassis was shipped from the United States to Hendon to receive its 31-seat two-compartment body and then again to Alexandria in Egypt for delivery to the Ramleh Electric Railway early in 1934. GMC was the marque name of General Motors Truck Co, based in Pontiac, Michigan. Duple had bodied a few GMC chassis for British operators in the 1928-30 period but the make had later dropped out of the British market.

Far removed from the glamorous world of style-conscious coach design, Duple built up a useful business in the supply of buses for use in the tough operating conditions of East Africa. Even so, it is noticeable that the rear panels were more carefully shaped than those on some of today's high-tech coaches. The vehicle shown was one of thirteen with body numbers 3812-24 for Kenya Bus Services Ltd, based on Albion Valkyrie chassis with Gardner 4LW engine completed early in 1934, being one of seven having 18-seat first-class compartments and a 14-seat unglazed second-class section at the rear.

Nairobi ordered thirteen Albion Valkyrie buses, completed early in 1934. This operator was part of the Overseas Motor Transport group in which Commander F. T. Hare was Managing Director, from which Duple was to obtain successive orders over the years – in the post-war period the group title became United Transport Ltd.

Apart from the bodywork, these Albions for Kenya were of interest in having Gardner 4LW engines and were among the first diesel models to have been bodied by Duple. With very rare exceptions, coaches were still almost always petrol-engined at that date and this often remained so until the end of the 1930s even though several experimental diesel buses were on the roads in Britain by 1930 and most of the larger bus operators were standardising on them for new additions to their fleets from around 1934-6. The Kenya buses had chassis basically similar to the contemporary home-market Valkyrie PW65 model, the chassis being numbered in the same series. The bodywork, generally seating 32, was somewhat utilitarian in style, some having first- and second-class interiors, the former with upholstered seats and the latter with wood slats. Special care was taken in the design and materials of the body structure, based on steel floor framing though using iroko, an African hardwood for the upper part of the structural framing, the aim being durability and resistance to attack by ants – this plus the rugged nature of the chassis and engine made them durable vehicles, some not being withdrawn until 24 years old despite the harsh operating conditions.

An alternative approach to the needs of operation in climates where the conventional ash body framing was unacceptable was to adopt steel framing, as in a 32-seat two-doorway bus body built in 1934 on an oil-engined Leyland TS6 chassis for operation in Mendoza, central Argentina, by the CITA concern, which was a subsidiary of the Buenos Aires and Great Southern Railway Co Ltd – it was Duple's first metal-framed body.

Less distant, yet quite exotic in its sense of unfamiliarity, was a further instance of Duple bodywork on French chassis, this time for a London-based firm, European Motorways, though registered in France and for use on Continental tours. The Citroen chassis was of bonneted layout and the body design showed French influence though, according to contemporary observers, had the benefit of the higher-quality trim by then expected of leading British bodybuilders.

One of the problems of a firm whose main business is coach bodywork is the seasonal nature of the trade. This was very much so in the 1930s, more so than applied in more recent years when efforts to even out the demand have succeeded to some degree. Many coach operators' virtually closed down during the winter months, delicensing most of their vehicles and selling off those at the end of their lives in the autumn. Ideally, operators did not want new vehicles until shortly before Easter or in some cases Whitsuntide yet prompt delivery when required was vital. A press reporter visiting Duple's works in the spring of 1934 was told that 130 coaches of widely varying specification were due to be delivered by Whitsun.

Duple's first metal-framed body was this one built in 1934 on an oil-engined Leyland TS6 chassis for CITA, operating in Mendoza, Argentina. In those days, the plate on the bonnet side reading 'El Omnibus Ingles – Leyland' conveyed a sense of pride. The body pillars were of U-section steel with ash filling; other framing was also mainly in steel. The vehicle had leather-covered seats for 32 and the livery was red with white roof.

Another case of Duple bodywork on French chassis was this Citroen coach for European Motorways Ltd, a London firm which operated in France. The floor sloped upwards towards the rear, a feature used increasingly on Duple coach designs – the seating was laid out in two-and-one fashion to carry nineteen passengers and a courier.

The sharp variation in demand over the seasons meant that although shift working was needed in the spring, after Whitsun many of the workforce were laid off and not re-hired until the autumn. Quite apart from the human problems – moreover, good craftsmen once laid off were liable to find work elsewhere – this meant that the factory and its equipment were under-used for lengthy periods, which was an uneconomic way of working. Bus bodywork was less seasonal, but in that field, Duple was up against strong competition from companies such as Park Royal and Weymann, to mention only two of the more important firms which happened also to be based in the area to the west of London.

The export orders also often helped to even out demand, but another solution was the construction of other types of bodywork. Among the most eccentric was the supply of five special passenger-carrying bodies built by Duple on Bedford WLG 2-ton chassis to the British Union of Fascists in January 1934. Ironically, they were part of a contract that had been intended for export to the USSR, and thus escaped from use by a communist regime only to become the property of a fascist organisation. At that date, fascism was in the ascendancy in Italy and Germany, in the latter case in the form of the Nazi regime led by Adolf Hitler. The British Union of Fascists, led by Sir Oswald Mosley, emulated the German or Italian blackshirts.

The Daily Mirror described the vehicles as 'armoured cars' with a sub-heading reading 'Like U.S. Gangsters – Bullet-Proof and Can Carry 20 Men at 65mph', which was certainly stretching a point save for the last part, since they were more in the nature of fairly crude buses with longitudinal seats for 20 occupants and having open sides normally protected by roll-down canvas side screens. They had steel panelling, but they carried detachable metal grids to protect the openings and there was a strong stone-guard fitted to the radiator, all of which implied a readiness for trouble, and indeed the fascists were involved in some scuffles, though never on the scale found in Germany, nor did their threat build up to anywhere near a similar level. Even so, within a few years even such a peripheral involvement was doubtless an embarrassment when the country found itself at war with a Nazi-controlled Germany.

Far more important were large contracts for the General Post Office. That organisation, in those days also responsible for the nation's telephone service, laid down precise body specifications which were then put out to tender. Competition was severe but Duple was becoming better adapted to the manufacture of standardised bodywork in quite large quantities. A major expansion in the use of small motor vans for postal delivery occurred in the 1930s, based on the early Morris Minor. This was supplied in chassis form, and a wood-framed body, simple in outline but to precise Post Office specification was purchased separately. Several of the well-known bus and coach bodybuilders tendered for this work but Duple was more successful than most in obtaining large contracts, to the extent that a special workshop was built to handle the work.

There were also small GPO telephone vans based on the same Minor chassis, though with different bodywork with windscreens having extra panels to facilitate inspection of telephone wires, and painted dark green rather than the red of post vans. The GPO was well satisfied with the Minor chassis and when Morris began standardising on its successor, the Eight, introduced in 1935 in van as well as car form, the GPO elected to stay with the previous model, updated in detail.

In those days most main roads had multiple telephone lines running alongside them, as well as the smaller numbers in more isolated areas, almost all carried by strong wooden poles, so the need for maintenance was considerable. When equipment to carry out heavier work was needed larger vans on Morris Commercial chassis were used, and Duple also built many of these.

Duple was also the obvious choice to build the streamlined bodywork for a special airmail collection vehicle, evidently produced mainly for publicity reasons, built for the GPO in the autumn of 1934. The chassis was a Morris-Commercial but the bodywork disguised its identity very effectively and was influenced in regard to the bonnet design by the Chrysler Airflow car introduced a year or so earlier in America, though also sold in Britain. The air mail vehicle was painted blue, like the special post boxes used for this pioneer service. In later years, air mail became incorporated in the normal mail though the blue air mail sticker persists as a reminder of the original scheme. For many boys of those days, the Dinky Toy model made of this vehicle did far more to popularise the idea than the full-sized vehicle, indeed later becoming a collectors' item.

The overall expansion of the business meant that the Edgware Road site, to which Duple had moved in 1926, by then completely filled with workshops, was becoming inadequate. At that stage, part of Cowleaze Farm, including the substantial house that had been the central point of the estate, survived. In 1934, a further 3½ acres, including this property, was purchased to add to the original 2½-acre site, giving space for further workshops added over the next few years and room for the parking of chassis awaiting bodying. This gave Duple quite a long unbroken frontage on to Edgware Road, although at first the house was retained for use as offices.

The compact Dennis Ace sold well, usually as a bus, but this 1934 example for Eames of Shanklin, Isle of Wight, had a short version of the taper-pillar style of coach body (Duple No. 4132).

The Maudslay ML3 had been in production since the mid-1920s, though mildy updated – its four-cylinder engine had an overhead-camshaft layout. Eclipse Coaches (R. Neal) of East Acton chose the 'plain' four-bay body for this one, AYH 349, in 1934.

This style of body introduced during 1934 and quite popular for a time gave a clear hint of future trends, with its curved roof line and the sloping pillars fast becoming fashionable. The stepped waist was also popular for a time, logical to some degree in relation to the gently ramped floor. James Sutherland of Peterhead was a regular Duple and AEC customer, this Regal with Duple body 4483 being an exhibit at the Scottish Show in November 1934. It survived until the operator was taken over by Alexander in 1950.

3 THE CURVACEOUS LATE 1930s

By 1935, Duple, as well as achieving greatly improved trading figures that year, was setting off on a new era of stylish design. Coach bodybuilders and, in many cases, operators were increasingly appearance-conscious. That was the era of streamlining, when aeroplanes were capturing the imagination, even though commercial air travel was still in its infancy, and the styling influence it fostered had far wider application in other forms of transport. Smoother lines were an obvious trend, but the adoption of curves was much more extensive than justifiable by aerodynamic considerations.

The motor coach, as a vehicle associated with pleasure travel, even when mainly engaged on relatively short-distance working, was an obvious outlet for such designs. The AEC Q coaches described in the last chapter were an early manifestation of this trend, and by the mid-1930s, the effects were very obvious in car design, especially in America, creating an expectation that not only the bodywork as a whole but such details as mudguard outlines should be formed from graceful curves.

In the car world, another trend was the positioning of the radiator further forward, primarily for reasons of better space utilisation, but also creating a different 'look'. Bedford had introduced a new 3-ton goods model, the WT-series, using similar principles and with a neat semi-forward-control layout at the 1933 Commercial Motor Show, the type going into production during 1934.

At first there was no bus version of the WT, and the WLB continued as the official standard Bedford bus or coach model for 1935, but a passenger adaptation of the longer-wheelbase WTL version was introduced at the Scottish Show of November 1934. Duple introduced a series of standard bus and coach bodywork designs seating up to 26 passengers for it, and it was an immediate success, selling more strongly than the WLB in many parts of the country. Apart from the more spacious bodywork, the coach version in particular looked much more in keeping with the latest trends as well as offering good value.

This body in the contemporary 'streamlined' idiom was built for the General Post Office in the autumn of 1934, mainly to publicise a new air mail service. It would hardly have been able to live up to its outline in terms of performance, being based on a Morris-Commercial 30-cwt chassis as widely used by the GPO for normal mail collection. It bore the registration BLB 444.

On larger models such as the AEC Regal, Leyland Tiger and Dennis Lancet, variety was still the order of the day in 1935, with numerous variations. Some users continued to favour quite restrained designs with vertical pillars and straight waistlines, but combinations of sloping pillars with various departures from horizontal lines at roof and waist, the latter sometimes stepped or partially curved, were becoming increasingly common, with various forms of curved mouldings applied to the side panels. The choice of half- and full-width

Bedford's WT range of semi-forward-control models began a new generation of types. Although basically a goods chassis, the longer-wheelbase WTL was offered adapted for passenger work in late 1934 and Duple-bodied versions immediately became popular. The rear entrance position was still widely favoured for coaches as on this early example, probably built for the Scottish Show that year.

These two Dennis Lancet coaches, both dating from the earlier part of 1935, illustrate something of Duple's freedom of approach to styling variations at that time – there is hardly a feature in common to indicate that their bodywork came from the same builder.

The example on the left, registered JT 2382, was built for Greyhound Coaches Ltd of Weymouth, and is an example of a surprisingly 'harsh' style found on a few Duple bodies of around that time, looking as though they might have been the product of a brash newly-recruited young designer. The angular outlines of the applied decoration and the straight-lined rearward extension of the mudguard outlines were not at all in keeping with usual Hendon styles.

More obviously a Duple product was this example, evidently a demonstrator, possibly for a dealer. In most respects, it was a fairly typical up-to-date Hendon product of the time, with more flowing curves in the waist and mudguard styling, though the turn-under at the rear would soon seem dated as the outswept tail became usual for coaches. The fleetname and destination box were to a typical Duple style of that time, and indeed the separate oval-topped units on the half-canopy front of the Greyhound coach were an equally typical Duple alternative, acting as almost the only styling giveaway.

canopy continued to be another point of variation. It was almost as if each design was like an individual artist's canvas, rarely exactly repeating what had gone before though with characteristic styles which resulted in most, though not all, products being readily identifiable to the practised eye as Duple products.

There continued to be variety of chassis makes and models too, with Albion, Maudslay and TSM (this being the marque name adopted for a time by what had been the Tilling-Stevens, later returning to that name) figuring among the makes of full-sized chassis bodied by Duple around 1935, even if some only in small numbers – there were occasional others, including even the odd Gilford, though by then that make was almost at death's door.

Although rebodying existing chassis was nothing new, the rapid changes in what were seen as acceptably modern coach styles and the widespread realisation from around 1935 that early Leyland Tiger chassis dating from say 1928-31, though having very low monetary value, still ran very smoothly and reliably, providing a good basis for an up-to-date seeming

coach, made fitting new Duple bodywork on this model quite common practice. Slightly later similar remarks applied to the AEC Regal of 1930 onwards, these two models being by far the most common choices for such treatment.

Maudslay introduced a new model called the SF40, with front-mounted four-cylinder petrol engine of similar pattern to that used in the ML3 which had been this maker's main passenger model in the early 1930s but having the front axle set back sufficiently to allow passengers to enter via a doorway at the extreme front even though the engine cover was between them and the driver. The body was thus full-fronted and although Duple bodied a fairly utilitarian bus prototype, the model accommodated coach bodywork of styles reminiscent of those built on the AEC Q, and Duple produced some quite glamorous bodies on this chassis. In practice several were of centre-entrance layout though, as with the Q, numbers were never large. In addition, the conventional ML3 was replaced by the more modern-looking ML5, though this was more a matter

Occasional rebodying occurred in Duple's early days as a coach bodybuilder but began to become more common when early Leyland Tiger chassis were increasingly thought too good to scrap despite outdated bodywork. This example was one of five TS2 dating from 1929 rebodied in May 1935 with another cocktail of contemporary Duple style (body Nos. 5115-9) for Shamrock & Rambler Motor Coaches Ltd of Bournemouth, by then a subsidiary of Keith & Boyle (London) Ltd, adopting its orange and cream livery – the chassis had come from that fleet, being registered UL 9580-4 but were re-registered as ARU 900-4 on rebodying. Similar bodywork (5120-1) was fitted to two new oil-engined Regal chassis for use by the latter fleet, BXO 208-9.

of a change to an up-to-date radiator and frontal style, not unlike that of the contemporary Leyland Lion LT5A and LT7, and Duple produced a few bodies on this chassis, which sold in very modest numbers to independent operators.

Duple was also still building both bus and coach bodies on several makes of smaller chassis in addition to Bedford, even though the latter greatly outnumbered the rest. Albion's Victor model was proving quite popular, both in normal-control and forward-control forms, the latter with half-cab layout being the basis of what often looked rather like a scaled-down full-sized coach, comments that also applied to the Leyland Cub. On the other hand, Commer and Dodge were more directly comparable to Bedford and often received very similar bodywork.

Coaches continued to be strongly in the majority among Duple's output, but the firm's clientele included some important exceptions to this pattern, in addition to the export instances already described. One was Barton Transport Ltd which, after taking small numbers of Duple coach bodies in 1933-34, placed the first of a series of orders for Duple bus bodies in 1935, although the specification was such as to make the word 'bus' seem unduly austere – perhaps a better one at that date might have been 'saloon', though in later years 'dual-purpose' was sometimes so used.

There were thirteen on Lion LT7 chassis in Barton's initial order, taking full advantage of that model's short bonnet by seating 39 passengers. They were of conventional straight-waisted design but had slightly ramped floors so as to allow all seats to face forward without problems of wheel-arch intrusion. Many details of the body were to coach standard, such as the clock mounted on the bulkhead and one item still fairly uncommon even on a coach at that date was the provision of a radio. They were thus suitable for occasional use on medium-distance excursion duty. There were also three 32-seat coach bodies, two on LT7 and one on a Tiger TS7.

Later in the year four more LT7 buses were supplied, and repeat orders for further Lion petrol-engined models with generally similar bodies having variations of trim detail followed each year until 1939, the later ones on LT8 chassis. The type thus became the standard Barton bus of the late 1930s and it is understood that a bulk order had been placed for extended delivery.

The Maudslay SF40 was more conventional than it looked, retaining a front-mounted engine and much of the mechanical design of the ML3. The passenger entrance could be ahead of the front axle but most of those bodied by Duple had the entrance to the rear of the front axle, as on this early demonstrator of late 1934.

The Albion Victor had been in production since 1931 but a new series of models with 3.9-litre four-cylinder petrol engines appeared for 1935, this early example of the PK114 long-wheelbase bonneted version being supplied to the King Alfred fleet of R. Chisnell of Winchester in June of that year as AAA 755. The model could seat up to 28 but this was a very spacious 20-seat coach – the sister vehicle, AAA 756, had a not dissimilar-looking body by Abbott of Farnham and survives in the care of David Hurley.

Gilford ceased production in 1935 but among the last was this Hera for Charles W. Banfield, of Herne Hill, London S.E., with stylish body of the stepped-waist, curved roofline type. It had a centre entrance position, then beginning a degree of following.

Barton Transport Ltd began to develop its own distinctive ideas on bus design in 1935, with the first of a series of batches based on Leyland Lion chassis. Seen when almost new, in May of that year, is one of the initial thirteen LT7 models, this being the successor to the LT5A, having vacuum-hydraulic brakes. Barton, despite having been a pioneer in the use of diesel engines, had reverted to petrol for its new Leylands, and this remained so for its single-deckers through the 1930s. The bodywork was of 39-seat capacity yet careful design made the standard of comfort acceptable for all but long-legged passengers while the appearance and standard of trim justified the description 'coach-type' buses.

The Bedford WTB model was announced in time for the November 1935 Show, and these pictures show the three body designs Duple introduced for it. The lettering on a side window of the bus (top left), evidently used as a demonstrator, emphasised the £290 chassis price, which even in those days represented excellent value – the complete bus cost £640 as a 26-seater.

More operators were attracted to coach versions, the rear-entrance 26-seat version, slightly extended from the WTL body of similar layout, at £735 being featured in Bedford advertisements. The example in SMT livery (above) was on the Bedford stand, though not delivered to that operator. The third type (left) was the 25-seat K. D. Special, devised jointly with Keith Davies of Orange Luxury, having a rear boot, folding roof and entrance at the front, at £795 – its body style was derived from that shown at the foot of page 34; the odd spare wheel position was soon abandoned. This design proved popular – SMT switched to it for 20 coaches delivered in the spring of 1936, and the idea of the rear boot soon became accepted practice.

At the November 1935 Commercial Motor Show, Bedford introduced the WTB chassis, which was to be its main passenger model until 1939, dominating the up-to-26-seat class and having Duple bodywork as standard. This was the 'official' passenger version of the WT series, with 10in longer wheelbase than the WTL, longer and softer-riding springs and distinguishable by a radiator having a grille with fine vertical slats, though otherwise very similar-looking. The chassis price was £290.

A batch of prototype chassis was produced, number 3 receiving Duple body No.5974, a rear-entrance 26-seater sold to Ayers of Dover as JG 6895, closely followed by chassis number 1, which received Duple body 5978 for use by Vauxhall, registered MJ 8563. Production chassis continued the series which had begun with the WLB, which by then had reached the 110xxx range and Duple-bodied examples were entering service from late 1935.

Duple introduced new body styles for the WTB, with initial attention largely concentrated on a design called the K. D. Special, produced in conjunction with Keith Davies, Managing Director of Keith & Boyle (London) Ltd, proprietors of Orange Luxury Coaches, which had developed and patented the idea of providing a much roomier rear luggage boot than had been thought possible hitherto – the first application had been on a Weymann 32-seat metal-framed coach body on an oil-engined AEC Regal at the 1933 Show. The boot was supported by a low-level rear extension of the chassis frame, akin to that on a contemporary double-deck model, and incorporated the space under the rear seat and the rear part of the floor, the latter being slightly ramped upwards from the level at the front entrance door towards the rear.

The K. D. Special body built by Duple for the WTB had a stepped waistline and folding roof, and, at first, an odd-looking offside mounting for the spare wheel – this latter idea was soon abandoned. It was offered as a 25-seat model at £785 complete, 'plus £10 for the patent luggage compartment' – evidently a patent royalty payable to Mr Davies. There were alternative Duple-bodied WTB models with a more conventional straight-waisted rear-entrance 26-seat coach body at £735 and a front-entrance bus body at £640, both offered from late 1935 and with bodywork much as built for the WTL apart from being a little longer.

So far as home-market independent operators were concerned, there was a strong swing away from bus bodywork, even where a local bus service was operated and, in practice, Duple built far more coach bodies on the WTB than buses, these being quite rare except for export. The reasoning was that coaches could be also used for hire or excursion duty and the modest extra cost of a coach was likely to be repaid by its more flexible earning power – in addition, the greater comfort was seen as desirable even for bus work on rural routes where journey times of over half-an-hour or so were common.

The 1935 Commercial Motor Show, the last to be held in the Olympia building in West Kensington, London, was the occasion for a particularly strong Duple display, with four exhibits on the company's stand, plus a total of eight more on the stands of six chassis manufacturers, all built for specific operators. All but two were coaches, the firm's dominance among British bodybuilders in this field being firmly established by that date. In addition a miniature show was held at the Hendon works, a tradition followed in many later years right up to the 1960s, including those years where no Commercial Show was being held in London.

There had been increasing use of curves on individual parts of Duple body designs during the earlier 1930s but the idea of combining continuous and largely matching gentle end-to-end curves for waist, window outlines and the roof with sloping pillars was something quite new when seen on this Leyland Tiger TS7 built in time for display on Duple's stand at the 1935 Show. Body number 5965 was for L. Adnams Ltd and entered service, registered CXL 695, the following spring. Gradually, the basic ideas became widely adopted, not only on many of Duple's later coach bodies but across much of the British coach body industry until the early 1950s. As often applies, many later versions, even among Duple's own output, seemed to lose some of the original's purity of line.

The trend-setting Adnams Tiger

Some of the advance publicity indicated that two of the exhibits on Duple's stand were intended as future standard products, and although this only proved so to a limited degree, one was a trend-setter whose main features were soon to influence almost the entire British coach scene until about 1950. This was a Leyland Tiger TS7 for L. Adnams Ltd, of Merton, chassis number 7736 with Duple body 5965, registered CXL 695. The key new feature was the combination of unbroken curved waist and roof lines with sloping pillars, a combination not previously seen, yet within two or three years being adopted by all the leading British specialist coach bodybuilders. It was a logical conclusion to the various tentative new design ideas involving the replacement of horizontal lines with curves that had been found in earlier coaches and, so far as can be judged, seems to have been an instance of genuine original thinking. Even though sweeping curves were to be found in some of the more advanced car designs of the day,

nothing comparable overall was in production.

As quite often the case with what could be counted as a classic design, the original concept was particularly graceful and well-proportioned, to a degree by no means always achieved in later derivatives, even among Duple's own products, and the effect was aided by an attractive mid-blue livery. Another feature to be widely adopted, particularly in later Duple products, was the use of alternate slim polished window pillars between the conventional painted ones, almost giving the effect of two large windows on each side. It had a half-canopy front-end, another feature widely adopted later, though by no means universally.

The other full-sized coach on the stand was a Dennis Lancet 6 for Windsorian Coaches Ltd, but this was in reality basically to the existing sloping-pillar straight-waist design. However, it picked up a touch of the growing emphasis on curves by the shaping of the polished mouldings on the side panels, an aspect of appearance on which much emphasis was being put in the mid-1930s. They were generally arranged so as to outline a

Duple's advertisements in the run up to the 1935 Show had featured this Dennis Lancet 6 for Windsorian Coaches Ltd. Basically, it was a straight-waist, sloping-pillar body much as had been built since spring 1934, to which an unusual form of arrangement of the relief colour had been applied.

Using virtually the same body structure, save for a slightly more upright tail, was this coach on Albion Valiant chassis for Red & White Services Ltd of Chepstow, also at the 1935 Show, marking the beginning of a period when this concern and its associate companies were major Duple customers.

A double-decker was included in Duple's 1935 Show exhibits, this being an Albion Venturer of type SpM81 for West Wales Motors Ltd, the 52-seat body, No.5963, being of lowbridge layout. The curved profile was quite an advanced feature at that date, Duple's designers possibly being influenced by the appearance of London Transport's standard STL as introduced the previous autumn.

Swan-song for the AEC Q as a Show exhibit was this one with Duple body on the chassis maker's stand at the 1935 Show. It was for Sutton's of Clacton, which had been a customer for the original production Duple style for this chassis with two, very similar to the Bracewell's coach shown on page 29, in the early summer of 1934. The basic design was much the same, although the profile was more strongly curved, but the outline of an elaborate fleetname lettering on the front panel gave an unfortunate 'fishface' effect as well as losing the clean look of the original Q front end.

The whole question of the appropriate styles for motor vehicles was quite controversial at the time, some organisations such as London Transport advocating an approach eschewing applied decoration of this type; where designed to suit the overall lines of what was, by its nature, meant to be a more flamboyant type of vehicle, they could, however, look well. Looking back with hindsight, some of Duple's efforts in this respect seem more successful than others, though inevitably the customer was the ultimate arbiter.

The chassis model of the Windsorian Show coach was a six-cylinder variant of the standard Lancet, on the point of becoming obsolete as a new Lancet II model was introduced at that same Show, which perhaps lessened the interest in this exhibit, despite it being featured in advance publicity. The third coach on the Duple stand was the Bedford WTB with K.D. body for Keith & Boyle, but there was also an Albion Venturer double-decker for West Wales Motors Ltd, of Ammanford, of up-to-date style, yet this type of business was still not one in which Duple had built a significant market.

The former Tilling-Stevens concern used TSM as a marque name in the early to mid 1930s and, no longer connected to the Tilling group, had gained a modest following among independent operators. The four-cylinder models, for which the model name Express was still used, continued to have mechanical design having much in common with the B10A2 type built in large numbers in 1928-31, including the four-cylinder side-valve petrol engine. Their appearance was modernised with a more square-cut radiator, and Duple was able to give this 1935 Show example for the Grey Coaches fleet of Wigg of Peckham quite a stylish appearance

Duple exhibits on other stands included an AEC Q coach for Sutton's of Clacton on AEC's stand, evidently still seeking to drum up more business for the type, but in fact its last Show appearance. Albion was entering a period when Duple bodywork was quite often associated with the make, and the Valiant coach for Red & White Services Ltd of Chepstow marked the beginning of a regular association of Duple with Red & White, one of the few operators counted as 'independent' and yet becoming quite a substantial group in its own right as well as being 'recognised' by joint agreements with companies within the big groups under the control of BET and Tilling which dominated company bus operation in England and Wales by then. There was also a repeat order for the Overseas Motor Transport group, for operation in Mombassa.

On Bedford's stand, there was a WTB rear-entrance coach for the Scottish Motor Traction Co Ltd, again marking an association that was to continue, SMT being the parent concern of the main company operators in Scotland as well as itself running services covering much of the south-east of that country. Dodge had a 20-seat coach and Maudslay a coach on the SF40 chassis for Lewis of Greenwhich, another long-term customer. T. S. Motors had two Duple-bodied TSM coaches on display, a four-cylinder model for Wigg of Peckham, and a six-cylinder evidently initially a demonstrator.

The variety of body designs represented by these twelve Show vehicles was immense, doubtless enough to give a modern production manager nightmares, yet Duple not only coped but took such variety in its stride, not merely at Show times but right through the 1930s. In those days, the customer was in control to a degree never to be repeated, and while many other concerns built a variety of designs in response to operator specifications, Duple was unrivalled in the variety of its coach output, despite many of the vehicles having readily recognisable Duple 'signatures' in detail features and, especially in the later 1930s, the characteristic flowing lines of much of its output. One can only marvel at the skill and artistry of the designers, having nothing more advanced than a drawing board at their disposal, and the craftsmen in wood and metal, often still largely relying on hand tools, in coping with a situation where quite often a

Red & White took delivery of sixteen Albion Valkyrie PW65 buses with Duple 38-seat bodywork in 1936. The characteristic staccato bark of the five-cylinder Gardner 5LW diesel engine would have been a familiar sound as they left the works. They were of functional but none the less well-proportioned appearance.

fresh order meant a fresh design. Yet prompt delivery, especially in relation to the beginning of the coach season, was vital and this variety had to be achieved without slowing production.

Even so, the output of larger batches was giving more opportunity for something approaching series production. It is also particularly noteworthy that when announcements in the trade press about the completion of the first workshops on the additional land were made in August 1935, reference was made to them being for the construction of double-deck **trolley** and motor bus bodies as well as long-distance coaches. No doubt the beginning of London Transport's large-scale conversion of tram routes to trolleybus operation then just beginning influenced that statement, and indeed a year later new trolleybuses were to be seen on the Edgware Road, passing Duple's premises, having taken over from trams. In fact, however, Duple never built a trolleybus body and indeed double-deck motor buses were to remain limited in numbers, save for special circumstances in wartime.

Bigger orders

These were partly the result of orders from larger customers, among whom Red & White became a regular large-scale customer. The Show exhibit was the precursor of a fleet of Duple-bodied Albion buses and coaches added to Red & White's own and associated fleets in Wales in 1936. An order for 33, composed of sixteen 38-seat rear-entrance buses on Valkyrie PW65 chassis with Gardner 5LW engines plus further Valiant coaches was completed early in the year, to be followed by a series of further substantial orders. By 1938, the total of Duple bodies built or on order for the Red & White group reached 110 and this pattern continued until halted by the war in 1941. Like several other bodybuilders at that time, Duple was quite prepared to build to operator specification, and it is understood that some at least of these bodies used teak framing to give better durability.

Petrol engines were still more usual for coaches, even among larger fleets where diesels were becoming standard at least for double-decker buses, and 50 coaches bodied by Duple for Ribble on Leyland Tiger TS7 chassis placed in service between January and July 1936 were petrol. This was the first order from this fleet for Duple, and although the vehicles had an outline which doubtless did not look out of place emerging from the Hendon premises, they were to a Ribble 31-seat design. A

batch of 50 almost identical coaches had been ordered from English Electric the previous year and the last examples of these were still entering service as the Duple batch began to arrive. They were slightly more reserved than many Duple coaches of the time in having straight waistlines and vertical pillars, but the roof line was slightly curved while the half-canopy cab was in line with a growing trend – indeed Ribble's adoption of the idea for its big new coach fleet undoubtedly encouraged its wider adoption.

The Duple examples had a 'reversed' livery of ivory and crimson and a revised design of side flash incorporating a sweeping rear wing outline, this looking as though it might have been drawn by a Duple draughtsman; both of these features were adopted as standard by Ribble. In addition ten further TS7 coaches having 28 seats and toilet compartments were built for Standerwick, these being to a design which had the Ribble front-end, with rectangular windscreen, but was of stepped-waist pattern, with a slight curve rearwards of the step. Duple continued as a supplier of part of Ribble and Standerwick's needs for coach bodies in 1937-9, again to Ribble design, though a curved waist was adopted for the 1939 version.

The early 1936 Ribble batch contributed to a total of over 500 coach and bus bodies that were planned for completion in the first six months of that year, as reported in the May 1936 issue of *Coaching Journal*, one of whose representatives toured

The 50 coach bodies on Leyland Tiger TS7 chassis built for Ribble (Duple Nos 6375-6424) early in 1936 were to the operator's design – that concern's Chief Engineer, Captain H. Betteridge, had precise ideas on appearance, internal as well as external. The Leyland 7.6litre six-cylinder petrol engine was quiet, smooth and lively; the author recalls these coaches as excellent vehicles in which to travel.

Duple continued to build the occasional 'exotic' coach, such as this Maudslay SF40 for Red House Motor Services of Coventry, registered BWK 48. Techniques of spray painting allowed the pillars to blend upwards from cream at waist level to red at the top. It is seen in Nottingham in October 1936 when a few months old.

Maudslay replaced the ML3 by the more modern-looking ML5 and this example was bodied for Ansell's of Peckham, London S.E.5, an established Maudslay user, in 1936, using a variation of the sloping-pillar straight-waist style – the roof luggage carrier was still common, in this case with folding steps in the side. It was registered CUC 770.

the works with W. E. Brown. Of these vehicles, 200 were Bedfords, the WTB proving to have immediate popularity – they included 42 for SMT and associated companies, plus a batch for Orange Luxury, following up the Show coach. Despite the installation of labour-saving machinery, the woodworking department had been working night shifts since Christmas to keep pace with the rate of construction – it was reported that it took about fourteen days to complete a typical body.

Output of passenger bodies was then running at the rate of 20 to 25 bodies per week and hence, in theory, the works showed the potential of producing over 1,000 such bodies per year. The demand continued to be seasonal, so the actual output of coach bodies tailed off from July, but big contracts for van bodies for the GPO and some for other Government Departments augmented the total numbers substantially, even though the

The Bedford WTB gained immediate popularity, though the Duple bus bodied version shown here was quite rare in Britain. This one, with body number 7251 seated only 20, an option offered to allow stage carriage operation without a conductor under the regulations then in force. It was supplied to Colson Bros of Carisbrooke, Isle of Wight in May 1936 but is seen here in 1939 after take-over by Southern Vectis Omnibus Co Ltd.

little Morris vans were far smaller and simpler – by then this work was being carried out in a separate department. Further factory extensions were in hand, planned to be ready for the 1937 season, though there was still sufficient watery wasteland behind the factory for a swan to return annually to rear a family of cygnets.

There continued to be considerable variety in the output in 1936 and indeed later, the hint of standardisation of full-sized models in the pre-1935 Show announcements not being borne out in practice, except for those on Bedford chassis, until after the 1939-45 war. Modest numbers of bodies to the original curved-waist outline with four bays behind the entrance pioneered by the Adnams Tiger TS7 were produced, notably for Barton Transport Ltd with four, plus two on Lion LT7; Christy of Bolton and East Yorkshire Motor Services Ltd, each of whom took three TS7. Other examples were largely on AEC Regal chassis, such as vehicles for Batten of East Ham, and Hadwin of Ulverston. A broadly similar style with full-width canopy and extra bay at the rear was built on a six-wheeled AEC Renown chassis for Bracewells (Colne) Ltd, and one on a Regal for Eastern Belle had five bays and a roof-mounted luggage locker neatly incorporated into the outline.

At that stage, more operators continued to favour straight or stepped-waist styles, though Duple's versions of the latter in this period usually had only a slight increase in level towards the rear, sometimes with a downward curving line on the rear portion. Such bodies were to be found on a wide variety of chassis, from AEC Regal and Leyland Tiger, down to smaller forward-control models such as the Albion Victor. Among major users favouring straight-waisted bodies at that stage were Red & White on the above-mentioned Albion Valiant coaches and Lincolnshire Road Car Co Ltd, the latter taking three Tigers. Although some chassis makes were fading from the scene, Duple was still building on some rare makes, the 1936 contingent including a Halley Conquerer for W. & R. Dunlop, of Greenock; Duple had provided a 36-seat coach body for a previous example in 1934 and this appears to have been a repeat order, though thought to be the last example of the model.

The new Dennis Lancet II, with taller but slimmer radiator than its predecessor and its four-cylinder engine housed in an unusually short bonnet, was offered with a stepped-waist front- or centre-entrance Duple body at an attractive price of £1,395 complete by Coaches & Components Ltd, originally set

The curved-waist body went into production soon after the 1935 Show. East Yorkshire Motor Services Ltd was among early users with a batch of three Leyland Tiger TS7 28-seat coaches with Duple body numbers 6787-9. The vehicle shown, EYMS No. 291 (BKH 472) entered service in May 1936 and was caught by Geoff Atkins's camera in Nottingham two months later. This choice of side moulding layout was to prove the more popular over the next few years though not standard for this body design.

Most of the 1936-season AEC coaches with Duple curved-waist bodies were on Regal chassis and generally followed the Adnams body style quite closely, but Bracewell's of Colne decided to follow up the eye-catching appeal of its Q by this 39-seat AEC Renown six-wheeler early in 1936 – it was one of only two of this model to enter service in Britain that year. It had a petrol-engined long-wheelbase 664-type chassis, number 664260, and it is noteworthy that it had the early semi-floating type of rear axles – 664T trolleybuses had switched to the fully-floating type the previous year.

A major part of Duple's output continued to be built to more conservative styles. This Leyland Tiger TS7 for Western Welsh dating from March 1936 was one of six built in the straight-waist sloping pillar idiom quite widely used for the previous two years and still being chosen by many customers. The shaping of the cab door window and that at the front of the passenger saloon was quite widely favoured for a time, though not usually associated with Duple. The placing of so big an emergency door opposite the front entrance door cannot have helped structural integrity. These vehicles were rebodied as buses by Burlingham in 1946, surviving in that form to 1957-8.

A means of smoothing out the flow of work in the Hendon factory over the year to compensate for the seasonal nature of coach bodybuilding was involvement in major Government contracts for van bodywork. Up to the mid-1930s, the mass-production of bodywork for cars had not spread into the van sector, and the General Post Office preferred to have its vans built to its own specification, becoming rather dated, not only in body outline but even persuading Morris to continue building the Minor chassis for GPO orders despite its replacement for general sale by the Eight model from 1935. There was strong competition for this work but Duple had secured enough to justify opening a special department to deal with it, as seen here. Most of the vans under construction in this view would emerge painted red largely for use in collecting mail from pillar boxes, but in the adjoining workshop some of the dark green GPO Telephone Department vans can be seen, these having glass panels above the windscreen to aid viewing of telephone poles and wires – the DXK and DYP registration letters visible date the view as taken in the early summer of 1937.

The economy of space given by the Dennis Lancet II's short bonnet is conveyed in this view of a Duple-bodied example dating from early 1936. Generally similar vehicles were being offered by Coaches & Components Ltd at an inclusive price of £1,395.

The standard bus for the Bedford WTB was built in left-hand drive export form, this example being one of eighteen built in 1936 for the Anglo-Iranian Oil Co Ltd – 32 further similar bodies were built in 1939 on the restyled 'bull-nose' version of the WTB.

up as a Gilford subsidiary but by then selling new Dennis and Bedford coaches with Duple bodywork. Dealer contracts were an increasingly important part of the new coach market, such providing for a bulk quantity of chassis and bodywork even though finishing instructions on matters such as paintwork and choice of internal trim were to customer choice, apart from a limited number of vehicles taken into dealer stock.

The body range built for the Bedford WTB was more standardised, Bedford publicity showing the Duple bus, rear-entrance coach and the K.D. coach as production models, although it is noteworthy that Grose, Thurgood, Waveney, Watson and Willmott were also quoted in small print as offering bodywork for the model in a July 1936 advert. By then Duple was regularly providing more passenger bodywork for home-market WTB chassis than all other coachbuilders put together. Hence it was well in front of any other bodybuilder in providing for this coach size range, in which it still built small numbers of bodies on other makes of chassis.

Duple took a share of the Bedford export business, too, for although many were shipped as chassis, there were some notable export orders such as one for eighteen WTB buses for the Anglo-Iranian Oil Co Ltd in 1936 which also included the provision of a passenger-carrying trailer.

As the coach output tailed off in the summer of 1936, Duple was doubtless quite happy to be involved in the design and construction of a mobile post office for the GPO. It was designed to provide full postal, telephone and telegraph services for use at outdoor events such as agricultural shows,

horse race meetings and the like. It was an articulated vehicle, using a Morris-Commercial Leader tractive unit and Brockhouse semi-trailer, on which Duple built the bodywork; this incorporated Post Office counters, mail boxes and telephones, the exterior being provided with a collapsible awning. The vehicle was given the registration number GPO 1, and indeed the whole GPO series, which normally would have been issued by West Sussex, was reserved for Post Office use.

The first Vista

In November 1936, the Scottish Show was again the venue for new productions. For Duple, the most important was the introduction of a new coach body design for the Bedford WTB – the choice of the Vista name was both logical for a coach with large windows and apt in the use of the initial letter V for a product based on a chassis made by Vauxhall Motors. The K.D. body had been quite popular but the concept of a largely folding roof was going out of favour and the sharply stepped waist design was no longer looking quite as up-to-the-minute as it had in 1935.

The Vista introduced the concept of curved waist and roof line and alternate slim polished pillars to the Bedford coach range, and had a sliding roof as standard. The design was not quite so generous in the use of curves, particularly at the front and rear, as the 1935 Adnams Show Tiger design but the overall effect was very stylish. The standard seating capacity was again 25; on this original version there was no attempt to provide a seat to the nearside of the driver, so the glazed panel

Dodge's answer to the Bedford WT series had an even more snub-nosed look. This RBF demonstrator with coach body of similar stepped-waist style to the K.D. but with sliding roof was produced in time for the November 1936 Scottish Show.

Another familiar sight of those days, and indeed well into the post-war era, was the GPO Telephone van, intended to deal with repairs to overhead wires, based on the Morris-Commercial 30cwt chassis. Among those Duple bodied was this one of 1937.

'Bedford Vista' became part of the language of the coach industry soon after the first production examples began to appear. This design inherited a fairly broad windscreen from the K.D., but the sides had the curved waist first seen on some of Duple's larger models the previous year and steadily becoming more popular. Shamrock & Rambler of Bournemouth received nine (body numbers 8919-27) in May 1937, the orange and cream paintwork gleaming on DEL 105, parked outside the operators premises at 77 Holdenhurst Road, Bournemouth. This operator still favoured a folding roof, though a sliding roof was standard, and had a policy of naming its coaches, this being 'Marcia'.

just ahead of the entrance door was quite slim. The Vista had strong appeal from the beginning, and by early 1937 was in production for numerous operators, the SMT group being among the first large users – the parent company's fleet of 30 had 20 or 14 well-spaced seats and were used for touring, remaining on this duty until the post-war period. There were also batches for Alexander and Western SMT.

Also at that Show, on AEC's stand, was a full-fronted curved-waist coach on a Regal chassis – AEC had been pursuing full-fronted versions of its front-engined models, maybe as a reaction to the failure of the Q in sales terms. The resulting coach was a very neat and stylish design, benefiting, in the author's view, by the retention of the distinctive AEC radiator in the frontal design, though perhaps a little surprisingly the four-bay layout of the 1935 design for Adnams gave way to a 'four-and-a-half' bay style. It was given the name 'Airline' in Duple advertisements at the time, though this seems not to have been continued. It was painted pale blue in a metallic finish – a new development at the time, possibly inspired by Vauxhall's introduction of such a finish for its cars – the liaison between the two firms was firmly rooted by then. It was sold to Leamington Touring Services of Blackpool. A few generally few similar bodies were built for various independent operators over the next year or so, some on Leyland Tiger chassis, but the full-width cab idea did not catch on widely at that date, largely on grounds of the

practicality of the half-cab in terms of easy access to the engine.

However, there was one small but prominent fleet which did adopt the full-fronted curved-waist Duple body for much of its needs, on Leyland Cheetah chassis, in the late 1930s, this being P. Hearn, of Grays Inn Road, London W.C.1, whose sightseeing coaches were to remain a familiar sight in London into the post-war period. The later ones had most of the non-opening roof area glazed to allow sightseeing of London's famous buildings and, to varying degrees, this was quite a frequent option on later pre-war Duple coaches. The Cheetah was a new model introduced in 1935, having a slim radiator similar to that of contemporary Lion models but was in fact based on components, including a 4.7-litre six-cylinder engine, from the lightweight Cub range. The Cub itself, in both normal- and forward-control forms, continued to figure in Duple's output in small numbers, the latter versions having scaled-down examples of contemporary full-sized coach bodies. A noteworthy export order completed later in 1937 was for six Cub bonneted coaches for use in Africa, three going to Cape Town. The bodies were not unlike the early Vista, but constructed to suit the local climate.

By 1937, there was wider though still far from universal acceptance of the curved-waist body, mainly with half-cab on forward-control chassis; generally the basic structure was of the 4½-bay style, though there were still plenty of

This full-fronted version of a curved-waist body was exhibited at the November 1936 Scottish Show; using the name 'Airline' it was for Leamington Touring Services of Blackpool, and was registered FV 8194. It was on a petrol-engined AEC Regal chassis, the body neatly surrounding the standard radiator – ventilating louvres were added above the front nearside mudguard. In general, operators found the half-cab more practical. More significant in terms of later designs was the switch to a 'four-and-a-half' bay layout instead of the previous four-bay style, not quite so clean-looking but perhaps more practical in terms of the full-drop opening windows used.

variations on the basic theme. That was the Coronation year of King George VI and Queen Elizabeth, (the Queen Mother), and the latest additions to quite a few fleets were christened 'Coronation coaches'. Among the best-known were those for SMT – eight Leyland Tiger TS7 with curved-waist Duple 30-seat bodies, for use on the two-day Edinburgh-London service, which was almost in the nature of a mini-tour, with overnight stop en route. They had full-canopy cabs and roof-mounted luggage carrier as well as a rear locker. These vehicles were oil-engined, the SMT group having adopted such power units as standard for heavy-duty models, even coaches, several years before most English operators.

Even so, the stepped-waist coach continued to have its adherents in 1937, Red & White continuing thus as well as the Coaches & Components standard offering on the Dennis Lancet II, though in both cases with a curving roof line. A new Duple user was the Bristol Tramways & Carriage Co Ltd, which sent six of its own-make JO6A chassis with AEC 7.7-litre oil engines and eight JO5G with Gardner 5LW to receive rear-entrance straight-waisted coach bodies that summer. Bristol was part of the Tilling group and at that time built most of its body requirements in its own workshops, as well as having Eastern Coach Works as an associated company, responsible for bodying most Bristol chassis for other related concerns, so the choice of Duple was somewhat of a surprise, though not as great as that of the AEC Regal chassis for a further eighteen coaches for BTCC with similar Duple bodies in 1938.

Red & White took further Albion Valkyrie buses in 1937, with similar rear-entrance bodywork to the previous batch, though seating 36, but a prototype centre-entrance body was

Duple was still building on a wide variety of chassis; this example of the then latest curved waist style of body is seen early in 1937 on a TSM for Sydney Smith Ltd, one of several firms which used the fleetname Black & White, this one based at Leyton, hence the Essex registration EPU 120. The chassis appears to have been of the six-cylinder type, then being phased out.

built for this fleet on an ex-Alexander 1929 Albion Viking Six chassis, this setting the pattern for later production batches on Valkyrie chassis in 1938-9.

Centre-entrance layout was also favoured for twelve Leyland Tiger six-wheel 43-seat single-deckers supplied to the City Coach Co Ltd of Brentwood, Essex early in 1937. Later that year another dozen Tiger six-wheel buses of largely similar appearance, but with seats for 41 and 7ft 10½in wide, were supplied to the C.I.T.A. fleet in Mendoza, Argentina. These were metal-framed, using what was described as W.A.S. steel framing and, in effect, a repeat order following on from the four-wheeled example of 1934.

The Hendonian

A more significant development of straight-waisted bodywork concerned the Bedford WTB. In 1936-7,

Widely publicised were the Scottish Motor Traction fleet of eight 'Coronation coaches' on Leyland Tiger TS7 chassis of April 1937. The bodies (8756-63) used the 4½-bay curved waist body in a form with full-width canopy and roof luggage carrier. Part of the relief colour was crimson, adding to the basic blue and cream then standard for SMT to give a tasteful version of patriotic colours appropriate to the high-class image of this fleet.

The Bristol Tramways & Carriage Co Ltd generally had rather conservative tastes in the mid-1930s and the fourteen Duple coach bodies (8825-38) built on Bristol J-type chassis in 1937 were of straight-waisted outline with rear entrance. This is thought to be one of the six JO6A models with AEC 7.7-litre engines, believed to be early examples of the direct-injection type. At that date BTCC used a dark blue and white livery.

Duple built to operator specification when requested, and a batch of AEC Regal 35-seat buses for Trent Motor Traction Ltd of early 1937 was shared with Willowbrook Ltd, a concern then having no connection with Duple, each concern building ten bodies to outwardly identical design. Originally there had been a darker red waistband curving down towards the rear but this was removed at the first overhaul. No 703 (RC 4604) is seen in Nottingham in August 1953 – it was withdrawn in 1955.

The City Coach Co Ltd of Brentwood, Essex, was in effect a continuation of the business of the City Motor Omnibus Co Ltd whose London-area activities and fleet, of which the last new buses were three 1933 Leyland Titanic six-wheel double-deckers, were taken over by London Transport in 1934. City retained a Wood Green-Southend service and chose the Leyland Tiger in six-wheeled form for a total of 36 single-deckers new in 1935-37, noteworthy in seating 43 passengers, the highest capacity among front-engined single-deckers in Britain of that era. The earlier ones had been bodied by Beadle but the last twelve, on TS7D chassis were bodied by Duple (Nos 8443-54) to similar style early in 1937, the vehicle shown, LT33, registered on 1st May of that year.

The Elliott Bros Royal Blue business had been sold to Tilling in 1935 and the express services were taken over by that group's Southern National and Western National companies. The body contracts for a new fleet of Bristol rear-entrance coaches of that year had gone to Eastern Counties, Beadle and Weymann, though there was an echo of an established Duple feature in the tapering pillars. For 1937, Duple got the contract for eight 31-seat bodies on AEC Regal chassis for the Southern National-owned part of the fleet, delivered in July. They were built to a similar style to the 1935 Royal Blue vehicles except for the choice of front entrance – later in 1937, Mumford of Plymouth built eight similar bodies for Western National's section. This particular vehicle, No. 1062 (ETA 996), caught fire at Tidworth in 1939 and was rebodied, as illustrated in Chapter Four.

There wasn't much doubt where CITA of Mendoza got the inspiration for its repeat order for twelve Leyland-Duple single-deckers built towards the end of 1937, choosing not only the Tiger six-wheeled chassis, then having moved on to the TS8D type, but also the centre-entrance layout as favoured by City – by coincidence, even the operating name was remarkably similar. However, metal-framed construction was again specified and the seating capacity was reduced to 41 to meet Argentine regulations.

Bournemouth Corporation had indicated a need for a body style for the Bedford WTB more functional than the Vista but more stylish than Duple's standard bus, taking an initial delivery in 1937. It led Duple to the introduction of the Hendonian style for more general sale. Ironically, Bournemouth decided to give the body order for further almost identical vehicles to Burlingham, including EEL 46 of the early 1938 batch seen here.

A general trend in regard to Duple coaches at the time of the 1937 Show was a general tidying-up of details, eliminating the rather fussy repeated small decorations of the valance strip between the front and rear wheels that had been in favour for the previous two or three years, for example.

However, the talk of the Show seems to have been the Tilling-Stevens Successor, a remarkable vehicle to be produced by what by then was a small-scale manufacturer which had concentrated on chassis of orthodox, even rather staid, design for the previous decade. It was a six-wheeled single-decker with amidships-mounted underfloor engine, Maybach seven-speed gearbox and independent suspension for the rear bogie. At that date, no British maker had put an underfloor-engined model into production, though Leyland, in conjunction with London Transport, had produced a prototype vehicle for what became the TF class. The Successor's engine was a flat eight-cylinder 7.45-litre diesel of Tilling-Stevens's own design, with a bank of four horizontal cylinders on each side of the crankcase (the firm never having produced anything but petrol engines, of simple design, previously).

For this remarkable model, Duple produced a stylish curved-waist full-fronted coach body with very spacious seating for 32 passengers, though a bus design for this chassis evidently drawn up in Duple's design office squeezed in 47 seats by dint of providing a very narrow entrance door at the extreme front. Unfortunately, though it looked very impressive, the Successor is thought never to have run under its own power. The engine is said to have had a wooden mock-up crankcase, and nothing more was heard of the project.

The Duple coach body on the Show example did survive, however, and eventually turned up on one of the LGOC's own-make CC-type six-wheeled chassis dating from 1930 which had run with double-deck body as LT1000, latterly being fitted with an AEC petrol engine and other units. It had been sold by London Transport in 1939; extensive modifications were needed to allow the body from the

relatively few of the Duple bus body or the rear-entrance coach on this chassis were built, this latter layout tending to go out of favour for small coaches by that date. During 1937, Bournemouth Corporation took some Duple-bodied WTB front-entrance buses to a style having a straight-waisted coach-like exterior and better-quality finish. It seems to have been these that led to the introduction of the Hendonian body for this chassis at the 1937 Commercial Motor Show, the first to be held at Earls Court, London. This was a straight-waisted front-entrance coach with 26-seat capacity, priced at £788 complete, a useful saving on the slightly revised 25-seat curved-waist design, now called Vista II, which cost £833. The Hendonian tended to be particularly favoured by country bus operators, and in many areas outnumbered the Vista models placed in service in 1938-9.

The remarkable Tilling-Stevens Successor six-wheeler with underfloor eight-cylinder engine and stylish Duple body (No. 3758 of Series 2*) was the talk of the November 1937 Earls Court Show. Thought never to have run under its own power, the body was saved and, after the 1939-45 war, was fitted to one of the almost equally rare LGOC own-build CC-type front engined six-wheeled chassis dating from 1930 for operation by White Heather Transport Ltd, Southsea. The body had to be modified extensively to suit the change of chassis, these views showing how the mudguards were repositioned to suit the longer wheelbase.

* Duple altered its body numbering system for the first of several times in mid-1937 when the first series ended at 9000. The second series then began at 1000, though the first PSV was 2250, this series continuing to 9999 in 1941.

This three-quarter front view of the 1937 Show body as running on the LGOC CC chassis for White Heather reveals the registration number GF 7254, the only obvious external clue to the source of the chassis, others of the GF 72xx series having been various AEC buses in the LGOC or related fleets. The radiator grille was from the Tilling-Stevens. An odd feature of the body is what can be described as the 'negative' vee angle of the windscreen, with the centre pillar set back slightly from the position of the corner pillars. The side pillar design was also unlike that of any other Duple coaches. The picture was taken at the time of the Coronation in 1953, an 'ER' plaque being displayed.

A more significant newcomer in production term at the time of the 1937 Show was the Vista II version of curved-waist body for the Bedford WTB, with 25-seat capacity as standard. The main difference was the slight setting back of the entrance position, the first side windows thus being broader than on the original Vista, apt to be called Vista I in retrospect.

A new Dodge coach chassis, type SBF, with 3.57-litre six-cylinder side-valve engine, appeared at the 1937 Show, gaining a sizeable share of the market. It had a wheelbase 10-in longer than the WTB and Duple's 26-seat body for it had the entrance set back from the front axle to an extent greater than the Vista II and pointing the way to the layout later adopted for the Bedford OB.

Successor to be fitted to a chassis with longer wheelbase and reduced front overhang but it entered service with White Heather Coaches of Southsea after the 1939-45 war.

Several chassis manufacturers again had vehicles with Duple bodies on their stands at the 1937 Show. Dodge introduced a new coach chassis, the SBF, and one was shown with a Duple 26-seat coach body akin to the Vista II (though the longer 14ft 9in wheelbase of the chassis resulted in a set-back door position much as was later adopted for the OB) – similar vehicles were built in modest numbers in 1938-9; a Duple bus version was also made but remained rare.

There were also examples of the Albion passenger range, including two Valkyrie coaches for the Red & White group. One was for Blue Belle, which acted as this group's outpost in London and had a 1½-deck coach body, in those days called an observation coach, a type which had been in favour among

a few coach fleets in the early 1930s and quite rare by 1937. For the first time Daimler exhibited a Duple-bodied coach, this being a COG5/40 model with curved-waist body for United Services of Upton, West Yorkshire – this complete vehicle was priced at £2,170, fairly typical of a full-sized 32-seat coach on heavy-duty oil-engined chassis at that date.

By 1938, the curved-waist coach was more firmly established for full-sized chassis although there were still a number of operators, quite often large concerns, which chose plainer styles. The output on Bedford WTB chassis was now split fairly evenly between the Vista II and Hendonian styles, accounting between them for the majority of the output for smaller independent operators. The Western and Southern National Omnibus Companies took delivery of 55 Duple coaches that spring, split between Bedford Vista and full-sized curved-waist half-

The Western and Southern National Omnibus Companies became major Duple customers in the late 1930s, largely for coaches used for local touring work in cream and green livery, as seen here, as well as some additions to the Royal Blue express-service fleet. Lined up in this scene at Truro in August 1950 are Western National 3528 (TR 9921), a Leyland Tiger TS1 chassis dating from 1931 (originally owned by Tourist of Southampton) rebodied by Duple in 1939, and 418 (ETT 973), a Bedford WTB with Duple Vista II body of 1938.

In July 1937, a 1929 Albion Viking Six PMB28, purchased as a used vehicle by Red & White and fitted with a Gardner 5LW engine, emerged from Duple's works to act as the prototype for a new generation of bus for that operator and its associates. The new Duple 37-seat centre-entrance body was numbered 2282 in series 2. Similar bodies were built for the group on new Albion and existing AEC and Leyland chassis from 1938 until 1941. Originally, SO 3551 had been operated by Scottish General (Northern) Omnibus Co., passing to W. Alexander & Sons Ltd where it had run latterly as E8. By 1946, it was sold by R&W to Scarlet Band Motor Services of West Cornforth, Co Durham.

canopy bodies, the latter rebodying early AEC Regal and Leyland Tiger chassis. Northern General Transport became a customer, ordering eleven bodies rather like the SMT Coronation batch, on Regal and Tiger chassis. The Red & White group's order that year amounted to 70 vehicles, including some double-deckers on Albion Venturer chassis (some SPM81 and others on the new CX19) which marked a modest revival of Duple's involvement in the manufacture of such bodies, and three observation coaches on Valkyrie CX13 for Blue Belle.

Barton Transport continued to take its characteristic 39-seat bus body on Leyland Lion chassis, ten being supplied in 1938, and a stylish 39-seat bus of similar outline was built as a demonstrator for Albion Motors Ltd on its Valkyrie CX9 chassis with four-cylinder engine, the high seating capacity made possible by its similarly short bonnet.

The proportion of curved-waist bodies on full-sized chassis was increasing by 1938, tending to become the generally-accepted choice on models such as the AEC Regal and Leyland Tiger, both new and rebodied – the latter were becoming quite significant in numbers around that time, as bodywork of pre-1932 or so patterns was becoming hopelessly obsolete for a self-respecting coach concern, yet the chassis were still good. The curved-waist style was also now more usual for models such as the Dennis Lancet II.

A new office block replacing the old villa came into use in the Spring of 1938, attention being given to customer reception with

display facilities to aid the choice of seats and moquette. This was an important step in the creation of the long facade so characteristic of the Hendon works in its later years.

The idea of operating something eye-catching has always appealed to some operators, and among Duple customers, Sutton's Crossley Coaches of Clacton and C. G. Lewis of Greenwich were in this category. In 1938, both took delivery of Leyland Tiger TS8 models with what were described as a new type of observation coach. Yet they were not of the true 1½-deck type normally associated with the name and of which Blue Belle was taking three more on Albion Valkyrie CX13 chassis at about the same time. The Lewis and Sutton vehicles had a gently ramped floor and seating for 32 passengers, little if any more raised at the rear than was standard practice by that time. The illusion of a stepped build was created by the shaping of the side windows and roof line, the latter not unlike that of a coach with roof luggage carrier. The side windows mostly followed normal contemporary fashion with sloping pillars and curved waist and cantrail lines but those towards the rear were raised to follow the roof line, the leading ones overlapping the rearmost lower-level windows. The effect was certainly striking, though it lost the purity of line that was becoming expected of Duple bodywork.

By August 1938, it was possible to report that the 1937-8 season had beaten all records, output exceeding that of 1936-7, itself a record and, apart from the sales success, reflecting the additional capacity made possible by the

By spring 1938 the curved-waist body was also being built on Dennis Lancet II chassis, though in this case with full-width canopy and 'plain' pillars. Most independents chose the 'Big Four' 6.8-litre four-cylinder petrol engine as on CUP 698 for Patterson & Bissett of Blaydon on Tyne, who jointly operated a Newcastle-Blackpool express service under the Primrose fleetname with Graham & Waddington, also of Blaydon. It seated 32.

Trent Motor Traction had chosen Duple's contemporary stepped-waist curved-roof style for six coaches on SOS ON chassis in 1935 and returned to it for six more, but on Daimler COG5/40 chassis, in 1938, No. 641 being seen here. Trent was unusual among BET-managed companies in choosing Daimler chassis for a large proportion of its new vehicles in the 1938-40 period. In 1942, all its COG5/40 fleet were rebodied as double-deckers, but these coach bodies were stored and fitted to new AEC Regal chassis in 1946.

The variety of Duple's output continued in 1938 – indeed as judged from 60 years on, it seems staggering. These four designs all on Leyland Tiger TS8 chassis represent only part of the range of ideas being produced. The Northern General Transport Co Ltd of Gateshead and its subsidiary Wakefield's Motors Ltd took six 30-seat bodies (Nos. 4910-5, Series 2) broadly similar to the batch delivered to SMT in 1937 except for having hinged entrance doors, favoured in these fleets for touring coaches – there were also two more similar bodies for NGT, on AEC Regal, these being petrol-engined. The first of the four for Wakefield's is seen, still looking very smart, at Scarborough in July 1953 – it was withdrawn two years later.

Yorkshire (Woollen District) Transport Co Ltd was, like Trent and NGT, under BET management but chose a quite different style to either for three oil-engined TS8 30-seat coaches for express duty. These were straight-waisted, with upright pillars, the basic structure of the body being not unlike the Ribble design, though with full-width canopy and roof luggage carrier having side access steps. Number 414 (HD 6613) is seen in Nottingham in May 1938.

Samuel Ledgard of Armley, Leeds, was a substantial independent operator and B & B Tours of Bradford had become a subsidiary of that concern. Earlier, the Ribble style of body had been adopted but in July 1938 four oil-engined TS8 coaches with Duple bodies 5289-92 of Series 2 were delivered. They were to the curved-waist half-canopy style but using vertical pillars, perhaps because of the porch-type entrance chosen. The last of the four, CKW 267 for the B & B fleet, is seen when ready for delivery.

Henry Coaches (H. C. Porter), a small excursions and tours business in Tottenham, London N15, took delivery of this TS8 coach, HMX 175, in the spring of 1938. The straight-waisted body design, a little conservative by that date among independent operators, used the taper-pillar idea much favoured about four years earlier. The author recalls riding in it about ten years later when it was one of the coaches hired by London Transport to overcome its shortage of serviceable buses, still in almost immaculate condition in grey/blue livery, with its petrol engine scarcely audible at stops and very quiet-running on the move.

None of the body styles shown on the previous page were considered sufficiently exotic by two of Duple's regular though small-scale customers, Sutton of Clacton and C. G. Lewis of Greenwich. Both chose this design for Leyland Tiger TS8 models in 1938, giving an illusion of being of observation coach style even though the seating layout was little if any different from that in most more typical Duple products of the day. As an exposition of the art of the bodybuilder they are remarkable, yet to most fleets, even in those uninhibited days, they would have been regarded as 'over the top'. Mr Lewis's EXH 14 is seen here.

Another approach was that taken by 'Patsy' Hearn, of Grays Inn Road, London WC1, who standardised on the Leyland Cheetah with full-fronted bodywork for his fleet of coaches mainly used for London sightseeing tours. Here the folding roof was still used, with most of the fixed roof panels glazed so as to give as unobstructed an upward view as possible. The chassis were petrol-engined, this model using the 4.7-litre six-cylinder unit of the Cub range, and with a modest weight, 5 tons 1 cwt in this case, and only 24 seats in a spacious two-and-one layout, performance was lively enough as well as very refined. This example dated from 1938 – several were still to be seen around London well into the post-war era.

Even when meeting the more conservative tastes of some operators, Duple's designers seemed to have a knack of imparting an air of 'style', as with the batch of eighteen rear-entrance 32-seat coach bodies (4939-56, Series 2) built for the Bristol Tramways & Carriage Co Ltd in February-May 1938. The element of surprise here was the choice of chassis, the AEC Regal, for Bristol was building its own chassis for most Tilling-controlled operators as well as its own fleet.

new buildings completed on the additional land acquired in 1935 – further construction was being contemplated. Orders were coming in earlier than usual for 1939 delivery, which was welcomed as an aid to smooth production. Examples of the new-style Bedford WTB with revised '28hp' engine and what later became known as the bull-nose radiator grille, rounded in plan and with horizontal grille bars, that had been announced the previous month were already at Hendon and for them the Vista III name was introduced, though the actual body itself seems not to have altered externally from the previous year's Vista II. However, it had been found possible to add a seat for one passenger opposite the driver in both Vista and Hendonian bodies, bringing the maximum seating capacity up to 26 although the extra seat was less than ideal in its position.

Possibly the most interesting vehicle then being completed was a centre-entrance 40-seat coach built for the City Coach Co Ltd on a Leyland Gnu twin-steering chassis, a model introduced at the 1937 Show, in that case with an Alexander front-entrance body. The City vehicle was of curvaceous style, but with vertical pillars. The original Gnu TEP1 chassis had the radiator offset to the nearside of the engine which meant that a full front with a wide decorative grille was needed to disguise the asymmetrical appearance, and something reminiscent of that on a contemporary radio set was used.

The combination of curved waist and vertical pillars was also found on some Tiger TS8 coaches for Ledgard of Leeds and an associated fleet – here there was indirect Ribble influence, this operator having taken English Electric bodies

The straight-waisted Hendonian body style for the Bedford WTB proved very popular in 1938-9, especially with independent operators who ran country bus routes as well as needing a vehicle suitable for hire or excursion work. The revised WTB chassis with 'bull-nose' radiator was introduced only a few months after the first Hendonians appeared so a high proportion of those built were as seen in this example used in an advertisement by W. S. Yeates & Co of Loughborough, already established as dealers though later to be competitors to Duple as bodybuilders, post-war.

The Vista body became Vista III when the face-lifted WTB chassis appeared, although in itself altering little if at all from the Vista II. Southern National placed eighteen in service in 1939, including 479 (DDV 45) seen here. With the closely-associated Western National fleet of ten, they were to be a familiar sight in the south-west of England until the early 1950s, 479 being among the first to go, in 1952, re-entering service with two successive independent operators. The windscreen style of the pre-war Vista bodies was significantly wider than the post-war version later to become so familiar on the OB chassis. SNOC and WNOC specified the non-standard double destination box layout shown instead of the usual side-by-side fleetname and destination panels and the glazing of the roof quarter panels was an option.

to broadly Ribble style on a previous batch of Tigers, though the Ledgard Duple bodies were not to the Ribble pattern and it seems that the key design factor may have been a desire to use a porch-style entrance (not compatible with the sloping-pillar structure), as favoured by several major Yorkshire company operators for their buses, the Ledgard vehicles being of dual-purpose character.

An improved bus body for the WTB had been evolved, more utilitarian than the Bournemouth version but more stylish than that offered for early models, with a smooth profile. Western Welsh

Omnibus Co Ltd, a major BET-managed operator took twelve arranged to seat 20 to allow one-man operation (although the normal capacity was 26) in the late summer of 1938. By 1939, it had been decided to call this style the Luton I bus body, though the name seemed to be forgotten almost as soon as it appeared; further examples were built for the Bristol Tramways & Carriage Co.

The Leyland Gnu twin-steering coach chassis as originally introduced in TEP1 form with offset radiator set something of a challenge to bodybuilders but Duple overcame the problem with this elaborate grille on the example built for City Coaches Ltd in August 1938, in whose fleet it was numbered G1. It had body number 5301 in Series 2, seating 40 in rather more spacious style than the 43-seat Tiger six-wheelers.

A noteworthy export order of which shipment began in September 1938 was for 38 two-compartment 31-seat buses on special Albion straight-framed chassis with Gardner 4LW engines for Uganda Transport Co Ltd, a new subsidiary of Overseas Motor Transport Ltd. for operation around Lake Victoria. Another familiar African-based customer taking a repeat order that month was J. N. Zarpas & Co, of Lagos, Nigeria, with four Daimler COG5 with single-deck bus bodies having partly transverse and partly longitudinal seating for 46 passengers.

An example of the Vista III, for David MacBrayne Ltd, was at the Scottish Show of November 1938, which was to prove the last major commercial vehicle exhibition in Britain until 1948. Also at that Show was an AEC Regal for James Sutherland (Peterhead) Ltd, to basically standard curved-waist style but with the hinged panel ahead of the bulkhead extended forward so as almost to give an illusion of a full-fronted body. This line of thought clearly preoccupied Duple designers at the time, a similar effect was evident on the special 'observation' Tigers for the Lewis and Sutton fleets. There were also Duple-bodied exhibits on Leyland and Dodge chassis.

The pattern of output in the earlier part of 1939 was much as before. Despite the welcome trend towards earlier ordering that had been evident the previous autumn, the factory was still working virtually flat-out a fortnight after Whitsun when visited by a *Coaching Journal* representative – he described the forecourt as being a blaze of colour as coaches of all sizes and designs were being made ready for delivery. It was anticipated that the works would be fully occupied up to 'the Bank Holiday', which in those days would have meant the beginning of August with an average daily output of five completed vehicles. It was considered 'worthy of note that, despite the international situation, Duple can place on record a greater output of coaches than a year ago'. By then, there had been a series of crises involving Nazi Germany and various surrounding countries from the spring of 1938, and there was a general air of unease, even though there continued to be general hope that the threat of war would again recede. In those days, factories worked a 5½-day week, so this implied delivery of fully 25 vehicles per week, even allowing for Saturday morning being largely a preparation and tidying-up time.

The general pattern of deliveries from around the beginning of 1939 was much as in the previous year, with large numbers of Bedford WTB with Hendonian and Vista bodies, plus the

Albion chose Duple to build this 39-seat bus body on a demonstration example of its new Valkyrie CX9 chassis in the summer of 1938. This model had a 6-litre Albion four-cylinder engine, its dimensions permitting a short bonnet and hence space for this seating capacity, although in fact it was also possible on the CX11 which had the five-cylinder Gardner 5LW as standard.

J. N. Zarpas & Co, of Lagos, returned with a further order delivered in September 1938, this time on Daimler COG5 chassis. For warm climates, Daimler continued to build the COG5 model in this form, with sloping radiator and longer bonnet, evidently to ensure adequate cooling, whereas home market examples from about 1936 were normally of the COG5/40 type with shorter bonnet.

Another interpretation of a coach intended largely for use in London, again on Leyland Cheetah chassis, was this vehicle for Orange Luxury dating from the summer of 1938, registered EYU 740. There was no external cab door, the driver gaining entry from the kerbside passenger door via an aperture in the offside of the bulkhead. This eliminated the hazardous business of opening an offside door in a busy street and may have been inspired by London Transport's prototype TF and CR types using a similar idea. The falling roof line superimposed on the by then usual curved-waist style had a faint echo of the early Duple AEC Q coaches but may have been intended to give extra internal headroom related to the method of cab entry.

The idea of extending the hinged 'trim' panel alongside the bonnet to give more of the illusion of a full-fronted coach recurred in several Duple coach designs in 1938. Minor service work could still be done from the front without disturbing it, though to swing back on its hinges about 4ft of space would be needed and the possibilities of minor damage making it not fit properly etc are obvious – the idea soon seems to have been dropped. Even so, a very elegant coach could result, as with this demonstrator of late that year on a petrol-engined Regal chassis owned by AEC. Another version of the same photograph was retouched by AEC to show the fleetname and livery of James Sutherland of Peterhead, publicity indicating that it was to be on the AEC stand at the Scottish Show of November 1938. In fact that vehicle, registered as AAV 785, with 32-seat body 5625 of Series 2, though basically similar, had the then recently announced A173 oil engine, entering service the following March and passing to Alexander as A92 in 1950, remaining in service until 1955 – it was one of a pair.

usual spread of larger models mainly on AEC, Leyland and Dennis chassis, most of the latter with curved-waist bodies.

There were still the occasional 'one-off' designs, and a notable one was a full-fronted coach on Leyland Tiger TS8 delivered early in the year to W. J. Mathias of Moriston, Swansea. It had curved contours with quite a pronounced downward sweep from the centre entrance, with emergency door directly opposite. What was unusual at that date was the elimination of the outswept skirt and the reintroduction of a pronounced turn-under at the rear, together with what appears to have been curved glazing for the divided rear window – this latter was very rare indeed at that date and it seems possible that Perspex might have been used in place of glass. The wing outlines used convex curves, in line with the latest car fashion, in place of the concave sweeps then usual at the rear. It was very controversial, even at the time, but forms a remarkable example of what would nowadays be called Art Deco design. A similar concept, slightly toned down except at the front (where there was a most elaborate winged grille design) was built on a Maudslay Magna chassis (the name by then given to the SF40 design) for Neath & Cardiff Luxury Coaches Ltd,

In general, however, there was a trend to less fussy design, sometimes with an approach to the original Adnams-style side 'flash' which came close to the style

which became so familiar as the early post-war standard. Also pointing the way to later practice was a fresh trend in rear-end design for what could be counted as more standard coaches. Duple had tended to hang on to the concept of one rear window, basically rectangular though with well-rounded corners, and rather 'heavy'-looking corner pillars, apart from

The late 1930s were a time when it was possible to indulge 'farout' ideas in occasional vehicles built for sale in a way quite impossible since. This voluptuous confection, body number 6032 of Series 2, was built in April 1939 for Mathias of Swansea on a Leyland Tiger TS8. The full front retained the standard radiator but narrowed to reveal more of the wings than usual – the traditional sidelamp seems to strike an incongruous note.

One of the batch of nine Leyland Lion LT8 39-seat buses of early 1939 for Barton, the last derived from the design first built in 1935, seen at Chilwell in 1948. Although quite simple in outline, the fleetname executed in polished brightwork and the side flash gave a touch of coach-style image. Number 336 (EVO 32) was showing some effects of nearly a decade of hard use, the offside headlamp being one of the wartime style still very common at that date.

occasional attempts at something 'different' such as the Mathias coach. Some 1939 Duple coaches, notably for Sheffield United Tours Ltd and the Plymouth Co-operative Society Ltd, had a divided rear window having a more curved outline and slimmer corner pillars, giving an effect close to the post-war Vista etc.

Early in 1939, Barton Transport Ltd took delivery of four Duple-bodied Leyland Titan TD5 oil-engined models, the first new double-deckers to be added to that fleet since the 1920s. At that date, Trent, Midland General and Mansfield District, which were the other major company operators in the area around Nottingham, tended to favour the front-entrance layout for their double-deckers. This had gained a fair degree of favour for a time in various parts of the country in the 1930s, but Nottinghamshire probably had the strongest concentration of users. In addition, in November 1935, Barton had acquired a 1934 AEC Regent with the business of F. W. Campion & Son, and this too had a front-entrance body, to a rather stylish design, built by Willowbrook.

It seems likely to have been the latter that triggered the basic concept of the Barton TD5 batch, but the talents of

Duple's drawing-office staff were reflected in the design that emerged. The buses were of lowbridge layout – in other words having sunken gangways on the offside of the upper-deck, as a means of reducing overall height, so as to be able to pass under bridges too low to accept full-height double-deckers. The staircase was arranged to run transversely just behind the front bulkhead, the entrance doorway being set back slightly to suit. Detail features largely conformed to the coach-like styles of Barton's Duple-bodied single-deckers of the time. Seating was for a total of 53 passengers, which was the norm for a lowbridge double-decker at that date. They attracted widespread attention in the trade press to an extent far greater than a mere four vehicles might have been expected to produce. Duple also supplied nine further Lion LT8 buses with 39-seat straight-waisted bodywork to Barton specification in its final form, and two Tiger TS8 coaches at about the same time as the double-deckers.

The Red & White group intake from Duple included the prototype Venturer CX19 double-decker, on which a 56-seat highbridge body was built, being very similar in design to 1938 deliveries to associated companies in the Swansea area – these latter had been amalgamated later in that year to form United Welsh Services Ltd. Other deliveries, in 1939, were Valkyrie CX11 centre-entrance buses (of which there were main batches of ten and six for Red & White and United Welsh, plus other smaller numbers), and CX13 coaches.

A significant development was the placing of an order by the Birmingham & Midland Motor Omnibus Co Ltd, for 25 full-fronted centre-entrance 30-seat coach bodies. They were on chassis made by BMMO to the specification of L. G. Wyndham Shire, that company's Chief Engineer. At that date its own-make vehicles were still known as SOS, the initials being displayed on the chromium-plated radiator grille attached to the front panel – the meaning of these letters has been a matter for debate since those days but a plausible version is 'Shire's Own Specification' – significantly it began to be replaced by 'BMMO' not long after Shire retired in 1940. The model designation was ONC, which was the coach version of the ON type introduced in 1934, though the directly equivalent bus version being built in 1939 was

Four double-deckers on Leyland Titan TD5 chassis were bodied for Barton in 1939, becoming well-known to an extent far greater than their modest numbers would suggest, though others were built later to very similar style. They were among the first double-deckers to be given coach-style external trim but the basic design had a touch of styling flair. They were of lowbridge front-entrance layout and seated 53. They were also noteworthy for having oil engines, the first in this fleet since a series of pioneer experimental installations had ceased in 1932. Number 348 (EVO 712) is seen in Nottingham in May 1948, still looking very 'modern', an effect admittedly heightened by the wartime Barton buses standing nearby, a 1942 AEC having a Northern Coachbuilders body and a 1943 Guy one by Northern Counties.

Production versions of Red & White's centre-entrance bus body began to be delivered in 1939. Number 404 (CWO 404), was one of a batch of ten 37-seat examples on Albion Valkyrie CX11 chassis – the CX11 had the Gardner 5LW engine as standard. In 1951, Red & White renumbered its fleet and this vehicle became S539, S signifying single-deck bus and 39 the year of manufacture. It remained in service until 1959.

Representative of the Red & White group's 1939 standard coach is this Albion Valkyrie CX13 with Gardner 6LW engine and Duple 32-seat body to a design peculiar to that group, with slight step in the curved waist and a more angular cab than Duple's usual curved-profile style of that era. This vehicle was one of a pair delivered to the London-based Blue Belle fleet, by then part of the group, and consequently had the London registration FLF 927. Soon afterwards, Blue Belle was absorbed into Red & White, its vehicles temporarily being given a B prefix to their numbers, hence B39 evident in this early wartime view, though the vehicle was later renumbered 739. This body style was also used to rebody early AEC Regal chassis in the group.

the SON, both having BMMO's own very compact 8-litre six-cylinder direct-injection diesel engine – the ONC differed mainly in having a five-speed overdrive gearbox.

The body design was to BMMO requirements, the basic concept being not unlike those on 50 petrol-engined SOS SLR chassis built in 1937 by English Electric, though those vehicles were of stepped-waist style. Many items were clearly of BMMO origin, yet there was a cleanness of line and tidy detail work which seemed to give indication of Duple drawing-office influence – no doubt the latter would have drawn up the detailed design from BMMO concept drawings. The end result looked strikingly modern and remained so into the post-war years. The first vehicle is thought to have acted as a prototype, possibly retaining the SLR style of red and brown livery but the batch as a whole introduced a distinctive colour scheme of red with black above the waistline which was to remain standard for

Midland Red coaches until the 1950s.

The Bristol concern also made a change of livery for its 1939 coaches, in this case reversing the previous colours to cream with dark blue relief. They comprised fourteen 32-seat vehicles, again straight-waisted but this time with front-entrance layout and on Bristol L5G chassis, with Gardner 5LW five-cylinder engine, which had become this maker's standard single-deck chassis.

However, Black & White Motorways Ltd chose the L6G, with the six-cylinder version of the same engine design for its fleet. This concern was jointly owned by the Bristol, Midland Red and Oxford companies, being based at the coach station in Cheltenham which had become a key interchange centre for coach services linking much of the Midlands and the West Country. It had settled on a Burlingham design for its coaches, initially on the previous-generation

Midland Red had the largest British bus and coach fleet outside London and had very distinctive ideas on vehicle design, making its own chassis though putting most body construction out to contractors even though specifying the design. There were many features characteristic of the operator in the ONC-type coaches bodied by Duple in 1939 but there were also a general cleanness of style, much less 'fussy' than on the previous SLR type, and neat detail work that looks as if Duple influence was at work.

Bristol JO6G, from 1936, though the first L6G batch of six had been bodied by ECW. In 1939, however, the order, again for six vehicles, went to Duple, still to the same almost unaltered style, looking very distinctive in the livery implied by the name, even if beginning to be a little dated.

The major part of Duple's output in 1939 was of more recognisably standard products, particularly the Bedford WTB in its final form, of which deliveries were being made to almost every part of Britain, from northern Scotland to the Isle of Wight, often to small operators but by no means always so. The Western and Southern National companies added 28 Vista III to the 22 Vista II supplied the previous year and the sixteen Vista I coaches of 1937, the type being judged well-suited to excursion work in Devon and Cornwall as well as augmenting express services at summer week-ends, a pattern that was to continue with later Bedford-Duple coaches in these fleets until well into the postwar era.

There was also still a small-scale demand for smaller-capacity bodies on Bedford chassis, seating 20 or less, and some were built on the 2-ton WLG goods model, notably for David MacBrayne Ltd and at least one independent operator based on the Isle of Lewis.

As had become usual, Leyland Tiger TS8 and AEC Regal chassis were prominent as the basis for coaches to Duple's own styles for various operators in 1939, such as Sheffield United Tours Ltd which took five new petrol-engined TS8 with curved-waist bodies and two rebodied TS6 chassis dating from 1934 with a straight-waisted version of otherwise similar style. This operator also took two 35-seat bodies rebodying Lion LT5A chassis and five new Leyland Cub KPZ4 normal-control coaches. A similarly mixed group of Leylands went to the Plymouth Co-operative Society Ltd, though in that case there was a full-fronted 32-seat TS8, a 26-seat Cheetah, also full-fronted, and three Cubs. Some reworking of Leyland's front mudguards helped to modernise the rather conservative Cub front-end, and the body design had more than a hint of the post-war Vista style. Among the Regals were examples for several London independent operators and one for Westcliff-on-Sea Motor Services Ltd, by then under Tilling control but continuing to favour the Regal for coach duty. Western & Southern National continued its rebodying of this model.

A new Dennis model was the Falcon, a lightweight chassis available in normal- or forward-control form. Bee-Line Safety Coaches Ltd of West Hartlepool chose the long-wheelbase normal-control version with optional Perkins P6 diesel engine for three coaches with 32-seat capacity, an unusually high figure for a bonneted coach.

The City Coach Co Ltd took a production batch of five Leyland Gnu 39-seat coaches, differing from the 1938 prototype in being on TEC2 chassis, and thus basically closer to the standard Steer twin-steering goods model, with the radiator placed directly in front of the engine, though it was again hidden by a decorative grille. They were first registered on 3rd August 1939.

By that time, war clouds were gathering.

A repeat order for three bodies on AEC Regal chassis came from Brown's Motor Co (Tunstall) Ltd in 1939, though this time on standard O662-type chassis whereas two earlier similar bodies were on the Regal Mark II model, type O862, in 1936.

Variety of output continued undiminished in 1939, as indicated by the examples on this page. There were clear hints of what were to be taken up as post-war styling features, especially the type of side flash, in this Leyland Tiger TS8 petrol-engined 32-seat coach, one of five for Sheffield United Tours Ltd, and a typically graceful example of Duple's output in the months before the war. SUT was a renamed former independent operator acquired jointly by three BET-group concerns and expanded by further takeovers – at the time 'United Motor Services' was used as its main fleetname.

Last of a succession of Dennis light bus models in the late 1930s, the Falcon was announced in 1938 – it was offered in alternative forms, including this long-wheelbase normal-control version. Duple fitted 32-seat coach bodies on three with Perkins P6 engines for Bee-Line Safety Coaches of Greatham, West Hartlepool in mid-1939, registered EF 7139-41. Rather confusingly, this particular coach was named 'Kestrel'.

There were more pointers to Duple designers' later thinking in this Leyland Cub, one of three built for the Plymouth Co-operative Society Ltd, one of several such organisations that ran coach fleets. The body design took up the vee-windscreen concept and other features later to be used for the post-war Vista for the Bedford OB.

The final standard bus body design for the Bedford WTB was called the Luton, an odd choice of name liable to confusion with the style of van often used to carry furniture – the name seems to have been used only rarely. This 26-seat example was supplied to Nash Estates, of Romford, using free transport as a means of attracting customers to a housing development.

A batch of five Leyland Gnu models was completed for the City Coach Co Ltd in August 1939, these differing from the 1938 vehicle in the type of chassis, now TEC2, and the seating capacity, which became 39. The radiator had been repositioned centrally and hence the grille design was simpler, even though still decorative with no obvious relationship to a recognisable Leyland outline. Seen here is G3 (HVW 214) with body 6707 of Series 2.

4 WARTIME AND CHANGE OF ROLE

The outbreak of war on 3rd September 1939 was to disrupt the lives of millions of people, yet many aspects of life did not change at once. Even Duple's production of luxury coaches did not stop immediately though it was sharply curtailed. Military vehicle production had already been stepped up and took priority as the country was put on a war footing.

Subject to the above, work in hand continued and indeed the provision of public transport for workers in factories engaged in war work was regarded as a priority. On the other hand, some vehicle makers virtually ceased civilian production almost at once. Bedford had introduced a new range of goods models in June 1939, the K, M and O series, with basically the same 'bullnose' grille, though now with external radiator filler and headlamps mounted lower, and a new pressed-steel vee-windscreen cab. The passenger version was the OB, with longer 14ft 6in wheelbase than the WTB, and Duple had built a modified Hendonian-style body for a prototype chassis by the swpring of 1939. The extra length enabled the seating capacity to be increased – the caption to a Duple Coachwork Annual illustration thought to have been intended for publication in late 1939 quotes the capacity as 29 seats, though a Vista, only shown as an artist's drawing, is given

as a 26-seater. In both cases the entrance door was set back far enough to allow a pair of seats to be fitted ahead of it on the nearside. The outlines were largely as the 1938-9 styles but with a vee-form windscreen clearly intended to emulate that of the new goods range.

However, only 73 of the OB chassis were built in 1939 before Bedford production was turned over to the war effort, and even of these only small numbers found their way to Duple. Among early recipients were two Scottish operators, Dean, of Findhorn, which took delivery of a 26-seat coach in March 1940, and Stark, of Dunbar, a concern which had a 'semi-detached' relationship to SMT, which took two 29-seaters placed in service in July 1940 and January 1941. Once again the Southern and Western National companies proved to be the main recipients, with ten and eight respectively, all with Vista 26-seat bodywork to the new design and placed in service in 1940. The body design retained some resemblance to the Vista III, though there was a marked difference in frontal appearance as a result of the adoption of a large vee-form windscreen. The effect was striking, yet for some reason seems to have been forgotten when the time came to reintroduce a Vista body after the war was over, for the postwar OB Vista design that was destined to become so familiar had smaller

The new Bedford OB passenger chassis with longer 14ft 6in wheelbase than the WTB had gone into production only a few weeks before war stopped further output. A prototype had been bodied with a straight-waisted body in the Spring of 1939 but this was one of the very few examples of the 1940-style Hendonian as planned for production, with slight dip in the waistline towards the rear, evidently photographed before the windscreen was glazed so that a picture could appear in the 1940 Duple Coachwork Annual.

The 1940 Vista body for the OB, not given a mark number, had a new front end, with large vee windscreen. As with the Hendonian, the extra length was added ahead of the entrance door and the rear window was of the new larger divided type but the sides rearward of the door were much as the Vista III. The vehicle shown was Western National 434 (DOD 532).

windcreen panels in a redesigned body front-end structure.

The late 1939 DupleAnnual included pictures of several of the coaches on larger chassis mentioned previously, together with a Dennis Lancet II with what was described as the Kenton body design – basically a normal curved-waist coach, but with hinged panel alongside the bonnet, as used on the 1938 Show Sutherland Regal.

Orders for new military chassis had already been stepped up in the year or so before the outbreak of war, and Duple found itself engaged in building bodywork for types such as the AEC Marshal, a 6x4 model that had been introduced in the early 1930s but was still a current type being added to the Army's fleet despite having what in retrospect seem curiously old-fashioned features. At that stage, the War Department body specification still called for a canvas-topped cab and the normal type of body was of wooden construction with a canvas tilt top, though Duple also built various types of special-purpose body.

Another activity in which many bodybuilders were involved in the early months of the war was the conversion of large private cars into crude ambulances for civil defence purposes by cutting off the bodywork immediately behind the front doors and building a very simple wood and canvas van structure at the rear. At that date older cars had little monetary value and among the conversions made by Duple was at least one of a Rolls-Royce Phantom which nowadays would be regarded as almost priceless.

Rather more substantial ambulance bodies were built on Fordson Thames forward-control 30-cwt chassis for the Anglo-French Ambulance Corps. The chassis were supplied complete with standard Ford pressed-steel cabs and the bodies were adaptable to carry four stretchers or up to ten seated wounded. Six vehicles with their crews took part in a hand-over ceremony at the Duple works but by the time a report appeared in the trade press on 15th June 1940, France had fallen to invading German forces.

Some civilian lorry bodies were also built, some on Chevrolet chassis, of which imports had resumed on a small scale shortly before the war, handled via Southampton, where there was a small General Motors factory. Most came in without cabs and Duple built both cabs and bodies, the latter mainly of straightforward dropside type. The cabs built for normal-control models could be described as intended to look something like the Bedford pressed-steel cab though the limited length gave it a more upright look. Some were of American-style cab-over-engine style. Amid the uncertainties of the early wartime era, such vehicles were soon snapped up by operators unable to obtain British-built vehicles.

The construction of goods bodywork on older passenger chassis was not new but there were fresh instances in the early war period. With little prospect of coaching work, some such vehicles were adapted as goods carriers, Duple building both van and lorry bodywork in such cases. On the other hand, there was a tendency for much of such passenger bodybuilding as continued at Duple during the first year or so of the war to be concentrated on the rebodying of existing chassis. Although new bus chassis were still being built by most makers in limited numbers, few seem

The outbreak of war created some strange vehicles. A need for ambulances had been foreseen and many bodybuilders were involved in a scheme for converting large private cars by cutting off the rear of the existing body and building very simple two-stretcher ambulance bodies. Few can have been more exotic than this Rolls-Royce Phantom II included in Duple's photo collection, probably dating from about 1930 and looking as if it might have been a sports saloon as built.

For military use, the Bedford range that had gone into production a couple of months before the outbreak of war received this style of full-width sloping bonnet though retaining the new vee-windscreen pressed-steel cab which had doubtless influenced Duple in its body designs for the OB. This was an OX 30-cwt model with a special body of which the canvas cover opened out, possibly for use as a mobile field headquarters.

Seen in the snow of early 1940 outside the familiar doors at Hendon is an AEC Marshal to War Department specification with open cab and a special-purpose body, possibly for bridge building.

to have been completed as coaches, although there were exceptions – Black & White put a final three Bristol L6G coaches with Duple-built Burlingham-style bodywork in service in 1940, and Wallace Arnold took three Leyland TS8 models with what could be described as standard curved-waist coach bodies. A more surprising instance

A handing-over ceremony outside Duple's works in the spring of 1940 which seems poignant in retrospect was of these six Fordson Thames ambulances to the Anglo-French Ambulance Corps - at least one was donated by the Durham Miners' Association as an act of solidarity to French miners. By the time the event was reported in the trade press, France had fallen.

This AEC Regal dating from 1939 and registered in Wolverhampton as CUK 823 was rebodied as a lorry for T. C.Cotton of Rugby.

Goods chassis of American origin were not uncommon in Britain around 1939-40. This was an International on which a semi-forward-control conversion was carried out (Duple had carried out similar work in the early 1930s) as well as the cab and body built - the giveaway to the conversion was the step behind the front mudguard, redundant as a result of the cab being moved forward. It was for Broadway Engineering Co, based nearby in Hendon. This view also shows the new office block which had been built shortly before the war.

direct all kinds of business as required by war circumstances, and this varied in its effects.

On the other hand, work in hand in Duple's works at the outbreak of war had been very much related to coach production. Although it may seem surprising to find some glamorous-looking coach bodies still being delivered in 1940 and even 1941, while the war situation deteriorated severely, leaving Britain virtually alone in a desperate struggle against the very powerful German war machine, it has to be remembered that the framing and other parts for many such coaches were probably already in hand in September 1939.

Barton Transport took its new vehicle bodywork from elsewhere in late 1939 and 1940, Lion LT8 and Cheetah LZ5 39-seat bodies to Duple-style curved-waist coach outline being built by Brush, while Willowbrook produced double-deck bodies almost identical to those on the 1939 TD5 batch for nine Titans of the latest TD7 type. However, in 1940-41 Duple built further 39-seat bodies again to curved-waist pattern to rebody twelve Lion LT5A chassis. In addition, some 27 further front-entrance double-deck bodies were built on Titan TD1 (and in one case a Tiger) chassis, all to basically the same stylish pattern as the 1939 TD5 batch. The chassis dated from 1929-31 and were drawn from a variety of sources, entering service as rebodied in 1941-42.

Red & White and its associate companies sent various early AEC Regal and Leyland Tiger chassis to Duple for

was Maidstone & District which received twelve Dodge SBF coaches with Duple 26-seat coach bodies in 1940-41, possibly a case of accepting stock chassis, even of a make rarely associated with a BET-controlled company; David MacBrayne, normally favouring Bedford for its smaller vehicles, also received two similar coaches. Although the centralised control of all forms of manufacture that was applied later in the war was not yet set up, the Government began to apply strong pressure to

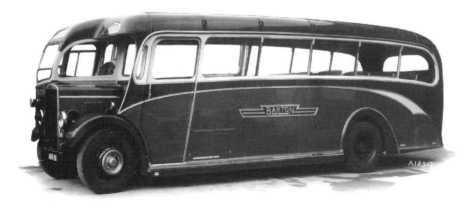

Despite the pressures of wartime, output of bodywork to Duple's elegant peacetime standards continued to be built for a couple of years. Barton decided to replace the original Brush bodies on twelve Leyland Lion LT5A buses of 1934 and Duple produced this style for them in 1940. By then, Barton had adopted the curved-waist as standard even for vehicles with bus seating, having had 39-seat bodies built by Brush on new Lion and Cheetah chassis to this Duple outline in 1939-40 and the same style was adopted for the LT5A rebodying, as conveyed by No.181 (ARR 181).

Barton needed more double-deckers to serve several war factories. An order for ten further new Leyland Titan TD7 chassis was not fulfilled and, instead, ten well-used examples of the TD1 type were obtained and reconditioned. In 1941 they and other similar chassis were fitted with 27 further new Duple bodies to the quite elaborate style of the four on TD5 chassis of 1939. The example shown was No.392 (KR 6407) of which the chassis had been new to Chatham & District in 1930. Unusually, it had received a radiator of the style fitted to TD3 or later models, requiring specially-adapted mountings. The only sign of wartime austerity evident in this view when newly rebodied in 1941 is that the various moulding strips, normally in polished aluminium, were painted.

Another surprisingly stylish product to be completed in spring 1941 was this replacement body, built on the Royal Blue (Southern National) 1937 AEC Regal No.1062 (ETA 996) illustrated on page 45, which had been the victim of a fire. The opportunity was taken to build the 31-seat body to a new curved-waist design which may have been intended for fleet renewals delayed by the war but instead acted as a styling prototype for the bodywork of post-war Royal Blue coaches on Bristol L6B and L6A chassis – in the event this work went to Beadle in 1947-49.

A batch of Albion Venturer CX19 lowbridge double-deckers was built for Red & White and its associate, United Welsh, delivered between January 1941 and February 1942, with sixteen delivered, these being among the first bus bodies (2299-2314) in a third Duple numbering series. By then, normal bus production had almost ceased. A new system of Government control and allocation was coming into effect; one further CX19 with body 2315 was supplied to Green's, Haverfordwest in January 1942. Further similar bodies intended for CX19 chassis were diverted to 'unfrozen' Bristol K5G chassis. Seen below is ex-R&W 440 (EAX 640) at Stroud depot after transfer to Bristol as its L4146 in 1950.

Red & White also rebodied various AEC and Leyland chassis in the earlier part of the war, often fitting Gardner 5LW engines. Seen below is 546 (WM 4615), a 1930 Leyland Lion LT2 – though having a Tiger radiator – which had been transferred from United Welsh in 1940 and rebodied with Duple 35-seat body as shown in 1942.

Remarkably, small-scale exports of buses had continued through some of the darkest days of the war, notably to subsidiaries of Overseas Motor Transport in Africa. This Albion Valkyrie CX11 with centre-entrance 33-seat body, built to a specification suited to its intended destination with the Uganda Transport Co Ltd, was built circa 1941 as part of an order for sixteen – some 77 Albion-Duple buses had been built for OMT by then. In the event they were diverted to other OMT concerns in Nairobi and Mombassa where some entered service in 1942.

rebodying in 1939-40, some at first receiving curved-waist coach bodies but most centre-entrance bus bodies, one of the latter also being fitted to a new Albion Valkyrie CX11 in 1940. In 1941, sixteen Albion Venturer CX19 were fitted with a lowbridge version of the same style of double-deck body as had been built for this group in 1938-39, of which twelve were for Red & White itself and four for United Welsh.

By that date new bus and, still less, coach body construction was becoming increasingly rare, but a significant exception was a rebodying exercise carried out on a 1937 AEC Regal chassis owned by Southern National but operated in the Royal Blue fleet. The express services operated under the latter name, together with much of the ex-Elliott fleet, had been taken over by Western and Southern National in 1935, though some of the coaches had passed to Hants & Dorset. In 1941, the 1937 Regal received a new curved-waist coach body, based on characteristic Duple outlines but with route display above the side windows. It acted as a prototype for the bodywork on the post-war Royal Blue fleet which proved to be on Bristol L-type chassis, some built by Duple.

Rather surprisingly in view of the war situation, Duple exports continued on a modest scale during the initial wartime years. Among early examples were some Commer Q4 models with 25-seat bus bodies built for ETB, Trinidad. A batch of Albion Valkyrie CX11 buses was intended for an Overseas Motor Transport branch at Kampala in Uganda that had been opened in 1938 but these vehicles intended for its expansion were diverted to Nairobi, which received six, and Mombassa four, arriving in 1942.

Bombers and utility buses

As the war situation became more critical, industry was drawn more tightly into the war effort. From 1941, Duple was a member of the London Aircraft Production Group, resulting from a scheme that had been proposed before the outbreak of war in which a group of concerns with appropriate engineering facilities in the London area were linked to Handley Page Ltd in the manufacture of the Halifax four-engined heavy bomber. Other members comprised Park Royal Coachworks Ltd, the bus body concern; Chrysler Motors Ltd, of Kew (which also made the British-built Dodge commercial vehicles); Express Motor Bodies Ltd, makers of goods vehicle cabs and bodies, and London Transport. Duple produced 750 fuselage front-end assemblies, contributing to the 710 complete aircraft produced between mid-1941 and April 1945. Duple's representative on the high-powered controlling committee was G. F. Watts; the importance given to the project is conveyed by the presence of Lord Ashfield as Chairman – London Transport, of which he was full-time Chairman, co-ordinated the whole exercise.

Duple, like almost all large manufacturing companies, was required to produce a wide variety of products for various military purposes, and a clue to the extent to which bus and coach work was no longer dominant lay in the body numbering system. A third series of numbers was in use by 1941, but it is possible that this was more of a job number system, there quite often being huge gaps between batches of bus bodies.

However, it was realised by 1941 that a supply of new buses was needed to provide adequate services, themselves essential to the war effort. New bus production had virtually ceased by that date, often set aside to allow more urgent war

A major part of Duple's wartime effort went into construction of 750 front fuselage sections for Halifax four-engined bombers, of which the other parts were produced by four other members of the London Aircraft Production Group put into operation in 1941. Such work was done to very precise tolerances although the Duple craftsmen's skills in producing complex shapes in aluminium panelling were of obvious value. In this view of the superstructure assembly and glazing section, the large notice instructing workers to save scrap rubber is a reminder of one of Britain's wartime problems – many of the normal sources of rubber were by then in Japanese hands. Another notice lists various types of air raid alert – the factory only shut down when imminent risk of attack was reported by roof-top observers, even when public warnings were in force.

A completed Halifax fuselage front-end leaves the Hendon works on a special trailer behind a Ford Thames lorry carrying other crated items. The Ford Eight car on the right, which would have been in the matt grey so familiar in wartime, was lettered Ministry of Aircraft Production and carried LAP markings to indicate its allocation to London Aircraft Production though the full name was not publicised. Note the barbed wire security fencing.

work to be done. Indeed, it had been much reduced since 1939, some firms turning to exclusively military work almost immediately, while Duple was among the few still managing to fit in a limited number of buses when circumstances allowed. Although many over-age vehicles were being kept in service, some operators needed new buses for replacements, including modest numbers for those destroyed in air raids, although remarkably often it proved possible to repair what seemed very badly damaged buses, often by rebodying. In other cases expansion of fleets was needed, for example to carry workers to new factories that were being set up in less vulnerable rural locations.

Production and allocation was under strict Government control, and as a stop-gap, chassis in course of production or for which parts existed were 'unfrozen'. These were largely double-deckers, mainly AEC Regent, Bristol K5G and Leyland Titan TD7. In some cases, bodies similarly held up were released, though quite often fitted to other chassis than those for which they were intended – some Duple bodies intended for Red & White group Albion Venturer double-deckers were fitted to 'unfrozen' Bristol K5G chassis, for example. In most cases, new bodies were built and these were to new Ministry of Supply 'utility' specifications, designed to economise on skilled man-power and scarce materials. Outlines were required to be simplified to eliminate panels having double curvature and, in general, construction was to use steel panels on wooden framing, with minimal standards of internal trim. On the 'unfrozen' chassis and other early wartime double-deckers upholstered seats were used, though of Spartan design. The completed vehicles were allocated by the Ministry of War Transport in response to operators' applications on a basis of need and quite often, especially in the early stages, the result was the arrival of types completely unfamiliar to the operators concerned.

Duple produced small numbers of utility double-deck designs of both highbrige and lowbridge types for 'unfrozen' chassis; seven highbridge TD7 buses and twelve lowbridge on K5G being delivered in 1942, although five more of the K5G buses received diverted bodies to pre-war pattern as mentioned above. A few single and double-deck buses were rebodied at this time.

More significantly in its longer-term implications, Duple was engaged in the development of what was to be the only new single-decker bus model on offer in Britain from 1942 to the end of the war in 1945. This was the Bedford OWB, of which the chassis was almost identical to the OB save for the

The circumstances of 1942 led to some bodies being reallocated both to different chassis and different users. This one was of the lowbridge style being fitted to Albion Venturer CX19 chassis for the Red & White group in 1941 but in this case, with slightly modified cab, on one of the 'unfrozen' Bristol K5G chassis, themselves built from parts in stock, this one allocated to T. Tilstone & Sons Ltd of Burslem, Stoke-on-Trent and placed in service late in 1942. Its body number, 31613, suggests completion after utility body output had begun as well as being separated from the Red & White CX19 batch by over 29,000 numbers, reflecting the wartime situation when serial numbers were basically job numbers in a factory busy with a multitude of items under Government contracts.

Among the first Duple bodies to the wartime 'utility' specification were seven of highbridge 56-seat type on unfrozen Leyland Titan TD7 chassis, body 30573 seen here being one of the six allocated to the Midland Red fleet as its No.2435 (GHA 789), seen here in 1950. This view shows the wide front upper-deck centre pillar characteristic of the early highbridge Duple utility design.

elimination of chromium-plated trim. The body was very different to the pre-war styles, conforming to the utility requirements, though the front-end retained the vee-screen concept and had quite a well-proportioned look, despite the squared-up lines. At the rear, as also the case on Duple's utility double-deckers, a 'shell-back' form of rear dome was adopted.

A prototype for the OWB was built, its chassis number, 10857, rather suggesting that it may have been in the series used for OB and other O-series models, as the early production OWB buses built from 1942 had substantially lower numbers, beginning around 8332, in an OW series which had been begun for the wartime variants. The body number was 28236, the first known instance of a five-figure Duple body number, the highest numbers of bodies built only a few months earlier being under 5000. Its design established the basis for the soon-to-be familiar wartime bus but it had upholstered seats and the emergency door on the offside. It was sold to Achnasheen Hotel Co in 1942, registered SN 9579.

The production version had the emergency exit in the centre of the rear panels and from the beginning had slatted wooden seats for 32 passengers. This was quite an achievement in a semi-forward control bus measuring only 24ft 4$\frac{1}{8}$in long. It involved the adoption of seat spacing at the minimum legal pitch, so the effect was far from luxurious – the interior finish was also Spartan, with white ceiling panels and lightly varnished woodwork.

Yet the OWB was not as austere a vehicle in which to ride as might have been thought, at least for people of medium height. The six-cylinder petrol engine was smooth, virtually silent at idling speed and not unduly noisy even when working quite hard, even if the gearbox was, and Bedford's skill in suspension design helped to mitigate the effects of the hard seats.

On the other hand it was a much lighter vehicle than most major bus operators favoured, and in any case, many preferred to make wider use of double-deckers, so the take-up of OWB models in such fleets was limited, amounting to barely a quarter of early deliveries and if anything even fewer subsequently. It was significant that prominent among the exceptions to this pattern were operators which already had fleets of Bedford-Duple coaches or buses, who knew of the type's merits, within its limitations, examples including Bristol Tramways, Western & Southern National and Western Welsh.

Duple built two batches of utility bodies on the early wartime Guy Arab, later known as the Arab I, all with Gardner 5LW engines. Thames Valley 418 (CJB 137) with body 31632 (left) was one of the fifteen 55-seat lowbridge buses, with sunken side gangway on the upper deck, while Maistone Corporation 49 (GKT 165) with body 31642 (right) was one of the twelve 56-seat highbridge. Note that

the wide centre pillar at the front of this early highbridge version, also found on those on unfrozen TD7, was not found on the lowbridge bodies on Guy or unfrozen Bristol. The 'chamfered' top rear corner to the cab door window was to be characteristic of almost all Duple double-deck utility bodies.

Many independent operators added OWB models to their fleets, most knowing the pre-war equivalents well. Some simply used them on their existing bus services, but others, including many whose normal activity was coach hire or excursion work, were engaged on special services to armament or aircraft factories – some quite large fleets were engaged on such work – and in both cases the larger seating capacity was of value in coping with the numbers of passengers to be carried on what were often restricted services. Others were supplied to Government departments, used by the armed services or other bodies having priority needs. A batch of twelve was supplied in 1943 to what was listed as Government Communications Headquarters, Bletchley Park, the true significance of which was highly secret at the time, for this was where the German Enigma code was broken, playing a major part in winning the war, so even the modest-seeming provision of transport for the staff there played its part in the outcome.

As applied to other utility types, the work was divided between various bodybuilders, but in the case of the OWB,

The shell-back rear dome of the Duple-designed body of the OWB made its 'utility' nature much more evident than at the front. The design was common to the bodywork from all firms under the wartime supply arrangements for this chassis, the example seen here being one of those built by SMT. It was W115 (WG 9864) in the fleet of W. Alexander & Sons Ltd, being one of a number in the maroon Perth City Transport livery used for vehicles running local routes in that city.

Duple's design was used in all cases. Of the 3,398 OWB chassis built up to late 1945, the majority received Duple-built bodies, and an indication of the scale of the exercise is given by the first order, which was for 540 bodies, numbered 31660-32199, delivered in 1942-3 at the rate of about ten per week. The first two examples from this batch in terms of body number and hence probably the first delivered were supplied to R. Grindle, of Cinderford, Gloucestershire, registered EDG 391 and 392 and on chassis 8414 and 8435 respectively. Duple's next batch of OWB bodies comprised 300 (33780-34079) in 1943-44, but in practice output was continuous.

These were supplied to operators in all parts of Britain but the output was augmented on a regional basis. The SMT concern, which had acted as Bedford dealers as well as operators, produced many of the bodies on OWB chassis supplied to operators in Scotland, both the SMT group itself and independent concerns there and also in parts of northern England. At first, Charles H. Roe Ltd built for an area covering other parts of the north and the Midlands, this concern producing 240 OWB bodies. Later in the war period, Mulliners Ltd took over from Roe, establishing an association with bus-type bodywork for Bedford chassis that was to continue after the war. There were very minor differences in such items as the ventilating louvres alongside the destination box that enabled the individual bodybuilders to be identified.

Double-deckers in volume

Production of new utility specification double-deck chassis began in 1942, the only make then available being the Guy Arab which was a wartime modernised revival of a pre-war model which had been built only in small numbers. The first Ministry contract was for 500 chassis, retrospectively known as the Arab I (all but 75 having the Gardner 5LW engine) and Duple played only a modest part in the body supply for them, with a batch of fifteen utility lowbridge (31621-35), among which as it happened Guy chose an early example supplied to Red & White for frequent use in advertisements, and then twelve utility highbridge (31636-47). It is noteworthy that these body numbers are lower than those for the utility bodies

Duple's production of bodywork on wartime Daimler chassis began when it was agreed it would build 30 highbridge bodies for the 100 CWG5 model chassis, deliveries beginning early in 1943. Swindon Corporation 50 (CWV 912) had the second such body, 34551, only slightly altered from its original form in this postwar picture. The body design had lost the wide centre pillar of early Duple highbridge utility bodies and the emergency exit was unglazed (as built) but the early examples were built with upholstered seats, and with the very effective flexible engine mounting inherited from the COG5 model, these were quiet-running buses in which to ride and perhaps the most 'civilised' of utility double-deckers.

built for unfrozen K5G chassis (31656-9 and 32200-7), implying that the Arab contract had been placed first.

The alternative engine for the Arab chassis was the more powerful 6LW and to avoid the need to modify bodywork, a projecting bonnet was used to accommodate this longer engine, the overall length being 4½in over the then 26ft limit for two-axle double-deckers by special dispensation. It was then decided to standardise on this length for the chassis, even with the 5LW, and subsequent chassis were known as Arab II although the 6LW continued to be rare, only small numbers being available at the time.

By that date, early 1943, Duple's double-deck output was being diverted to Daimler chassis, that firm having restarted bus production from temporary premises in Wolverhampton, the initial model, the CWG5 being a mildly modified version of the pre-war COG5, also with 5LW engine but retaining the combination of fluid flywheel and preselective gearbox found on all Daimlers of those days. For the 100 chassis of

There was one further small batch of nine Duple utility bodies on Guy chassis built soon after the CWG5 buses, these being of lowbridge layout on the Arab II chassis with projecting radiator. The arrangement of louvres over the windows changed several times on Duple's utility double-deckers, this batch introducing them over the upper-deck front windows. Barton Transport 431 (GAL 390) was one of five in that fleet, all with 5LW engines.

this type built, Duple's share of the CWG5 body supply was 30 highbridge bodies, numbered 34550-79, and under wartime arrangements these were allocated to operators in the south and midlands of England.

The CWG5 was superseded by the CWA6, which had an AEC 7.7-litre engine and was to be the main type of wartime Daimler bus. There was also a CWD6 model, with a new Daimler 8.6-litre engine, built in much smaller numbers from the spring of 1945, and some of these intermingled with the CWA6 until the end of the wartime allocation system, final deliveries reaching operators in the Spring of 1946. The contracts let for these by the Ministry of Supply were in smaller batches than for the OWB, the initial ones for the CWA6 being for 65 lowbridge (37170-37234) and 60 highbridge (37235-94), though the proportion of highbridge bodies increased considerably for later batches as the authorities responded to the level of applications. Overall, just over 25% were lowbridge.

Duple built bodywork on about 509 CWA6 and 53 CWD6 under the scheme, thus being the largest supplier of bodies on this pair of models and representing nearly half (45.8%) of the 1,227 chassis involved. They were to be found in almost all parts of Britain, from Aberdeen to Exeter, and included 107 supplied to London Transport.

Only nine more wartime Guy chassis received Duple bodies after production on Daimler chassis had begun, these being Arab II models dating from late 1943. In addition, from mid-1945 Duple took over production of highbridge bodies for the Bristol K-type chassis, of which production had been restarted the previous year, though at that stage of K6A type, with AEC 7.7-litre engine. This was a smaller-scale operation, there being 38 bodies on the W1 and W2 series chassis with tall radiator and 45 on the W3 with low radiator, some of these latter being K5G.

Supplies of good-quality timber for the framing were a problem for almost all British bodybuilders in wartime, but Duple's utility double-deck design, despite what looked rather spindly construction, with slim pillars and side framing, proved among the most durable. The secret seemed to lie in the use of deep waistrail sections, helping to give rigidity to the structure as a whole.

The association of Duple with the Daimler CWA6 began with an order to build 65 lowbridge 55-seat bodies (37170-234), the first of which went on to the first production chassis of this type, delivered to Richmond Motors, of Neath on 31st July 1943. More in the news were the batch of six for London Transport, the first new Daimlers for that undertaking, simply numbered D1-6 and placed in service in May-June 1944. Lowbridge bodies were rare in London but wartime had increased the need. Seen here when newly in service from Merton garage is D4, with body 37221, looking smart in the red and white livery of the time, though the anti-blast netting on the windows is a reminder of air-raid dangers. Note the raised cab waist, characteristic of Duple bodies on the CWA6 from about this date (though not early ones), and the individual louvres over opening windows, also found on some Duple bodies for other fleets at the time.

Deliveries of an equivalent 56-seat highbridge batch (27235294) began on 1st October 1943 and this view of Bradford Corporation 476 (DKY 476) with body 27240 which entered service just a month later conveys how many of them looked when new. Many utility double-deckers were delivered in grey, Duple's standard shade being quite dark, and they often entered service thus. At that stage, the continuous louvres over all windows were still standard though soon to switch briefly to the individual type, but wooden seats had become part of the specification. The taper pillars on the nearside at front and rear bulkheads neatly blended into the valance were a new feature found on most later Duple wartime bodies.

The characteristic rear-end of Duple double-deck bodies of the period between mid-1943 and about two years later is seen in the lower view of the former Douglas Corporation No.52 (FMN 955), a Daimler CWA6 with body number 40577 delivered in February 1945. The shape of the windows in the emergency exit, with well-rounded top outer corners, was a good Duple recognition point among utilities, and the shell-back rear dome was distinctive too; although Brush used a quite similar shape, its emergency exit had a single smaller rectangular window. The CWA6, with its AEC 7.7-litre engine and preselective gearbox, was quite a lively bus though the lack of sound absorbency of the wooden seats made the noise level from the rigidly-mounted engine fairly high.

The wartime Duple double-deck body design altered slightly at various stages in its production. The early highbridge examples on Titan TD7 and Guy Arab I had a slightly clumsy look, with a wide centre pillar at the front of the upper deck, but gradually the design improved and, to the author at least, the typical Duple-bodied CWA6 seemed among the better proportioned of wartime designs, even before the 'relaxed' specification, removing the most austere features, came in from about April 1945. The subsequent versions had the benefit of quite

a shapely rear dome and were among the most attractive double-deckers then available that still conformed to the Ministry specification – gradually departures from it became more common among some other bodybuilders, though Duple made no further changes before the scheme ended.

Overall, Duple double-deck bus production under the 'utility' scheme between 1942 and early 1946 added up to about 730 bodies, including a few on reconditioned chassis. This was vastly greater than the occasional orders for double-deckers, generally of no more than half-a-dozen at a time,

spread over the previous fourteen years, and was never to be achieved again, although several noteworthy post-war double-deck contracts were fulfilled.

The overall Duple war effort, with over 2,600 utility bus bodies, 750 heavy bomber fuselages, large numbers of bodies for military vehicles and trailers, and the more normal if restricted bus and coach output in the first couple of years, gave an indication of the capacity of the Hendon premises. Some of the lessons learned were applied to the new challenge of the post-war years.

When production of Bristol K-type chassis resumed in mid-1944, highbridge body supply was at first entrusted to Park Royal but in mid-1945 Duple took over this role, building 38 bodies (41203–40), mainly on the second W2 sanction of chassis though 41202 was on a late W1 series. These batches retained the tall radiator of previous Bristol models but in adapting the cab design, Duple reverted to a straight waistline and also changed the 'chamfered' cab door window to one with rounded top rear corner. Colchester Corporation 46 (KEV 331), a K6A of the W2 series seen above, had body 41214.

The W3-sanction Bristol K-type, seen below, introduced the low radiator standard on post-war examples of the make. London Transport was the first recipient with the earlier deliveries of 20 K6A with Duple highbridge bodies (41705–24). Here a deeper windscreen lined-up tidily with the waist level and the overall effect was of a neat-looking bus. The vehicle posed for a picture outside the Hendon factory seems likely to have been that with the first body, 41705, which became B11 (HGC 236) on the second chassis of the type, W3.002, delivered in December 1945 – the complete batch was B10-29 but the body numbers were not in sequence. They operated from Hanwell garage, which was very close to the AEC works, the author often travelling in them in 1951-3 during his days working for that maker – all were sold to Tilling group companies in 1953, B11 being one of seven running with Lincolnshire Road Car Co Ltd until 1959-60.

5 THE POST-WAR YEARS

The utility body for the Bedford OWB did not go through a 'relaxed specification' phase in the same way as most utility body types, save that upholstered seats were introduced within the otherwise unchanged body from the spring of 1945. However, from August of that year, just as the final stage of the war ended with the surrender of Japan, it was confirmed that a completely new 32-seat bus body was to be built by Duple, initially still on the OWB chassis. It was called the Mark II and although this might have been taken to imply that the standard OWB body was 'Mark I' though never quoted as such, even retrospectively, it could also be considered as the successor to the bus design for Bedford chassis of 1939, which briefly had been called Luton I.

The layout and pillar spacings were similar to the utility version but all external traces of its austerity vanished, save that at first these buses continued to be supplied in the same overall brown paintwork, though most were soon put into their owners' normal colours – supplies of paint were also getting back to normal.

The front and rear of the body incorporated a pleasing blend of curves in typical Duple manner, the windows had radiused corners, and a sliding entrance door replaced the folding type. At the front, the vee windscreens extended almost to full body width, with only a slight inward taper in the foremost side panels.

However, within, the Mark II was still quite an austere design, with tight spacing of the rather basic upholstered seats and no overhead racks for luggage. Despite its much better looks, it was still built to Ministry of Supply contract, the first order being for 200, and allocations continued to be made by the Ministry of War Transport though in a manner which was becoming more responsive to operators' choice.

This was a time of transition and deliveries moved from OWB chassis with utility body, through a spell from late 1945 when the OWB chassis was supplied with the Mark II body and then, at about the turn of the year though there seems to have been some overlap in deliveries reaching operators, resumption of supplies of OB chassis (which in practice meant little more than a return to normal headlamps and chrome trim) fitted with the Mark II body. Just to add to the complexity, the RAF took delivery of some OB chassis with the utility-style OWB type of body, though these differed slightly from the civilian version in not having the large front destination box, and it is believed that some, at least, had Mulliner-built bodies. There were also Duple-built export examples, some with left-hand drive.

The availability of additional makes and models of chassis meant that more normal trading conditions were returning, though the Government-controlled production system continued to operate well into 1946. The effect was to group chassis and body makes in a manner similar to wartime even though the vehicles were to peacetime specification, including coach bodies for a time.

The demand for new coaches was particularly strong, as they had not been included in the utility scheme so none were built from 1942 to 1945, and indeed very few of any type had been built since 1939 – Duple's very limited output of such bodies in 1940-41 was itself a rarity. In addition, many coaches had been acquired compulsorily for military or civil defence use and few of these returned with bodywork in a fit state to resume normal use without a major rebuild (many being too far gone to make this worthwhile) or not being returned at all.

Despite quite widespread continuation of an austere life-style in Britain because of continued scarcities in the early post-war years, express services were restored during 1946. Permission was given for the resumption of coach manufacture from about the beginning of the year and this meant that supplies of materials, though still limited amid the immense demand for all types of products, were made available. As part of a reorganisation to suit the needs of the times, the title of the firm was changed from Duple Bodies and Motors Ltd to the simpler form Duple Motor Bodies Ltd in the spring of 1946.

The appearance of the first post-war coach bodies was quite a dramatic event after so long a spell when anything not

The body for the OWB did not go through a 'relaxed utility' stage as generally understood. Instead, the Mark II body, as seen here, with no trace of utility outline, went into production in August 1945, at first still mounted on the OWB chassis with its military-style headlamps. They were built to Ministry of Supply contract and delivered in the standard brown paintwork, the initial order consisting of 200, though others followed in 1946. This example was registered in Kent as BJG 534.

Deliveries of the post-war Bedford OB with Duple Vista body began in the early spring of 1946, before any of the other main types of coach resumed production. Although continuing the tradition of a curved-waist, sloping-pillar design, there were many differences from the Vista III of 1939 or even the few OB Vista coaches of 1940; there was more in common with the style built on Leyland Cub chassis for Plymouth Co-op of 1939, as seen on page 57. Though at first seeming very stylish after the wartime years of austerity, the type was soon to become familiar all over Britain. West Yorkshire Road Car Co Ltd used these two Vista coaches dating from mid-1947 for tours of the City of York though seen here on excursion duty in Scarborough in 1950. The leading vehicle, 646 (FWW 596), is one of the many examples still in existence half a century later as a preserved vehicle.

strictly utilitarian was banned. The first production model to appear was a new version of the Duple Vista on Bedford OB chassis, its curved-waist sloping-pillar design seeming astonishingly glamorous in a way difficult to understand even a few years later, when the model became so commonplace. One of the first was supplied to Taylor Bros, of North Shields, registered FT 5651, of which photographs were used for publicity in the trade press. The author happened to have the good fortune to see it standing outside the main Bedford dealers in Newcastle, Adams & Gibbon Ltd, ready for delivery, in March 1946. After the years of war and all its austerity and gloom, when nothing comparable had been built for five years, and very little since 1939, it made an impression hard to understand today.

The new design had a different design of windscreen to that used on the 1940 Vista deliveries, still being of vee-style but with rather smaller panels and having squared top corners. It had the effect of making the front of the body narrower, the front portion of the side panels tapering in more sharply and altering the overall appearance considerably. The spacing of the side pillars was also revised, giving four approximately equal bays behind the entrance.

As announced, it was quoted as being available in 26-, 27- or 29-seat forms, the first following on from the pre-war practice as usual on the WTB. A change in the vehicle taxation system meant that instead of being increased in steps of 20, 26 or 32 seats, etc it was graduated more precisely in relation to the actual capacity. In response to the high level of demand for travel at the time, there was a widespread tendency to choose higher capacities, often by making the rearmost seat take five rather than four or adding extra pairs of seats where practicable. In practice, the 29-seat capacity soon became established as the post-war Vista standard, with the 27-seat version chosen by a minority favouring a more

spacious layout; the 26-seat version almost immediately disappeared from the quoted range, though later very occasional examples were produced with non-standard low capacities.

This was to be the standard Duple coach body for the OB until it went out of production towards the end of 1950 – the last completed examples were delivered in the early months of 1951. A few minor changes in appearance occurred during that time, though the characteristic outline was unaltered. The first 46 had the enclosed rather than concealed type of entrance door. There was a slight reversion to austerity for a time in 1948-9 when a shortage of the polished extrusion used for the side flashes led to these being omitted for a brief period and later the rear-end mouldings were updated. The Hendonian straight-waisted coach body for Bedford chassis was not revived post-war despite its pre-war popularity.

Demand for the post-war Vista was strong from the beginning, and the Mark II bus soon became relatively rare, although not quite so much so as for bus versions of the WTB. Before long, new Vista coaches were being added to independent operators' fleets all over the country and it was not long before they were to be seen in large numbers in seaside coach parks at summer week-ends as well as on country bus services. The traditional larger operators which had favoured Bedford-Duple coaches pre-war, such as Southern and Western National, generally added OB versions to their fleets but there were also many more operators not hitherto associated with vehicles of this character, among which Southdown was perhaps the most notable.

The typical larger coach became of 33- or 35-seat capacity in the post-war era, the traditional 32-seater heavy-duty forward control coach soon becoming fairly rare in the post-war scene, particularly among production coaches as supplied to independent operators via the dealer network, though some larger fleets still stuck to the traditional figure or less.

The Mark II bus body continued in production for the Bedford OB, with a modest increase in brightwork. The numbers produced were soon dwarfed by the demand for the Vista and Mulliners took over production to allow Duple to concentrate on coaches. This Duple example began life with Enterprise of Scunthorpe early in 1947 but in 1950 was taken over with that fleet by Lincolnshire Road Car Co Ltd, already running a fleet of Bedfords.

A temporary material shortage led to the deletion of the characteristic 'flash' from the side panels of standard OB Vista coaches for a brief period in 1948-49, producing a markedly different appearance - with some liveries, the effect was quite agreeably 'clean', as with KNN 314 in the fleet of the South Notts Bus Co Ltd seen above in July 1949 soon after delivery.

The standard style of coach seat used in Duple's immediate post-war production, both for the Vista and on larger models, had a polished metal frame, similar in construction and finish to some contemporary metal-framed bus seats, with exposed fixing screws, though having a deeper back-rest than the bus version. Even so, the overall standard of internal finish of these vehicles, with overhead parcel racks and traditional-style polished wood trim, was a welcome contrast to that of wartime buses.

The first type of full-sized chassis to receive Duple postwar coach bodywork was the AEC Regal, reintroduced in a model with specification very like that of standard oil-engined models of 1939, with the 7.7-litre engine – no petrol model was offered, this omission being usual with post-war heavy-duty chassis. In post-war form it was called the Regal I to distinguish it from a new version then about to go into production.

Duple's initial post-war body design for the Regal I and generally similar chassis from other makers was virtually a repeat of the curved-waist sloping-pillar design, much as being built in 1940, save that for the first year or so it had the slightly austere metal-framed seats as mentioned above. In post-war form it was called the A-type, although also known as FS1 in a new series of 'Full Size' drawing numbers used to identify main body types in the period from 1946. Although not strictly-speaking a new design, the A-type seemed particularly striking in the post-war world, with its graceful curves set off by a relatively simple side 'flash', in essence reverting to the original concept much as seen on the pioneering Adnams coach of 1935.

Deliveries of AEC Regal I chassis with FS1 bodywork began in May 1946, customers including both familiar and less familiar names, partly because early examples had been

Production of larger Duple coach bodies resumed in May 1946, initially on AEC Regal I chassis. The flowing lines of the FS1 body design, also known as type A, suited the Regal well; such products as this and the Vista make a remarkable contrast with the bomber fuselage sections and austere wooden-seated buses that formed the output of the factory only a little over a year earlier. This 33-seat example was supplied to A. Skill of Nottingham, a long-standing Duple customer, in July 1946, registered HAU 695.

The demand for coaches was strong in the immediate post-war period. Hall Bros, of South Shields, ran a Newcastle-Coventry service which proved very popular. This line-up in Nottingham in August 1949 was led by CU 4741, one of a pair of AEC Regal I coaches with Duple A-type 33-seat bodywork dating from 1947, the other vehicle very possibly the third in line here. The second vehicle, in non-standard livery, may have been a similar coach acquired second-hand from Lily of Tottenham. Duple bodies were fitted to nearly 300 Regal I models dating from 1946-48, the majority being of the A type.

The Leyland Tiger also continued its traditional popularity, though the new PS1 model had altered considerably in design, with a new 7.4-litre diesel engine, lively in performance but noisier than the pre-war 8.6-litre unit. Here also the A-type body was the usual choice for independent operators, and it was no surprise that Sutton's of Clacton was again a user with this early 1947 example, though now accepting the standard production job rather than the exotic designs built for this fleet in the 1930s. Leyland created a problem for coach bodybuilders by mounting the driver's instrument panel at the top outer corner of the front dash on the PS1, making it impossible to trim to suit the body style, as was common practice and this led Duple to adopt a horizontal bottom edge for the windscreen for this model, giving a rather harsher look.

allocated to operators under a continuation of the wartime Government scheme. Even though choice was increasing, speed of delivery was often the crucial factor when operators were in desperate need of new vehicles. For example, the Grey-Green fleet of George Ewer & Co Ltd, generally a strong Leyland user, was among the first customers for the Regal I with Duple A-type body.

In addition, many concerns had gained experience of previously unfamiliar makes or models in wartime, and pre-war loyalties sometimes changed. Duple's order books, as well as starting the post-war period with a healthy initial collection of advance orders for coaches, soon filled up for several years ahead.

Deliveries of other chassis makes gradually appeared in ensuing months until there was quite a wide choice and Duple

seems not to have attempted to limit its output to any particular make or model. Coach bodies based on the A-type design or derived from it were built on new AEC, Albion, Bristol, Crossley, Daimler, Dennis, Foden, Guy, Leyland and Maudslay chassis during the 1946-50 period, though AEC, Leyland and Dennis were again predominant in much the same manner as in the 1930s. In the lightweight range, the Bedford OB had a clear run.

In addition, rebodying once again became common practice, partly because of the long waiting list for new chassis, but also because of the substantial number of sound pre-war chassis with bodywork which was beyond economic repair or considered too outdated for operators' needs. Although rebodying was never a large-scale activity, Duple was willing to accept orders for A-type bodies on most of the

The Dennis Lancet III set a different type of problem with its high bonnet level, but even so Duple's designers managed to produce a neat-looking vehicle. The model was put into production as Dennis's post-war standard single-decker in 1946 and had the Dennis O6 engine, a particularly smooth-running 7.58-litre unit. With the standard overdrive five-speed gearbox, it offered more refined travel than either of the market-leading AEC or Leyland models of the immediate post-war era. This one, PRE 294, for Well's of Biddulph dated from May 1948. Over 180 Lancet III models had Duple bodies, generally standard A-type as shown.

The Red & White group continued to favour the Albion Valkyrie CX13 for coach duty in 1947-48, though this was now available only with Albion's own 9.0-litre engine. Among the first post-war examples were an initial three for United Welsh Services Ltd dating from August 1947, including 922 (EWN 22) seen here. Eight more followed in 1948, and Red & White itself had a similar batch. The CX13 with Duple A-type body was also favoured by a number of independent operators based in Scotland.

Maudslay began post-war production in 1946 with two new identical-looking coach chassis. The Marathon Mark II had a Maudslay 7.4-litre six-cylinder petrol engine, a remarkable twin-camshaft unit, much as had been used in the ML6, together with a five-speed gearbox, the only 'big' petrol coach model available in Britain at that date. The first chassis, number 60001, for Samuel Johnson (Supreme) Ltd of Stourbridge, Worcestershire, is seen here with 33-seat A-type body 42437 when new in October 1946, the first of six supplied between then and a year later. The Marathon Mark III, with chassis numbered 70001-up, had the AEC 7.7-litre diesel engine and AEC four-speed gearbox, both as used in the Regal I, and was more numerous if less interesting. Duple A-type bodies were fitted to a high proportion of the early Marathon II and a modest share of Marathon III.

well-known AEC and Leyland chassis types going back to about 1930 despite the differing dimensions involved, which must have required individual attention to a degree which seems surprising at a time of high demand in a firm very conscious of the economies of large-scale production.

Hence, although the Duple A-type became perhaps the most familiar of all British coach designs for heavy-duty chassis in the early post-war years, there was considerable variety in the complete products that emerged from the Hendon works even within this group, quite apart from the existence of several other quite different Duple body designs.

Taking into account other orders both for what could be regarded as further Duple standard types and for what to Duple were nonstandard designs received in the early post-war period, the output was still remarkably varied despite the absence of the individuality that had been allowed in the 1930s.

Some operators had orders still outstanding from when normal production ceased in the early war period or had

placed orders for post-war delivery during the period up to 1945, and this is also reflected in the pattern of body numbers, with some of the last utility batches intermingled with post-war products and the actual order of manufacture often far removed from the numerical order. As the aftermath of the war receded and up to 1951, Duple adopted a new policy of allocating blocks of body numbers to makes of chassis, not necessarily all of the same pattern even from a bodybuilding viewpoint and often issued well out of order, possibly as a consequence of filling-in blanks left by cancellations, though often leaving many numbers unused, so again they tend to obscure the actual pattern of production.

In addition to the standard A-type coach body, Duple offered alternative styles also regarded as production options and also denoted by alphabetic code.. The B- and C-type bodies could be regarded as dual-purpose – i. e. suitable for bus as well as coach duty – in character, both having upright pillars and a full-width canopy allowing use of a larger destination display. The B-type body had a curved waistline and was also known as FS4, while the C-type (FS3) had a straight waistline. Type D (FS8) was Duple's own design of standard bus body, yet still quite stylish in looks. Type E was an export design for the OB and F was allocated to the Vista, though this last designation was very rarely used.

There were also further designs, as well as variations of those mentioned above, given other FS numbers, some having a measure of characteristic Duple appearance and others built entirely to operators' specifications.

The FS numbers

Duple's early post-war production was more orderly than in prewar days with greater standardisation on clear-cut designs, a few types seen as standards for general sale being identified by an alphabetic system and almost all in the FS series. The principal types, mainly for forward-control chassis can be summarised in tabular form, as shown:-

F S No.	Type letter	Description	Main customer	Chassis (main)
FS1	A	Coach, curved-waist sloping pillar, half-canopy	(Standard)	Various
FS2	-	Bus, rear-entrance	NIRTB	Regal I
FS3	C	Coach, straight-waist, vertical pillar, full canopy	SMT	Regal I
FS4	B	Coach, curved-waist vertical pillar, full canopy	Alexander	Guy Arab
FS5	-	Coach, special, rear-entrance	Southdown	Tiger PS1
FS6	(A)	Coach, curved-waist (four-bay, to suit longer bonnet chassis)	(Standard) Leyland TS1,	Bristol L6G, TS2, TS4 etc
FS7	(A)	Coach, curved waist (to suit short bonnet chassis)	(Standard)	Lion LT5A, Cheetah, etc
FS8	D	Bus	(Standard)	Regal I etc
FS9	-	Export bus (Bulawayo)	OMT	Arab 19ft 6in
FS10	-	Special Vista	Overseas Motor Tpt	Bedford OB
FS11	-	Double-deck front-entrance	Barton	Titan PD1
FS12	-	Special coach	BMMO	BMMO C1
FS13	-	Bus, special	Guernsey	Guy Vixen
FS14	(A)	Coach, curved waist (four-bay)	(Standard)	Regal III
FS15	-	Bus	(Standard)	Regal III

Note that the standard body types built for Bedford chassis did not have FS numbers. In this period, these were the Mark II bus, the Vista coach and the Almet metal-framed export bus.

The A-type FS1 body was offered in the period from 1946 up to the beginning of the 1950s (the actual periods varying as the various chassis models came into production) on new AEC Regal I, Albion Valkyrie CX13, Crossley SD42/6, Daimler CVD6, Dennis Lancet III, Foden PVSC6, Leyland Tiger PS1 (also later the PS2), and Maudslay Marathon (both Mark II with petrol engine and Mark III with AEC 7.7-litre oil engine). In addition there were FS1 versions for models such as pre-war AEC Regal chassis (including the 17ft wheelbase version as built before 1932), and the Leyland Tiger TS6, TS7, TS8 and TS11. Generally these models were offered in 33- or 35-seat form and the designation covered versions with minor variations to suit the various chassis types – the cab length could vary slightly to suit the chassis (for wider variations see FS6 and FS7). The version for the PS1 and PS2 had a horizontal bottom edge to the driver's windscreen instead of the normal curve because of the position of the Leyland instrument panel which precluded trimming the chassis front dash panel as was standard practice on other types.

A version of the A-type body adapted to suit chassis with a longer bonnet or chassis front end was produced as type FS6, these including both the Bristol L6G in its post-war form, rebodied Leyland Tigers of types TS1, TS2 or TS4 and also the Tilling-Stevens K6LA7 which, like the Bristol L6G, had the lengthy Gardner 6LW engine (the Foden PVSC6, though also so powered, was counted as an FS1 body, evidently because of slightly more compact cab design, even though the type was offered only in up to 33-seat form). The FS6 body, slightly shorter in its passenger-carrying length, had four rather than five bays rearwards of the entrance.

A four-bay version of the A-type coach which did not have as long a bonnet was the FS14, as built for the AEC Regal Mark III chassis, this evidently responding to AEC's strong association with four-bay double-deck body styles for the equivalent double-deck Regent Mark III, not least in its London Transport RT form.

Yet another variant of the A-type coach was the FS7 design for short-bonnet models such as pre-war Leyland Lion LT5A and LT7 and Cheetah LZ2 and LZ2A models, as well as the Albion Valkyrie CX9 and the Foden PVSC5, this last with an unusually compact installation of the Gardner 5LW engine.

In practice some of these variants on the A-type were much more widely used than others, and the order of production was not necessarily related to the design number – in particular the four-bay FS14 version on AEC Regal III chassis was in regular production from 1947. There were also minor variants, Black & White Motorways Ltd choosing a full-width canopy variant of the FS6 for its first post-war order on Bristol L6G chassis of ten coaches, delivered in 1948 – the seating capacity was 30, some of the major operators tending to be more conservative in this respect. In 1949, a further ten basically similar coaches had full-fronted cabs, and versions based on the FS1 but with full fronts were built on some AEC, Leyland and Maudslay chassis.

The B-type body, with curved waist and roof line but upright pillars, a full-width canopy, half-drop opening windows and folding door at the front entrance, was intended to be suitable for bus as well as coach duty. The main user was W. Alexander & Sons Ltd, which ordered a batch of 30 on Guy

The B-type body, also known as FS4, was intended as a dual-purpose design, the first and main customer being W. Alexander & Sons Ltd with an order for 30 (body numbers 42533-62) on the Guy Arab III single-deck chassis with Gardner 5LW engine, the first three of the type being registered in August 1946 and the rest, including G7 (AMS 537) seen here, in March 1947. The curved waist, seats of Duple's standard coach type of the time for 35 passengers and Bluebird livery all conveyed a coach image, even if hardly a luxurious one, while the folding door and half-drop windows were more bus-like (at that time, 'proper' coaches had full-drop windows operated by a winding handle).

The C-type body (FS3) had a straight waist (save for the rearmost bay), yet a gently curved roof line gave quite a stylish effect and the sliding door was more widely accepted as appropriate to a coach. The Scottish Motor Traction Co Ltd took 50 on AEC Regal I chassis, between July 1946 and April 1947 but while these were in course of delivery the City Coach Co placed nine on Leyland Tiger PS1 chassis in service, the first four, including LS2 (LHK 413) seen here, in December 1946 and the remainder in March 1947.

The D-type body (FS8) was a bus, but of characteristically stylish looks, as was to be expected of a Duple product of that golden era. Enterprise & Silver Dawn, of Scunthorpe, had twelve 35-seat examples on AEC Regal I chassis dating from 1946-7, including No.13 (DFW 776) shown here. They were included in the take-over of that organisation by Lincolnshire Road Car Co Ltd in 1950. The appearance could be altered slightly by details of trim. Midland General having four on Regal and two on PS1 having a rather more 'corporate' look with wider destination display with separate route number and side route boards.

Arab III chassis in 1946-7, though 20 of these were supplied to David Lawson Ltd of Kirkintilloch, which was run as an Alexander subsidiary. The chassis were to the standard early post-war Arab single-deck design with 5LW engines and low bonnet line. Some very similar vehicles were supplied to Moore Bros of Kelvedon, though a number of independent users favoured the A-type FS1 body for this chassis despite it being more generally considered a bus rather than coach model.

The C-type FS3 body took the dual-purpose concept a shade further in having a straight waistline yet had a sliding entrance door. The SMT concern placed 50 on AEC Regal I in service in 194647 as its initial post-war fleet intake, and although these were hardly luxurious vehicles, with 35-seat capacity, some became a familiar sight on the Edinburgh-

London service for the next few years. A version on Leyland Tiger PS1 chassis was adopted by two well-known independent fleets, the City Coach Co of Brentwood and Ledgard of Leeds.

Type D was the standard post-war bus body for half-cab forward-control chassis, with full-width canopy, front entrance and 35-seat capacity as standard. It was of more functional style than the coaches but even so shared in the stylish Duple look, with such details as the curved windscreen pillars and trim details. The main type was FS8, offered on much the same range of chassis as the A-type FS1 coach though built in much smaller numbers. Again the AEC Regal I was prominent, being the basis for ten early examples supplied to the Newbury & District and two for Venture of Basingstoke concerns in 1947,

Southdown Motor Services Ltd was a much-respected BET-group concern running a substantial coach fleet, mainly on express services linking London to South coast resorts. It continued to prefer rear-entrance layout and a special body design was produced for 40 coaches based on Leyland PS1 chassis, ordered in two batches, Duple body numbers 42563-82 and 45854-73, the vehicles entering service between June 1947 and December 1949. The overall effect was an attractive blend of Southdown's traditional dignified good taste with Duple stylishness, as indicated by No.1345 (HUF 945) with body 45867 dating from June 1949 seen at Victoria Coach Station on a wet day in September 1950.

both at that stage part of the Red & White group. The designation FS15 was taken out for a version on Regal III, again including examples for these operators but in practice the examples built on this chassis were of outwardly similar basic design to the FS8.

The other early FS numbers were taken up by bodies built to operators' specifications. The FS2 was a rear-entrance 36-seat bus for the Northern Ireland Road Transport Board, which ran most services in the province outside Belfast at that date, being a predecessor of the Ulster Transport Authority. There were 20 on AEC Regal I and seven on Leyland Tiger PS1, all delivered in 1946.

The FS5 was a 'special', built to the requirements of

Southdown Motor Services Ltd which had purchased the majority of its coaches dating from the 1930s from Thomas Harrington Ltd, based at Hove and thus near Southdown's headquarters in Brighton, as well as being one of Duple's major rivals in the general market for coach bodywork. Some bodies to Southdown's specification had been built in that period by other concerns, notably Beadle and Park Royal, but in the early post-war period the net was cast wider, with six bodybuilders for the 125 Leyland Tiger PS1 coaches placed in service between 1947 and 1949, and Duple proved to be the largest supplier.

Southdown's preferred specification was a rather restrained style of rear-entrance coach with traditional 32-seat capacity. Some variation of design was accepted but Duple's FS5 version showed evidence of the bodybuilder's involvement in the interpretation even if the outline, with curved waist but straight cantrail was basically Southdown's own choice. A total of 40 such coaches were built by Duple over that period, the largest share of the total.

Overseas Motor Transport was the customer for whom the FS9 body design on export long-wheelbase Guy Arab was produced, intended for service in Bulawayo. The FS10 was a special 14-seat touring coach on Bedford OB chassis, also for

In 1947-9, Barton Transport expanded its double-deck fleet with 40 new vehicles on Leyland Titan PD1 chassis with Duple body numbers 42686-710 and 45905-19 – No. 453 (JNN 793) is seen here. The design (Duple FS11) was broadly similar to the original 1939 version but included recessed driver's windscreens, an idea doubtless influenced by Midland Red having adopted it for its post-war vehicles; double sliding doors were another new feature. The pre-war curved external trim was replaced by horizontal strips of a style later adopted for other Duple double-deckers. In addition, Barton fitted two further new PD1 chassis with 1940-41 bodies transferred from the TD1 chassis on which they had been built.

The standard early post-war Barton single-decker was a Leyland Tiger PS1 with Duple A-type body, some with chassis modified to allow the body to seat 39 passengers in the manner of the prewar Lion LT8 etc, as in the case of 550 (KAL 147) seen here.

Midland Red adopted the underfloor engined layout for all its post-war single-deckers, the first British operator to do so, aided in freedom of action by producing its own chassis, by then called BMMO, and the progressive ideas of Donald Sinclair, the firm's General Manager. When the first coach version, type C1, appeared in 1948, Duple was asked to provide the bodywork, coded FS12 by Duple. Seen in this view in Llandudno in August 1949, No.3315 (KHA 315) conveys the stylish result, which enabled these vehicle still to look up to date well into the motorway era – most remained in service until 1965. Although the body design was basically also by BMMO, Duple influence in the neat detailing and flowing lines is not hard to detect, as on the 1939 ONC type, of which FHA 410 is also visible here.

OMT.

Duple's first post-war double-decker was the FS11 front-entrance lowbridge design for Barton Transport Ltd, closely related to the original batch of four on Leyland Titan TD5 of 1939 but this time on the PD1 chassis, with seating capacity of 55 and modernised in detail. Like many other operators, Barton had greatly increased the scale of its double-decker operations and 40 bodies of this type were built in 1947-48. By this date the front-entrance double-decker had very largely gone out of favour in Britain, and in the early post-war period only two operators, both independent, revived the type, the other being Birch Bros, an old-established London firm, though in that case with that concern's own-make bodywork.

Midland Red was the first British operator to standardise on underfloor-engined single-deckers, using chassis made in its own workshops and by then using the BMMO initials as the marque title, the first production examples being the S6 bus, of which 100 entered service in 1946-7. For the C1 and C2 coach derivatives based on largely similar chassis with the horizontal version of the BMMO 8-litre engine, coupled in these cases with an overdrive five-speed gearbox, Duple was again chosen as bodybuilder, the resulting design being coded FS12 at Hendon. As with the front-engined ONC of 1939, the body design shows evidence of co-operation between Midland Red and Duple designers. To the author at least, the result was visually superior to subsequent designs produced for this operator by other coachbuilders, the Duple's designers' almost unfailingly good 'eye' for outlines and proportions being a key element in the overall effect.

The combination of curved waist and upright pillars was in essence similar to the ONC of 1939, and that model's full-fronted style was now even more logical with the engine no longer at the front. The centre entrance was retained but the set-back front axle gave a quite different look, set off by revised contours and detail features giving a more modern effect. There was evidence of American influence in some details, one being the recessed driver's windscreen, inclined to reduce unwanted reflections at night. On the 45 C1 coaches with 30-seat capacity built in 1948-9 for express service, only the driver's side of the screen was of this pattern, the nearside one being flush-mounted. Twelve more basically similar coaches with 26-seat capacity built in 1950 for touring duties and designated C2 had both sides of the screen recessed in this way, giving more of a 'frowning' look to the frontal appearance. Another trans-atlantic touch was the original style of radiator grille, shaped almost exactly like that of Buick cars of a few years previously.

An altogether more conservative design was the FS13, a plain though well-proportioned 35-seat bus body built on the Guy Vixen chassis for the Guernsey Railway Co Ltd which had given up rail services in favour of buses in 1934. Nine vehicles were delivered in 1948 and a tenth, to similar design, built for Guernsey Motors Ltd the following year. The Vixen had been introduced in the 1930s as a lightweight range of goods and passenger models, the latter not generally seating more than 26 but here in long-wheelbase form much as sometimes used for furniture vans, though in rare half-cab form. The type was chosen partly because the chassis design made it possible to comply with a requirement for operation in Guernsey that

By contrast, the FS13 design, of which ten were built for service in Guernsey at about the same time as the BMMO C1 coaches would hardly have caused any surprise had it appeared in about 1935. They were on Guy Vixen chassis, a model of pre-war origin chosen partly because of a width limit of 7ft on that island.

Metal framing had tended to be considered as an 'export' option at Duple. This Bedford OB with Almet body was a typical metal-framed export bus as built during the 1947-49 period – construction was such that it could be supplied in c.k.d. (completely knocked-down) form where preferred.

The use of a bought-in metal-framed structure was another method of meeting the demand for such vehicles. This left-hand drive Leyland Tiger LOPS4 (a long-wheelbase export equivalent to the PS2) for Gibraltar Motorways proudly posed outside Duple's works in 1949 was one of a batch with body framing built by Park Royal Vehicles Ltd. The latter had built various complete export bodies with side framing of similar construction but Duple used more stylishly contoured front and rear outlines.

overall width was not to exceed 7ft.

A move to metal framing

Duple had built occasional metal-framed bodies as far back as 1934, but on a limited basis, for export markets for which wood framing was considered unsuitable. After the 1939-45 war, interest in this form of construction broadened partly because of a shortage of satisfactory timber and partly because of the greater durability shown by some, though by no means all, metal-framed bodies. For a time, a confusing collection of different designs were produced, though some seem to have been delayed or not built at all – export projects were often speculative in character around that time.

The Almet bus body built on the OB for export markets used a Duple design of framing section. However, one by Accles & Pollock Ltd of Oldbury, also known as AP, was chosen for a design for a prototype 32-seat coach on Bedford's proposed new SB passenger chassis, then under development. This design was given the number FS16 in Duple's series, thus coming before others built in time for the 1948 Show, indicating that the project was under way at least two years before the model was announced in time for the 1950 Show, in line with the usual long-term planning of Bedford and General Motors products. Another application of AP framing of around the same time was a 34-seat coach design, type FS17, on left-hand-drive AEC Regal III with 20ft wheelbase for the South American market and accordingly using the ACLO marque name.

For a time, a rather surprising limited-scale collaboration also took place with Park Royal Vehicles Ltd, in one sense a competitor as a major bodybuilder based in the London area, though concentrating largely on bus work and thus catering mainly for a different market. Its Managing Director, W. R. Black, tended to take an open view in such matters and another factor may have been wartime contact between Duple and Park Royal as fellow members of the LAP joint venture in building bombers. In 1949 Park Royal joined the ACV group, in which AEC was the principal chassis maker, though continuing to build on non-group chassis.

A Duple list of FS numbers shows FS20 and FS23 as further South American export projects, this time using Park Royal-built framing. FS20 is recorded as a 39-seat bus on ACLO Regal III 21ft 6in chassis and FS23 as a 39-seat coach

on either Leyland Tiger LOPS or AEC 21ft 6in chassis.

Park Royal records show frames for sixteen coaches as being built in 1949 on Leyland LOPS4/3 chassis for completion by Duple, mainly for sale to operators in Buenos Aires, the exception going to Gibraltar Motorways. A Duple export demonstrator bus on Regal III chassis was to have been built on Park Royal framing at about the same time but was cancelled; however another, with 9631E chassis, was produced as a 39-seat bus in 1949 and sold to Viacao Cometa, of Sao Paulo, Brazil. No further use of Park Royal framing seems to have occurred.

Duple had meantime strengthened the potential for its own

Colin Bailey, Leyland's double-deck body designer, was particularly interested in glazing methods and the Leyland Farington body design had been developed shortly before he left to join Duple in 1948. This example was one of 35 on Leyland Titan PD2/3 chassis supplied to Manchester Corporation in 1950 – the resemblance to the Duple version by then being built was striking, particularly in regard to the windows with sliding panels.

Duple's new design of metal-framed double-decker had the stylish looks to be expected from the firm in that period. It seems clear that the appearance was an amalgam of Duple's designers' usual flair, with touches carried over from the Barton PD1 design and of London RT influence, with evidence of Colin Bailey's arrival in the design of the opening windows. Red & White No.877 was the first of the total of 31 lowbridge 53-seat buses on Guy Arab III chassis with Gardner 6LW engines placed in service by that concern in 1949-50. Note the Southdown PS1, and the tail of an export Albion in the background.

capabilities with the appointment of Colin Bailey as Director and General Manager in 1948. He was an almost legendary figure in relation to bus bodywork, having developed Metro-Cammell's highly successful steel-framed bus body structure from that company's railway-carriage design in 1930. As well as proving the basis for Metro-Cammell's own fast-growing bus body business, an agreement made with Weymann led to the formation in 1932 of Metro-Cammell Weymann Ltd, which held the metal body patents and allowed their use by Weymann, further expanding the scale of their use.

Then, after Leyland Motors Ltd ran into difficulties with its early ventures in metal-framed body construction, Colin Bailey was recruited by Henry Spurrier in 1935 with a virtually free hand to develop successful designs. The outcome was the development by Bailey of a new pillar section, initially to get round the MCW patent but which proved equally successful and led to the creation of another family of very successful metal-framed bus bodies, notably the curved-profile double deckers built on successive generations of Leyland Titan from the later TD4 models of 1936, continuing with only minor alteration though later TD and PD series to the PD2 from 1947. Bailey was also interested in the development of rubber glazing, and the Farington version of the PD2 body introduced in time for display at the 1948 Show embodied this feature.

By then, however, Bailey had joined Duple and set about the development of metal-framed designs for more general sale than the specialised export types to which this form of construction had been restricted hitherto.

The first to go into production were double-deckers, for which demand was very strong at the time, and no doubt Bailey's experience and Leyland's success in this field encouraged this move. Rear-entrance layout was still all but universal and new standard designs were developed in both lowbridge and highbridge forms, adopting the four-bay layout which was then beginning to come into wider favour following its adoption by London Transport. The flush-mounted rubber glazing and style of sliding windows showed clear resemblances to the Leyland Farington style and although there was continuity with previous Duple practice in the general styling of the new designs and also the use of polished beading reminiscent of the Barton double-deckers, there are hints of how Leyland's double-deck bodywork might have developed had Bailey stayed with that firm.

Duple had continued to supply the Red & White group with most of its bodywork needs since the 1930s, but its early post-war double-deckers had been bodied elsewhere. In 1949 a phase of standardisation on Guy Arab III chassis with Gardner 6LW engines and Duple bodywork to the new design began with a pair of lowbridge 53-seat buses for Red & White, soon followed by 29 more delivered in 1949-50. Other group bus-operating subsidiaries also placed batches in service, United Welsh having five highbridge 57-seat buses in 1950, with four similar buses for Cheltenham District Traction Co, two lowbridge and one highbridge for Newbury & District and four highbridge for Venture Ltd of Basingstoke.

Another early customer for basically similar lowbridge bodywork was the Scottish Motor Traction Co Ltd, which ordered 20 on AEC Regent III 9612E chassis. They were delivered between September and December 1949, by which

Contemporary with the Red & White batch, the 25 AEC Regent III buses for SMT, also of lowbridge 53-seat type, had obvious similarities. Yet they differed slightly in that the lower deck was of 4¼-bay layout, resulting in a longer rearmost upper-deck side window, and the curve of the profile was carried right through to the top of the upper-deck pillars. The batch had body numbers 51509-28, and BB77 (GSF 668) with body 51510, was one of the first to be completed, in September 1949 – the operator's full title 'Scottish Motor Traction Co Ltd' shown in the legal lettering was to become obsolete before delivery was complete.

date the bus operating side of that concern had been transferred to a new company, Scottish Omnibuses Ltd, as a result of its sale to the State-owned British Transport Commission that had been formed the previous year (though SMT continued to be used as the fleetname). The SMT Vauxhall/Bedford dealership, including the bodybuilding department, was not included in the sale.

Despite these early successes in sales of the new metal-framed double-deckers, this venture did not attract any more customers at that stage, apart from a small number of bodies mainly on Daimler CVD6 chassis for independent operators. Many major bus operators had already placed their main contracts for fleet renewal or expansion in the aftermath of the war years, and although most bodybuilding factories were still very busy, there was growing competition. Hence a firm less well-known in this field was under a handicap when competing with leading firms better known in the bus side of the industry.

Smaller numbers of lowbridge double-deck bodies were also built on Daimler CVD6 chassis with the smooth-running Daimler 8.6-litre engine, a model also figuring in Duple's output in single-deck form with A-type coach bodies. This 1950 example was for Skill's of Nottingham; two similar vehicles were built for A. Gash & Sons of Newark.

Coaches in the late 1940s

Thus Duple's main business remained much as it had been for 20 years, concentrated mainly on coaches. By 1948, the OB with Vista body and the standard A-type body were such familiar sights all over Britain that they attracted little attention in the trade press, yet the Hendon works continued to be very busy, mainly with just such vehicles.

Figures relating to the five years between May 1946 and April 1951 quoted by John Woodhams in his book on the OB published by DPR in 1986 give a total of 8,720 bodies on all types of chassis built by Duple in that period, representing an average output rate of 1,744 per year, never equalled before or subsequently. Of these, 3,864 were Vista coaches on OB chassis, representing about 44% of Duple's total output in that period, and by far the largest number built to a single design. In fact, deliveries of post-war Vista bodies had begun a couple of months earlier in 1946, so the overall Duple-built total would be slightly higher. In addition, demand was such that SMT had reopened its bodybuilding facilities in time for the 1947 season and augmented the Hendon output by producing further Vista bodies to Duple design, these being supplied mainly to Scottish operators in a manner not unlike that used for the wartime OWB.

Overall home-market post-war OB chassis deliveries totalled 7,200 and although small numbers of Vista bodies went to overseas users, the Vista body comfortably outnumbered all other types on this chassis supplied to British operators added together.

In addition, the bus body designs for the OB, both home and export, augmented the flow of Bedford-Duple products – output of the Mark II body, at first on OWB chassis began at a production rate of 50 per month, but this dropped back considerably once the Vista became available, and from 1947 manufacture of this type was transferred to Mulliners Ltd in another effort to cope with overall demand. Only a small proportion of the 5,493 postwar OB chassis that were exported were shipped with bodywork, but Duple built a few batches including 30 bodies for Uganda in 1946 using a teak-framed design two-compartment design with front-end like a Mark II, and others went to Kenya, in both cases to Overseas Motor Transport subsidiaries. The Almet metal-framed design also contributed to the export Bedford output.

The Mark IV (FS18) bus body for the Bedford OB differed considerably from the Mark II. There are indications that some, at least, were of metal-framed construction. The frontal appearance had more of an inward sweep each side of the windscreen in a manner a little like the post-war Vista, and the outswept skirt gave a slightly more coach-like external appearance. Bristol Tramways & Carriage Co Ltd took twelve with 30-seat capacity in 1949-50, as seen here, although a larger user had been Trinidad Government Railways, with 20 early in 1948.

A new Duple-built bus body design for the OB, called the Mark IV, was in production by 1949 – although broadly similar to the Mark II in overall concept, it differed quite extensively in design, with a windscreen shape and inward-tapering front, producing a frontal appearance rather closer to the Vista. There was a sliding entrance door and the external finish was a little more stylish with such details as outswept skirt panels. However sales were relatively limited, with Bristol Tramways & Carriage Co Ltd as perhaps the best-known British bus-operator user with twelve 30-seat examples delivered in 1949-50, though the Metropolitan Police took a batch in 1950, used mainly to transport police to major sporting events etc.

On the various larger chassis, the proportion of Duple bodies to overall output was not so high, yet some substantial figures were built up. For example, Duple contributed 294 of the bodies on home-market AEC Regal I chassis in the period between 1946 and early 1948, mostly coaches though 50 were quoted as bus or dual-purpose, the combined total representing just under a quarter of home-market sales of this immediate post-war model, and Duple continued to be a major supplier on the subsequent AEC Regal III range. The number of Dennis Lancet III J3-series chassis with Duple

bodies, almost all A-type coaches, was over 180, representing a similar proportion of this model in the 1946-50 period during which it was in production.

Similar patterns applied to other chassis, even though the Duple proportion was usually rather less, and some were built in substantial numbers. Most notable in this way was the Leyland Tiger PS1, which was Leyland's standard home-market single-decker until 1950, the PS2 with O.680 engine being built only in small numbers for operators in Great Britain during the period from 1948 to 1950. To these were added the numbers of models such as the Albion Valkyrie and Valiant (the latter name re-introduced from 1948 for a new CX39 model with 9.9-litre engine replacing the Valkyrie CX13), Daimler CVD6 and the Maudslay Marathon II and III, for all of which quantities of Duple bodies, almost all A-type coaches, were built.

The 1948 Show also brought further new types to the range, notably coach bodies for new lighter models from Albion and Leyland, built in modest numbers. The Albion was the Victor FT3 and FT39 full-fronted forward-control chassis, for which the Duple FS21 body was introduced for the Show and subsequently a standard 31-seat coach body, type FS27, was added to the range. The Leyland Comet in its

The A-type coach body continued to be Duple's main product on full-sized chassis through the 1946-50 period, though there were quite a number of variations. For the AEC Regal Mark III, a four-bay version was introduced, type FS14, paralleling the association of four-bay double-deckers for the corresponding Regent III, including the RT. This design went into production in 1947, though the five-bay version continued for most other chassis – in a sense, it revived the original curved-waist four-bay concept first seen a dozen years previously. These two examples of what AEC then designated as its O962 chassis (9621E from 1948), with 9.6-litre engine and preselective gearbox, are seen posed in the AEC works drive at Southall in August 1947 before delivery to Brewer's Motor Services, of Caerau.

original semi-forward-control form was the basis for the FS28 standard coach, with body similar to a slightly extended Vista, with 32-seat capacity – there was also a metal-framed design, type FS29.

Further FS numbers issued in the period from 1948 to the earlier part of 1950 can be summarised as follows:-

FS No.	Type letter/ name	Description	Main customer	Chassis (main)
FS16	-	32-seat coach (prototype, using AP-section metal framing)	Vauxhall Motors Ltd	Bedford SB
FS17	-	Export coach, 34-seat, AP metal framing	S. America	AEC (ACLO) Regal III LH (20ft wb)
FS18	Mk IV	30/31-seat bus	Vauxhall	Bedford OB
FS19	-	Export bus	O.M.T. (Kenya)	Guy Arab (17ft 6in wb)
FS20	-	Export 39-seat bus PRV metal framing	S. America	AEC (ACLO) Regal III LH (21ft 6in)
FS21	-	Bus and coach, 30/33-seat	Albion Motors	Albion Victor
FS22	-	Coach	(Project deleted)	Guy Vixen
FS23	-	Export coach 39-seat (PRV metal framing)	S. America	Leyland LOPS & AEC (ACLO) Regal III LH
FS24	-	Double-deck, lowbridge	SMT	AEC Regent III 9612E
FS25	-	Double-deck, lowbridge	Red & White	Guy Arab III
FS26	-	ditto, highbridge	ditto	ditto
FS27	-	Coach, 31-seat	(Standard)	Albion Victor FT3 and FT39N
FS28	-	Coach, 32-seat	(Standard)	Leyland Comet
FS29	-	ditto (metal-framed)	ditto	ditto

By about 1948 interest in full-fronted bodywork was beginning to grow, partly as a reaction to the advent of underfloor-engined models, on which the full-width front end was the most obvious outward sign of the different layout. The adoption of this type of vehicle by Midland Red helped to heighten interest and although only one maker, Sentinel, exhibited an underfloor-engined model at the 1948 Show, it was widely known that AEC, Leyland and others were developing such designs. Hence full-fronted bodywork on what were then conventional front-engined chassis began to find favour – for example, Maudslay had a Marathon III with a full-fronted version of the Duple A-type body on display on its stand at the Show, and examples on AEC, Leyland and other chassis began to form a still minor but significant and growing proportion of output over the next couple of years. Usually, the bodywork was built round the standard radiator of these models and, to the author at least, this helped in retaining their 'high-quality' look.

To sum up, the five years 1946-50 formed what was in many ways a golden age for the bus and coach industry, and not least Duple, with demand for its products at unprecedented levels. The firm's standing in terms of matters such as coach styling was underlined by the number of other firms, often new to the industry, which adopted styles reminiscent of the Vista and A-type – "the sincerest from of flattery is imitation". The demand for new vehicles and the rebodying of old ones was such as to have attracted many new entrants to the business but as the 1950 Show approached with the promise of many new models, there were also the first signs of a forthcoming fall-off in demand as the post-war shortage of new vehicles was overcome.

By 1950, scenes such as this view in Slough, with a line-up of coaches of contemporary Duple designs were becoming commonplace. This one was led by a Windsorian Motor Coach services Ltd Dennis Lancet III, No.40 (DMO 240), which was numerically the first of this model to have Duple bodywork (chassis number 106J3 in a series beginning at 101J3, the preceding examples all being buses for Aldershot & District). It was delivered early in 1947 as the first of a batch of three. Windsorian was traditionally both a Dennis and Duple user.

Despite much greater standardisation, there was still plenty of variety in the 1946-50 period, as conveyed on this page. The post-war Albion Victor was more closely related to goods models of similar size than had applied pre-war. This FT3AB model, with six-cylinder side-valve petrol engine, was displayed at the 1948 Commercial Motor Show, being for export to the Delhi Motor Transport Co.

Leyland's post-war lighter vehicle range was called the Comet, originally of semi-forward-control layout, the passenger version generally being of type CPO1, with 5-litre six-cylinder diesel engine. For it, Duple introduced the FS28 coach body style, having obvious affinities with the Vista but longer and seating 32 passengers – this one dating from early 1950 was for Orient Coaches of Bristol.

Crossley had largely been associated with municipal buses but became quite a strong competitor in the coach business, mainly with its SD42/7 chassis – the Crossley 8.6-litre engine seems to have been more successful as a coach power unit than in an urban bus. Duple bodied about 40 in the period up to 1950, Robinson of Great Harwood having seventeen. The example shown dating from about late 1949, and with non-standard slim side flash, was being used as a demonstrator, the legal lettering recording the owner as Scottorn Ltd, New Malden, Essex.

Foden entered the coach market on a commercial basis just after the war, immediately adopting a full-width bonnet with concealed radiator of the type later adopted by several makers. It presented some problems from a styling viewpoint, but Duple adapted the A-type body to it quite successfully, as indicated by this example with body 46045, one of two on the PVSC5 chassis with Gardner 5LW engine for Osmond Bros of Curry Rivel, Somerset, delivered late in 1947.

A number of operators turned to full-fronted bodywork from about 1948 and at first glance these two Duple-bodied AEC Regal 33-seat coaches in the fleet of Morley's Grey Coaches of Mildenhall, Suffolk, might be taken for new vehicles of this period. In fact both were, at least nominally, extensive rebuilds of much earlier Regal chassis, BCF 648 (with new body 45586) being re-registered from HX 1270, having begun life as an AEC demonstrator in 1930 while GO 1148, registered in 1931 and originally operated by E. Paull of Forest Hill in London, (now with body 51458) was about to become BGV 553. The way in which the original Regal model of those days had been altered by successive interchangeable items up to the post-war Regal I specification meant that it was possible to use later parts to update them, both mechanically – sometimes including new frames – and in appearance. Even so, the extent of renewal in some cases seems to suggest that the objective had more to do with overcoming the big delays in delivery of new chassis at that time.

6 THE EARLY 1950s – AN ERA OF CHANGE

The introduction of metal-framed construction for double-deckers from 1949 mentioned in the previous chapter was the first outward sign of a fundamental review of Duple's designs and production methods made in 1948. It was partly a conscious effort to adopt fresh ideas and partly a reaction to the problems then being experienced in meeting the level of demand, even though also influenced by changing trends in vehicle layout and legislation. There was at first comparatively little sign of this to the outside world as the Hendon works was busier than ever through the late 1940s, with an output largely of designs basically as introduced in 1946, mainly the Vista body for the Bedford OB and the A-type coaches for larger models.

Yet the very level of success was part of the problem. Production was not far short of the maximum possible within the limitations of existing methods and the factory space available on the Hendon site, by then fully occupied and surrounded by other factories. The need for an increase of capacity seemed clear at the time, even though the level of demand for bodywork was far above normal mainly because of the after-effects of the war, and hence bound to decline as a normal pattern of fleet renewals resumed.

The labour force employed had grown to 1,200, compared to the 800 reached by 1939 and a greater degree of standardisation had helped to boost output. The demand for skilled wood and sheet metal workers was particularly strong in and around the western outskirts of London and labour costs were rising. This effect was being accentuated by trade unions which had grown in strength during the war years, when many of their demands had been conceded in an effort to increase war production. The high level of demand locally led to the more militant agitators in the unions having greater power than applied in most other parts of the country and the objectives of some, quite often members of the Communist Party, went far beyond securing better pay and conditions for workers. Deliberate crippling of what they saw as part of the hated capitalist system was apt to be regarded as a welcome side-effect, so negotiations with them were very difficult.

In August 1948 it had been announced that G. R. (Gerald) White, Herbert's son, who had been working as Acting Managing Director, was confirmed as Managing Director. He felt the need for a change to more modern technology and considered that although the traditional timber-framed body was well suited to medium-scale output and allowed flexibility, Duple's needs were moving beyond that point. The same announcement reported the appointment of Colin Bailey, initially as a Director and General Manager, already mentioned, and the two events were directly linked.

The plan was to introduce what was intended eventually to be a large-scale turnover to metal-framing, taking advantage of the more economic and speedierw production methods this would allow, though it was planned to introduce new body designs of both metal-framed and composite construction.

It was known by Duple management by that time that Bedford had a new model range well advanced for introduction in 1950 and indeed already Duple had designed a body for a prototype SB passenger model, using a proprietary form of metal framing. It was relevant in this context that Bedford was part of the General Motors empire which had been a pioneer in the large-scale adoption of the pressed-steel car body two decades earlier, and a standardised coach had obvious possibilities for obtaining some of the anticipated manufacturing cost savings. The makers of several of the larger and heavier-duty types of chassis were also known to be developing underfloor-engined chassis, for which new body designs would be needed.

Ideas on vehicle styling were also under review, as was also the case in the car industry, with both American ideas and aeroplanes as sources of fresh thought. The basic sloping-pillar and curved waist concept that had served Duple very well for almost 15 years was becoming regarded as over-familiar in a business which, in the view of some operators at least, depended on novelty in external appearance as a means of attracting passengers.

The first clue to a fresh styling approach at Duple to become evident to the outside world was the building early in 1950 of a new design of coach body on a Leyland Tiger PS2/3 chassis for the fleet of Wallace Arnold Tours Ltd of Leeds. It was sent to a special British Motor Show in New York in April of that year, part of a motor industry export drive.

It was the first example to be revealed of a new range of full-fronted body designs given the name Ambassador. These were of composite construction and this early FS35 version for front-engined chassis was to the 27ft 6in by 7ft 6in dimensions then still in force as the maximum for general use in Britain – 8ft width had been legal for specifically approved routes since 1946, but this was of no practical use for a coach intended for general use. This vehicle, registered NUG 1, was a touring coach seating only 21 and after the Show was sent on a promotional coast-to-coast trip in an effort to find American customers for the operator's tours in Britain.

This initial Ambassador design for front-engined chassis had centre-entrance layout. The radiator was hidden by a decorative grille using a pattern of polished strips which, like many of the type, seemed rather bland and lacking in character. The body design as a whole also departed from many existing Duple characteristics and although the familiar curved waist was still evident, the pillars were vertical. The overall effect was 'different' in the way doubtless intended yet, to the author at least, much of the previous distinctive elegance was missing.

The windscreen and cab side windows were shaped to form a related wrap-round unit, though the main screen panels were made from flat glass – the large-scale manufacture of

Coach design was in a state of flux as a new decade began. The prospect of new vehicle designs and of increased dimensions, coupled with changing tastes in appearance meant that what had seemed settled practice was being challenged. An early manifestation in the search for a 'fresh' look was this coach built for Wallace Arnold Tours Ltd early in 1950. It was built to the maximum length then in force for a two-axle single-decker for general use in Britain of 27ft 6in and was on a front-engined Leyland Tiger PS2 chassis (itself still quite rare in Britain by comparison with the smaller-engined PS1) but was to a new style having little in common with Duple standard products of that date but with clear indications of some that were to appear a little later. The seating capacity, in a two-and-one layout, was 21 and there was no internal bulkhead. Body number 53867 to design FS35 was the first example to be revealed of a new style called the Ambassador, appropriately enough since in April 1950 it was sent to a special Motor Show in New York and used for tours promotion work in the USA. It was registered NUG 1, though it was not licensed for service in Britain until January 1951. The body was transferred to a 1947 Tiger PS1 chassis, KUG 667, in 1954 and sold off in 1958.

curved glass for such use was in its infancy. Styling emphasis was put on the side pillar immediately behind the cab, with a dip in the cantrail moulding at this point. The side mouldings were arranged to give the impression of one continuous mudguard outline embracing both front and rear wheels. This design was built only in small numbers and can be counted as a transition pointing towards what was to follow. It was also available on AEC Regal III chassis with almost identical appearance, one such being supplied in the summer of 1950 to

J. Boddy & Son, of Bridlington, to carry the Hull City football team. It too seated 21, this time without the extensive roof glazing – the basic design could seat up to 33.

Yet more dramatic new developments were already under way as a result not only of the new chassis types already planned but also the changes in maximum dimensions for use in Britain. Slight changes were expected but the unexpected announcement early in 1950 that two-axle single-deckers entering service after 1st June could be 30ft long instead of 27ft 6in sent drawing offices into

More typical of production in 1950, Royal Blue's standard design, elegant in an older style, was that first seen on an AEC Regal rebodied by Duple for this fleet in 1941, though Beadle had bodied 45 new Bristol L6B and L6A coaches in 1947-49. Duple got the order for a further ten L6B coaches but it became clear that a new longer limit on length would be in force when they were to be supplied in the latter part of 1950, though the chassis had the 17ft 6in wheelbase to suit the old limit. It proved possible to build the bodies (type FS34) to an overall length of 28ft 2in, the seating capacity going up from 31 to 33 – the extra length was neatly added to the rearmost side window. One of the five owned by Southern National, 1260 (LTA 889) with body 54572, is seen at Victoria in July 1952.

Another case of responding to increase in permitted dimensions was that of Ribble which switched from the old 7ft 6in width to 8ft when a second batch of 20 A-type 31-seat coach bodies was ordered for pre-war Leyland Tiger chassis for delivery in 1950, following an initial batch of 34 to the old width in 1949. The 8ft version was designated FS33 by Duple. These vehicles also received new 7.4-litre diesel engines similar to the type used in the PS1 in place of their original petrol engines, an alteration which doubtless made economic sense but increased the internal noise level considerably. Here No.1497 (RN 7747), a TS7 chassis dating from 1936, is seen with new Duple body No. 53824. It remained in service with Ribble until 1960.

a flurry of activity, not least at Hendon. A little later, general approval for use of 8ft width was granted, further adding to the complexity of the variations.

A new series of FS numbers was issued in rapid succession in response to the new situation, as listed herewith, and even though the actual order of vehicles being produced to them in 1950-51 was not always as implied by the numerical order, the list shows how output was moving into a new pattern. A new system of denoting minor variants on a basic theme by a stroke or suffix number, Leyland-style, seems quite likely to

have been a Bailey innovation. The FS31 series ran to some 31 such variants, many of which were never built, though in fact FS31/31 was to prove one of the most important, covering the version as built on Guy Arab UF chassis for the Red & White group. The following list gives only the basic numbers.

Of the types listed below, types FS33, FS34 and FS36 were continuations of existing designs, though the fact that their numbers were higher than some of the new types indicates that they were put in hand from a design viewpoint after some of the new-generation models. The FS33 was an 8ft-wide adaptation

FS number	Type name	Description	Main customer	Chassis (main)
FS30	Luxury Land Cruiser	Coach, composite, metal pillars	AEC demo.	AEC Regal IV prototype
FS31	Roadmaster	Coach, metal (30ft x 8ft std)	Standard	Underfloor engine
FS32	Vega	Coach, metal, 27ft 7in	Standard	Bedford SB
FS33	A-type	Coach, composite 8ft wide	Ribble	Leyland TS7
FS34	–	Coach, composite 28ft 2in x 7ft 6in	Royal Blue	Bristol L
FS35	Ambassador	Coach, composite 27ft 6in x 7ft 6in	Standard	Front engined
FS36	National	Coach, composite 30ft	Standard	Front engine
FS37	–	Double-deck normal height	–	Guy or other
FS38	–	Double-deck low height	–	"Any chassis"
FS39	Ambassador	Coach, metal 30ft	Standard	Underfloor engine
FS40	Duple-Metsec	Bus, metal	Standard	Bedford SB
FS41	Provincial	Bus, metal 30ft	Standard	Underfloor engine

End of an era. To meet the possibility of demand for 30ft coach bodies on conventional chassis, Duple introduced the FS36 design for the 1951 season, basically an extended version of the A-type or FS1, with six bays behind the entrance door rather than five. The individual bays were thus rather shorter, contrary to the general trend of the times – even so, the result was a handsome coach in what up to then had been the accepted style. As it turned out, the only substantial orders came from the Southern & Western National companies, and that only because a new underfloor-engined Bristol model was not yet ready for production. They were on Bristol LL6B chassis having the 8.1-litre Bristol AVW engine, and of 7ft 6in width, partly because of some unease about 8ft coaches negotiating narrow Devon roads. Seen here is Western National 1302 (LTA 740) with body 54593, one of the fourteen coaches in cream and green livery supplied in 1951 seen in almost new-looking condition in Minehead in May 1958 – by that date, such a coach was bordering on the unacceptably old-fashioned. The Royal Blue equivalent was identical up to cantrail level but had the style of roof traditional to that fleet, with full-width canopy and luggage carrier.

of the FS1, chosen by Ribble for its 1950 batch of rebodying of 20 pre-war Tiger coaches (19 TS7 and a TS6), plus four TS7 for Standerwick, when it was realised that the restrictions on the general use of wider vehicles were to be lifted. Some 34 generally similar bodies of 7ft 6in width had been built on TS8 chassis for Ribble the previous year. All these vehicles continued to use the 31 seat capacity favoured by Ribble for its coaches since prewar days.

The FS34 design was an intermediate-length design for Bristol L chassis, taking such advantage of the relaxation on length on chassis intended for the 27ft 6in limit as was possible without infringing the maximum permissible overhang, the result working out at 28ft 2in. In general by then the Tilling companies were required to standardise on Bristol chassis with ECW bodywork, save for light vehicles. However in the 1946-50 period when ECW was not producing coach bodywork beyond the dual-purpose 'express' type based on the bus body shell, it was agreed that vehicles in this class could be bodied elsewhere. The Southern and Western National Omnibus Companies obtained their requirements for the Royal Blue coach fleet from Beadle in the earlier post-war years, using a 31-seat capacity, but returned to Duple for the 1950 and 1951 deliveries.

The design was very similar to that built by Beadle but the slight increase in length was used to accommodate an extra pair of seats taking the capacity to 33. The basis for all these was a

1941 prototype body built by Duple on a pre-war AEC Regal chassis. As a result of the short notice given in regard to the changes in permitted dimensions, manufacturers found themselves producing interim designs, although many operators wished to adopt the new limits as quickly as possible. In the event, Duple built ten bodies to this design on L6B chassis, five each for SNOC and WNOC, in 1950.

The FS36 body design was basically an extended version of the FS1 type to suit the various types of front-engined chassis which were produced to fit the 30ft overall length permissible from June 1950, allowing seating capacities of up to 37 or 39. Most of the chassis in question were basically longer-wheelbase versions of the various maker's models, much as had been produced in 27ft 6in form apart from minor changes to tyres and springs etc, and were apt to be regarded as a stop-gap until underfloor-engined models were put into production. Versions for both 7ft 6in and 8ft width were designed to suit Bristol LL, Foden, Daimler CVD6, Dennis J10A, Crossley, Guy, Maudslay, Leyland, AEC and Tilling-Stevens chassis, to quote the rather surprising order in which they were listed in an internal Duple list of FS variants.

In this list, 'National' is used as a type name for all of these designs, but this was probably no more than a reference to the Southern and Western National companies being the source of the initial enquiry, and indeed they proved to be the main users – it was not until nearly two decades later that

Sales of FS36-type 30ft-long half-cab bodies were generally on a very small scale. A pair of 37-seat examples on Daimler CVD6 long-wheelbase chassis were delivered to west of England operators in July 1951. The CVD6, with smooth-running Daimler 8.6-litre engine and fluid flywheel transmission, had been quite popular as a coach and its appearance suited the Duple body well, though the combination had never been common even in 27ft 6in form. The vehicle shown, LFJ 931, was supplied to Taylor's Central Garages of Exeter, though seen here arriving at Victoria Coach station, London, probably as a Royal Blue relief, after takeover by Greenslade's of Exeter in 1954. As was often so at that time, the body numbers, this one being 50209, were among a sequence of numbers more related to chassis make than precise date.

'National' was to take on a quite different significance with the formation of the National Bus Company.

The actual order of FS36 suffix numbers was further complicated by the addition of 8ft versions part-way through the process and by the fact that what were produced as a continuation of the Southern & Western National orders mentioned above were given their own numbers because they incorporated other features. The FS36/7 was a 37-seat design built on Bristol LL6B chassis for use on these companies' own coach duties, largely local tour and excursion work, painted in cream and green livery and having half-canopy bodies with glass roof quarter lights, whereas the FS36/15 version was the Royal Blue version with full-width canopy and

the traditional row of destination displays above the side windows, again on the LL6B. There were seventeen of the Royal Blue version making up the balance of the 1950 deliveries plus seven more placed in service in 1951. There were fourteen of the half-canopy cream and green type, all delivered in 1951.

Duple had also continued to supply Vista bodies on Bedford chassis to these two companies, as had applied most peacetime years since 1937, there being a final 23 such in 1950. However, Southern and Western National, like Tilling companies generally, turned exclusively to Eastern Coach Works for bodywork, including that for coaches, in succeeding years, so an important pair of customers was lost to Duple. Even so, this final set of orders for coach bodies on Bristol L and LL chassis was a substantial parting contract, amounting to 48 bodies built in 1950-51 – clearly they were ordered together as the body numbers run in sequence as 54571-618.

Sales of all types of half-cab coach bodywork underwent a remarkable collapse after the 1950 Show period, when the combination of the underfloor-engined models being shown on almost all the heavy-duty makers' stands and the full-fronted forward-control Bedford SB made such vehicles suddenly seem outdated. Very few new coaches of this type on any make of chassis were produced by Duple in 1951. Heavy-duty front-engined chassis were henceforth rarely seen at Hendon, even to receive full-fronted bodywork, although there were a few cases of rebodying in subsequent years.

The FS30 design was produced for one of three pre-production AEC Regal IV chassis, this being that maker's initial underfloor-engined model, using units derived from those of the Regal III. The body could itself be counted as a pre-production version of the Ambassador, the general fairly curvaceous style and centre-entrance layout being not unlike the Wallace Arnold body for PS2 chassis. The construction also appears to have been of a transitional form, using metal pillars.

The Roadmaster

The FS31 metal-framed Roadmaster body was quite dramatically unlike any previous Duple coach design, with a straight waistline set at an unusually high level, not merely due to the higher floor-line because of the underfloor engined layout of the chassis, but even in relation to the seats. Its appearance conveyed an impression of sturdy construction and the apt nickname 'Iron Duke' given by Duple staff recalled a battleship as well as the form of construction. The front-end incorporated a pair of windscreen panels set in a vee formation, the waist being stepped down slightly to suit.

Overall, the outline was more angular than any standard Duple coach since the mid 1930s, with only the well-rounded rear dome and a more localised softening of the outline around the top corners of the windscreen having an echo of previous practice.

The name Roadmaster had a distinctly American ring to it, having been used for a successful range of Buick cars from 1938 and into the early post-war period. There were instances where this type of duplication led to hasty withdrawal of the second user. Whether or not Duple got the name from this

Duple was in at almost the beginning so far as the AEC Regal IV underfloor-engined chassis was concerned, bodying one of three production prototypes. The body style, FS30, had resemblances to the Wallace Arnold Tiger PS2 and could also be counted as a prototype for the production Ambassador. It was used for development work, including test-running on the punishing pave roadway at the Motor Industry Research Association proving ground at Lindley, before being sold to Berry's Transport of Bradford-on-Tone, near Taunton, and registered NYD 509 in 1952.

source, it seems unlikely that would have wished to court displeasure from a General Motors concern when so much of its business was in building on Bedford chassis made by a different branch of that group. The use of '-master' was quite a fashionable idea for various products around that period and London Transport's choice of 'Routemaster' for its bus design introduced in 1954 may well have been influenced by Duple's choice four years earlier.

Roadmaster body designs were drawn up in both coach and bus forms for quite a variety of underfloor-engined chassis, including the AEC Regal IV and the Leyland Royal Tiger in home market (both 7ft 6in and 8ft wide) and export forms as well as the Dennis Dominant, Daimler Freeline, Guy Arab UF and Sentinel. There was even a Roadmaster design of composite construction for the front-engined Dennis Lancet III in 30ft J10A and J10C full-fronted form but this and indeed many others of the combinations listed were built only in very small numbers or not at all.

The Leyland Royal Tiger PSU1 series was the first and most widely chosen model on which examples were built, and indeed the second production chassis of this type, a 7ft 6in wide PSU1/11, received a Roadmaster 41-seat coach body for Scout Motor Services Ltd, of Preston. A batch of six PSU1/15 8ft-wide 41-seat Roadmaster coaches supplied to

Standerwick in 1951 for that operator's services linking Lancashire and London received widespread publicity and may have been the inspiration for the Dinky Toy model of the type. Others went to various independent operators, a PSU1/11 for A. & P. McConnachie Ltd, of Campbelltown being notable as being a 45-seat bus version with an unusually narrow folding entrance door.

Red & White Services Ltd had the first PSU/15 from a large order for Royal Tigers fitted with a Duple coach body, being completed late in 1950, though most of the others were bodied the following year by Lydney, which was a Red & White subsidiary. However, the Roadmaster body with spacious 37-seat layout was chosen for a fleet of Guy Arab UF coaches for this group. Fourteen were supplied to Red & White in 1952-3 and seven for United Welsh in 1952, thereby creating the largest collection of Roadmaster bodies.

However, this could be counted as the swan-song at the end of a long period when Red & White had been among Duple's most important and regular customers. The group had sold out to the British Transport Commission in 1950, the various bus and coach subsidiaries then being placed under the control of the Tilling group, itself a BTC concern since 1948. Red & White and United Welsh adopted the Tilling policy of standardisation on Bristol chassis with ECW bodywork

The announcement shortly before the 1950 Show of a new range of larger Bedfords, at first marketed simply as the Big Bedfords, was a dramatic event in itself. Duple was closely involved in regard to the SB passenger model from an early stage and although the front-end design of the resulting Vega body was closely related to that of the truck cab, it was produced at Hendon so as to merge with the body contours. Here there were plenty of curves, with styling that was bold to the point of being brash, with a strong American flavour in the contours and detailing. Other parts of the body showed some affinity with the Ambassador in the shaping of the pillar behind the cab, the continuity of wing treatment and at the rear, but the overall effect was unlike anything else on the road at the time. This example, representative of most of the 33-seat version built in the first two years, was supplied to Yellow Bus Services of Guildford early in 1952.

from 1952 or 1953, and the same also applied to the smaller ex-Red & White group concerns, which were placed under the wing of various Tilling operating companies and gradually lost their identity in succeeding years.

Overall, demand for the Roadmaster thus proved quite limited and it faded from the scene by 1953, a rather wider spread of operators preferring the Ambassador described below.

The Vega

The first production body for the new Bedford SB chassis was equally startling to eyes that had become used to the Vista. It was much more curvaceous than the Roadmaster but in a bold almost voluptuous way, the front end having a rather transatlantic flavour with a hint of air-liner styling from the waist up. It was coded FS32 and given the type name Vega, continuing the use of names beginning with V for bodies intended for chassis built by Vauxhall Motors Ltd.

The whole concept was based on some bold policy decisions taken by Bedford, the model being part of a new S-type range introduced in time for the 1950 Show and known collectively as the Big Bedfords. The goods models were capable of carrying 7 tons, compared to the 5 tons maximum of the existing O-type range, to which the OB had belonged, and were of forward-control layout, using a new 4.9-litre six-cylinder petrol engine and other units to suit the weight range.

The SB had been designed to suit the 27ft 6in by 7ft 6in dimensions and there was no way that the manufacturing setup of Vauxhall Motors, geared to large-scale and long-term planning, could respond to changes which became known just before production was in process of being set-up. As announced, the overall length was just over the former limit at 27ft 7in and the width 7ft 6in, though an FS32/3 design with 8ft body width was added slightly later.

In any case, the step up in size from the OB to the SB was already considerable, putting the latter into the 33-seat class which hitherto had been the preserve of the heavy-duty coach. One of the boldest decisions, and one which might be open to question in some of its effects, given the benefit of hindsight, was that the OB was to be dropped even though it was still selling very well. This certainly helped to boost SB sales, since the former OB user had nowhere else to go, and the SB Vega package was again one of exceptional value, just as the OB Vista had been – the complete 33-seat coach was priced at £2,190, which was no more than some heavy-duty chassis. The purchase and running costs were increased compared to the OB, though not by a huge margin, and there was the revenue from four extra seats to pay for them.

The Bedford designers had been very weight-conscious from the beginning and this was still so with the SB, with a chassis weight of 2 tons 8 cwt 1 qr; Duple played its part in keeping the unladen weight of the complete Vega coach to around 4 tons 15 cwt. This contrasted with many of the new underfloor-engined models which turned the scales at around 8 tons (admittedly with a greater seating capacity), and the SB, returning 11 miles per gallon or so, thus often used no more fuel than such vehicles despite being petrol-engined in this early form.

The body design as initially offered was described as of Duple 'truss-framed' construction with rolled and folded steel framing. The front-end styling had a close family affinity to that of the S-type trucks, with a similarly bulbous front panel and decorative horizontal bars across the radiator opening, though in fact the panel was shaped to suit the greater width of the body as compared to the truck cab. The main windscreen panels were in a vee formation and set back slightly in a similar manner, but the curved glass cab side windows were deeper and shaped to produce an overall wrap-around shape in a somewhat similar way to the initial Ambassador on PS2 chassis for Wallace Arnold, though using more rounded outlines.

The rest of the body had much more of a recognisable Duple look than the Roadmaster, with gently curving waist and slender polished metal pillars, though these were vertical, and the rear curved in traditional manner, though the lower edge of the skirt panel was no longer outswept. The SB Vega sold well from the start and soon became a familiar sight in most parts of Britain, though the body design did not continue unaltered long enough to rival the ubiquitous nature of the Vista models built over the previous five years.

A new system of classified body numbering was introduced, coming into effect from 1951, although the transition from the previous one took two years or so to complete, with a rather confused interim period when both were in use. Under the new system, a production batch number was followed by an oblique stroke and then individual serial numbers. Batch numbers from 1000 up were at first reserved for Bedford production. A clue to the scale of manufacture was that the first major batch for the SB, number 1006, ran to 1006/500. Although delivery of these extended through 1952, followed numerically by quite a number of much smaller batches, some evidently covering variants, a regular pattern emerged of the main output of bodies on SB chassis each production year running to several hundred units and rising to over 500 in the later 1950s. Standardised production at this level, with little more than paint and seating moquette differences, was something in which Duple was unrivalled in the coach business in Britain.

There was also a bus version of this initial body design for the SB, FS32/1 (or FS32/2 in 8ft form), officially called the Mark VI and priced at £1,960, but this retained the Vega body shell, differing essentially in having bus seats and lacking interior luggage racks as standard. It was a rare choice, most independent operators reasoning that the extra £220 would buy a vehicle that could be used for both bus and coach duties, just as they had with bodywork for previous Bedfords back to the WTB era.

Further variants of the Vega body design (FS32/4 to /7) were based on the latest version of the Dennis Falcon, with 5-litre six-cylinder Dennis diesel engine. These had the Vega

This austere-looking metal-framed bus body was produced for the SB chassis in 1951 for military or other non-public use. It used a front cowl of even more bulbous shape than the Vega, similar to the truck version. The 'official' Mark VI bus of that period was quite different, being based on the Vega coach structure but was sold only in small numbers.

This Vega demonstrator, KBM 60, was built for Vauxhall Motors Ltd towards the end of 1951. The body appears to have been 8ft wide, an option from about that date and one soon taken up quite widely. It seated 28, with a row of seats just behind the rear axle reversed and another row removed.

body structure married to the Dennis full-width front panel giving a more orthodox profile. All were 27ft 6in long and there were coach and bus versions each available in 7ft 6in or 8ft width, but only a handful were built.

The Duple-Metsec was a rugged export bus for the SB using Metal Sections framing aimed at a similar market to the 'All Metal' body for the OB, this FS40 design being in alternative widths and lengths with various entrance positions.

A new version of the Dennis Falcon was bodied by Duple in 1951-52 with a variation of the Vega design of body but incorporating the Dennis front panel assembly, basically as used on equivalent goods models, giving a very different overall effect despite the similarity of the grille design to that used with the Bedford. It seated 33 and this example weighed 5 tons 3 cwt 2 qr.

The production Ambassador for underfloor-engined chassis, type FS39, had a pronounced downward sweep in the window line at the front of the side panels. Ideas on appearance are inevitably a matter of opinion but, to the writer at least, there seemed to be some loss of the sureness of eye in the choice of curves that had been evident in previous generations of Duple styling even though the overall effect could be quite impressive. The Leyland Royal Tiger, with horizontal 9.8-litre Leyland O.600 engine and a synchromesh gearbox, was the main model on which examples were built. Among early examples were five on PSU1/15 chassis for Scout Motor Services Ltd of Preston, placed in service in 1951. Seen here is DRN 358 with body 67/13, the first of the batch. Scout's cream and plum livery suited the design well.

The Ambassador

The more popular choice among Duple body styles for early production underfloor-engined chassis proved to be the Ambassador, and it is this version, initially type FS39, that springs to mind when the name is mentioned rather than the rare examples of the FS35 for front-engined chassis already mentioned. It was offered in both 7ft 6in and 8ft wide forms on Leyland Royal Tiger, AEC Regal IV, Dennis, Sentinel and Daimler Freeline chassis, but the Royal Tiger was the most popular.

The basic concept of centre-entrance layout with curved waist and roof lines was much as on the prototype Wallace Arnold vehicle built early in 1950 on PS2 chassis for the New York Show, but for underfloor-engined chassis the window line fell much more sharply at the front end. The windscreen sill line also drooped quite sharply from the centre and, to the writer at least, these features combined to give an effect curiously like a sad facial expression and the overall effect lacked the flowing gracefulness of the earlier Duple bodies.

Duple was by no means alone among well-known bodybuilders in evidently experiencing difficulty in establishing satisfactory front-end designs for underfloor-engined models, as if the absence of the discipline set by a well-proportioned traditional radiator left body designers somewhat adrift – in most cases, they seemed to find creating grille designs having any strength of character especially difficult.

Even so, the Ambassador proved to have a wider appeal than the Roadmaster. Southdown chose it for a batch of ten touring coaches with luxurious seating for 26 passengers on

Leyland Royal Tiger chassis delivered in 1951 and then 20 more with 41-seat capacity for express duty in 1952. Scout Motor Services Ltd of Preston took four similar coaches in 1951, followed by six in 1952 – in those days, Scout was still an independent operator although operating jointly with Standerwick, Ribble's coach subsidiary, on the London services. The distinction of Scout's new Royal Tigers being mainly Ambassadors while Standerwick's were Roadmasters suited the desire to be 'different' in the atmosphere of friendly rivalry between the two.

Some well-known London-area customers also chose Ambassador-bodied Royal Tigers, including two who were virtually neighbours of the Duple concern, Venture (Hendon) Ltd and Lewis Cronshaw Ltd, also with a substantial business in Hendon though the firm's origins were in Blackburn and in those days its vehicles were registered there – Cronshaw also took two on Daimler Freeline chassis. Another London buyer of the type was Samuelson New Transport Co Ltd, which was owned by London Coastal Coaches Ltd whose main activity was running Victoria Coach Station, and for a time Samuelson became a regular Leyland-Duple customer.

The Ambassador body was to be found on other chassis, notably ten AEC Regal IV for A. Timpson & Sons, an old-established coach operator based at Catford, London S.E.6, which had come under joint BET and Tilling control. However, Duple bodywork was less common on the Regal IV than on earlier generations of AEC chassis, there being only small numbers supplied to various independent operators. A few were also built on other makes of chassis, such as the Daimler Freeline and Sentinel STC6.

This Royal Tiger PSU1/15 with Ambassador 37-seat body, LYP 425, had body number 36313 – the 'old' numbering system was still in use for a time alongside the new. It was one of a pair built in 1951 for Samuelson New Transport Co Ltd, whose garage adjoined Victoria Coach Station and, since 1936, a subsidiary of London Coastal Coaches Ltd, proprietor of the coach station and itself jointly owned by the major operating companies using it. Samuelson's acted as a servicing facility and, sometimes, overflow departure point for them. Its small fleet, painted green and cream, had been composed of second-hand coaches from these fleets, but a policy of running new coaches had begun, sometimes for air travel hire work, as here.

Underfloor-engined buses

The FS41 body design catered for this market, widely seen as potentially very important. Some people in the industry saw the 30ft-long single-deck bus, perhaps with provision for a large number of standing passengers, as having the potential to succeed the double-decker. In practice, this did not happen, British passengers being unwilling to accept the loss of comfort this implied if even a 56-seat double-decker's capacity was to be equalled. Even so, the potential for 44-seat capacity with an all-seated layout did have quite widespread appeal.

Early work on this project was carried out with the co-operation of Daimler, based on that concern's new underfloor-engined model, the Freeline. A leading advocate of the 'standee' bus at that time was Moris Little, General Manager of the Edinburgh City Transport undertaking. The second Freeline chassis to be built, a G6HS model with Gardner

More traditional body styles continued in small-scale production, though sometimes with new rather bland front-ends. These two Albion Victor FT-series coaches, DBV 318 & 319, were bodied early in 1951 for Lewis Cronshaw Ltd of Hendon, NW4 (whose vehicles were still registered at the original base in Blackburn). Similar bodywork – a short 31-seat version of the A-type – had been built with the rather handsome Albion radiator exposed, much as on the export bus shown on page 83, but this was evidently thought outdated here. Cronshaw had quite broad tastes in terms of chassis, taking Ambassador bodies on both Leyland Royal Tiger and Daimler Freeline. Slightly earlier there had been Crossley and Daimler CVD6 coaches, all with Duple bodywork.

Duple introduced the FS41 bus design for underfloor-engined chassis, and gained plenty of publicity as a result of its choice for a Daimler Freeline demonstrator, LRW 377 with body number 95/1, designed to try out the concept of the 'standee' bus, in which most passengers had to stand when it was fully laden, as widely accepted in Europe. This was largely at the instigation of Moris Little, then building up a reputation as one of the more adventurous of municipal bus managers in his post with the Edinburgh undertaking. After a spell operating in that city, it went on a demonstration tour and is seen here working for Nottingham City Transport in February 1953, but no orders resulted.

The BET group of companies, mostly running large fleets of single-decker buses, was an obvious target for sales. Duple's FS41 design had a general resemblance to the BET Federation standard single-decker as delivered to several of them, though with the front-end outline simplified to a degree and giving a somewhat crude-looking effect. J. James & Sons Ltd of Ammanford had been taken over by BET in 1950 and this Leyland Royal Tiger PSU1/13 was fitted with Duple body number 103/1 as an initial venture into this market. It had semi-coach seats for 40 and a repeat order for two basically similar vehicles seating 44 a year later had the distinction of having body numbers 57409/1 and 57409/2, thus applying the 'new' system to a number in the 'old' series.

6HLW engine, was sent to Duple in March 1951 to receive a body of this type, with two doorways, that at the rear being the entrance and the exit being alongside the driver – a conductor was carried, it being illegal at that date to operate a bus of this size without one. Its seating capacity varied between 30 and 36 in the course of experimental operation. It was completed in Edinburgh livery with the fleet number 800 though owned by Daimler and used for demonstration work as well as being displayed at the 1951 Scottish Show, then entering service briefly in Edinburgh before making an extensive tour of operators, though without success in sales terms – the Freeline used a power-hydraulic brake system, which was regarded with some suspicion, quite apart from the controversial standee aspect.

Nearer mainstream thinking was a front-entrance version of the same body design aimed particularly at the BET group. The FS41 body broadly resembled the BET Federation standard design, as built, mainly by Brush, on Royal Tiger chassis for several BET subsidiaries, with windscreen having both sides of the upper portion recessed, though the Duple version lacked the original's subtlety of line. One was built in 1951 on Royal Tiger chassis for J. James & Son Ltd, of Ammanford, which had come into BET control. A further

Competition became a major worry for a time as the drop in orders led to a struggle for survival in an industry which had expanded to meet the extra demand just after the war but was faced with a much smaller market. Particularly galling to Duple's management was the success for a period in the early 1950s of Windovers Ltd, a near neighbour in Hendon, with its bold Kingsway body style, here seen on a rear-engined Foden built in 1952 for Biss Bros of Bishop's Stortford, Herts – there were seven Windover bodies and six Duple in that fleet in 1957.

pair of similar vehicles for James followed in 1952, but no large-scale order was forthcoming from the BET group, and there was little interest in the type from elsewhere though four special bus bodies on Royal Tiger chassis were built to Government order in 1953 for use at Windscale.

A turn for the worse

During the early 1950s, the bus and coach manufacturing industry, and particularly bodybuilders, went through quite a difficult time, even though most other sectors of industry were still very busy. Duple also suffered some more specific problems not applicable elsewhere. The basic problem arose because the process of catching up with the backlog of demand created by the war ended in most fleets at around that time. The combined effect was one of a quite rapid drop in orders.

Not only did overall demand fall to more normal levels, but there was considerable excess capacity in the industry, especially among builders of coach bodywork, due to the many firms that had started building them when demand was so high that the older-established firms could not cope. Many of these were small concerns which soon went out of business or turned to other work, but some were substantial, having grown quite strong over the previous few years.

Inevitably, competition became intense – on underfloor-engined chassis, Burlingham attracted many orders for its stylish Seagull design, pushing it well in front in terms of numbers of coach bodies from the specialist coach bodybuilders on the leading first-generation underfloor-engined chassis, the Leyland Royal Tiger and AEC Regal IV. Duple was not far behind on the Royal Tiger, but bodied a curiously small share of the Regal IV, in contrast to earlier generations of that model name, with fewer examples than Plaxton (then beginning to become a serious competitor), Windover or Harrington.

Windovers Ltd, also based at The Hyde, Hendon, was a firm that had built high-grade car bodywork pre-war but which had turned to coaches post-war. Despite being a much smaller concern, it attracted several orders from former Duple customers and it is not hard to imagine the frustration this must have caused. Windover established effective relations with the BET group in particular as soon as it entered the coach business, gaining orders from several of that group's subsidiaries. For underfloor-engined chassis, its boldly-styled if controversial Kingsway body had caught the imagination of quite a number of such operators, the best known case being a fleet of 32 on Regal IV chassis built up between 1950 and 1953 by Sheffield United Tours Ltd, in those days run by a very publicity-conscious General Manager, Ben Goodfellow, and for a time Windover gained strongly from this.

Another factor was the loss of other major customers such as the cases of Red & White and the Southern and Western National concerns already mentioned. Both were related to the build-up of bus companies in State ownership, where the sale of the Tilling, SMT and Red & White groups to the British Transport Commission. Its subsidiaries were still free to purchase vehicles from outside suppliers, but Bristol and ECW were no longer free to sell to non-State concerns, which resulted in Tilling (and ex-Red & White group) operating companies standardising on those makes even more strongly than previously, virtually closing the door for some time to concerns such as Duple, which had supplied Vista coaches to several such companies.

Yet the biggest problem for Duple lay within its own walls. Reorganisations are never easy and the new ideas Gerald White had on becoming Managing Director in 1948, conceived at a time of high demand, were proving troublesome to put into practice, particularly when demand was falling and competition becoming more intense. By the time the Vega, Roadmaster and Ambassador bodies were in production early in 1951, the team under him had been expanded and redeployed. It included Colin Bailey, by then as Technical Director, Ron Brown as Sales Director, F. Hogg, Works Manager, and G. Lynch, Chief Engineer.

As indicated earlier, labour relations in manufacturing firms in the area to the west of London were often among the most difficult in Britain, despite wage rates which were significantly higher than in the provinces. The trade unions' often very militant line, built on the high demand for skilled labour, was further hardened by the expansion of London Airport at Heathrow, with many highly-paid new jobs on offer.

At Duple, it was inevitable that the move to wider use of metal framing was liable to run into trouble. It was up against opposition from skilled craftsmen in wood as well as opportunistic pressure from the metal workers keen to seize any

Further variants of the Vega body were prepared for a new lightweight Tilling-Stevens model with Meadows four-cylinder engine, L4MA8, reviving an old name with the title Express Mark II. In this case, a wrap-round effect for the mudguard outline gave a different look. The example shown, for Cliff's of Eltham, dated from 1953.

opportunity for action to boost pay. Stoppages played havoc with deliveries, soon a matter of great concern in a very seasonal trade. More catastrophic was a strike lasting some 36 weeks.

In the short term, there was little room for manoeuvre and it is significant that some new or revised designs introduced by Duple from 1951 reverted to composite construction. The distinction between 'composite' and 'metal-framed' is by no means always as clear-cut as the names suggest, the former almost always incorporating metal parts, sometimes quite substantial, to reinforce the strength of the joints of the basically wooden framing. Conversely, timber packing within the metal pillar sections of metal-framed bodies is commonplace as a means of securing the panels, yet in some cases also helping to stiffen the framing quite considerably.

Some aspects of Duple's metal-framed designs were continued in the new-generation composite designs – in particular what were described as steel racking and truss panels were used in both, though the earlier reference to riveting as the method of attachment is dropped. The composite body also retained the feature of connecting pillars and bearers with high-tensile bolts, which would not have been practicable in a purely wood-framed structure.

In the FS series, FS42 was issued for composite versions of the Vega 33seat coach and corresponding Mark VI bus for the

The Vega had a lengthy series of design revisions and from early in 1952 an increase in seating capacity to 35 or 37 was made possible on the FS46 version by increasing the rear overhang to the maximum permissible, giving an overall length of just under 29ft while retaining the original SB's 17ft 2in wheelbase. The original version had quite a short overhang and the new one still looked quite well balanced as well as showing only a modest increase in unladen weight to 4 tons 16 cwt 2 qr, so performance with the refined petrol engine remained lively. This picture of an early 37-seat example bore the name of W. S. Yeates Ltd, the Loughborough dealer, as legal owner – in those days it was also a bodybuilder but was happy to sell the Vega.

Doubtless this line-up of coaches about to leave the factory was posed for the benefit of the photographer, but Bedford SB Vega coaches were regularly leaving the premises in substantial numbers in much the same way as OB Vista models had earlier. This picture dating from early 1952 shows three of the new Vega 37-seat version for Wessex Coaches of Bristol, led by OHY 395, the first of six for that fleet (body numbers 1011/6-9 and 15-17); in this view the way in which the 8ft-wide body overhung the SB axles, still of 7ft 6in width, is evident. They were being followed by five Leyland Royal Tiger Ambassador coaches for Southdown, part of a delivery of 20 (body numbers 111/1-20, fleet numbers 1600-19) for that operator's express service fleet. In the background, the rows of trolleybus poles which then lined Edgeware Road are visible. The preponderance of Vauxhall cars was part of the usual Duple landscape.

SB and the related designs for Dennis chassis, the latter bodies now being recorded as 'Falcon', thus restricting the use of the Vega name to Bedford products – this was a pattern that was to be repeated in later years, although the Duple internal records are not always consistent.

It is not clear just when the foregoing designs were issued, but FS44 was used for a further set of Vega-based designs, this time for a lightweight 30ft-long front-engined Tilling-Stevens model, type L4MA8 with four-cylinder Meadows engine, produced in 7ft 6in and 8ft coach and bus forms, in this case all metal-framed, seating 37 and 39 respectively. The body had a windscreen rather like the initial version of the Ambassador as built for Tiger PS2 chassis. All the FS44 entries in the list of FS types quoted 'Festival of Britain'. This event took place during the summer of 1951 and thus helps to date the FS42 entries as preceding that event. Subsequently, another set of designs for the L4MA8 was prepared under the number FS47, this time of composite construction, but the total of all types built barely reached double figures.

The next development in relation to the Vega series of body was the introduction, in time for deliveries in the spring of 1952, of a lengthened FS46 version for the Bedford SB chassis. This latter was still of the same 17ft 2in wheelbase as when introduced in 1950, but by extending the body rear overhang to the maximum permissible, it was possible to extend the overall length to 28ft 11 3/4in, thereby allowing the seating capacity to be increased to 37, although there was an alternative of 35. There were optional widths and bus versions, as previously, but a new option was the Super Vega, with improved interior trim.

The external design was largely as on the original Vega, retaining the bulbous front panel, but the cab side windows were not quite so rounded as previously, evidently in an effort to improve the driver's sideways vision at road junctions.

A new composite body design for underfloor-engined chassis appears in the FS list simply as 'Ambassador' (FS49) but when it was realised that 1953 was to be Coronation year, the full name adopted was Coronation Ambassador. In this case, there was extensive visual redesign, in which elements of both the original Ambassador and the Roadmaster were evident. The high-waisted look, stepped down at the front, was rather reminiscent of the Roadmaster but there was an Ambassador-like, though more modest, degree of curvature in both waist and roof lines. The windscreen arrangement was more orthodox but there was extensive use of polished metal trim strips.

Overall, the styling seemed more self-confident but sales were relatively modest. Southdown took an initial batch of five, one being exhibited on the Duple stand at the 1952 Commercial Motor Show though none entered service until 1953. Also at that Show was a basically similar body on Daimler Freeline chassis for Northern Roadways of Glasgow. Scout of Preston was another user, receiving three Royal Tigers in 1953.

Evidently the form of decorative trim of the original Ambassador was preferred by Southdown, for later deliveries to that fleet were of a compromise style, basically with the 'Coronation' outline but with the cab side window line curving downwards more like the earlier style and reverting to its type of grille and external brightwork – the latter features were even adopted for

The Coronation Ambassador was a new centre-entrance design, seeming to regain a little of the old Duple self-confidence in its styling though the rather heavy use of polished trim strips was not to everyone's taste. East Kent took delivery of two as 32-seat touring coaches on Royal Tiger PSU1/15 chassis in 1953, with body numbers 154/1 and 2, the latter, registered HFN 2, being seen here.

subsequent bodies built to Southdown specification by Beadle.

A new customer was the East Kent Road Car Co Ltd, another BET company, in this case hitherto generally favouring Park Royal for both bus and coach bodywork but switching to Duple for a pair of Royal Tiger chassis with Coronation Ambassador bodies in 1953 and then 30 coaches on Dennis Lancet UF chassis, model LU2, this being the underfloor-engined equivalent to the Lancet III delivered in March-June 1954. The LU2 had a low-set driving position and the body design was modified to suit, having a more marked step in the waistline.

Coronation Ambassador-style designs were also drawn up for front-engined chassis (FS52) and one was built on a stock Crossley SD42/9 chassis in 1953 for Benfleet. Rebodying of existing chassis continued as a small-scale activity, and around 1954 a few early post-war front-engined models such as the AEC Regal I and III or Leyland PS1 were fitted with full-fronted bodies of similar pattern.

Another fringe development was the first of a series of what could be called 'Vista revival' exercises. The Bedford OB 29-seater had met the demand for a small coach so effectively that

its absence from the market left a sense of loss. There were calls for its revival, and the nearest approach came in 1952 when a coach body seating up to 25 was mounted on the equivalent Bedford OLAZ 3-ton goods chassis then still in production, in effect seeking to revive the situation that had applied in 1935, when the WTL 3-tonner had been quite a popular choice for passenger bodywork. The initial FS50 body design with 25-seat capacity and 22ft 3in length was called the Sportsman, a rather curious extension of the idea of the estate car (or what the Americans called a station wagon) with exposed woodwork, to this size of vehicle. It failed to appeal, but a conventionally panelled FS50/1 version was taken up by David MacBrayne Ltd for its services in the Highlands and Islands of Scotland, a fleet of 22 entering service in 1952, some of types FS50/2 and /3 with smaller capacities to suit local needs. A slightly longer version (FS51) measured 24ft 3in and could seat 26.

(Left) A late 'jazzed up' version of the original Vega for the Bedford SB is represented by Yeoman's of Hereford No.85 (KCJ 802) with 31-seat body 1030/24 dating from May 1953.

(Below left) The FS52 version of the Coronation Ambassador was used to rebody a few front-engined chassis in 1953-4, including this Leyland Tiger PS1 originally dating from 1948 for Lloyd's of Bagillt.

(Below) The dropping of the OB left a sense of vacuum and the Sportsman body, FS50, of 1952 on Bedford OLAZ 3-ton chassis was a first attempt at filling it – this is the 1952 25-seat demonstrator, MXV 578. Few were sold but MacBrayne took 22 of a conventionally panelled version.

7 HELP FROM THE MIDLANDS AND A RETURN TO TRADITION

The cost of operating a manufacturing business in the London area was becoming an increasing problem in the 1950s. Labour costs were significantly higher than elsewhere in Britain, land for expansion increasingly expensive and skilled staff often difficult to find. The growth of air travel and expansion of Heathrow airport, with its associated aircraft maintenance industry, put particularly strong pressure on companies which depended on engineering skills in the western outskirts of London and this had its effects even ten miles or so away at Hendon.

Perhaps the most crucial factor of all was the deterioration in labour relations – trade union branches in London seemed to take on a particularly 'bolshie' character in the 1950s, and coach bodybuilding, seasonal in demand and dependent on prompt springtime delivery, was badly affected by the resulting uncertainty. Duple was beginning to lose significant amounts of business, and competitive firms such as Burlingham and Plaxton, based respectively at the seaside resorts of Blackpool and Scarborough, where alternative work was less easy to find, especially in the winter months, had a clear advantage.

Nudd Bros & Lockyer Ltd

The problems with the planned switch to metal-framed construction at Hendon were also doubtless in mind when the possibility arose of acquiring a business based in the Midlands. Nudd Bros & Lockyer Ltd was one of several firms which had grown largely on the basis of rebuilding pre-war bus bodies. Such work requires plenty of space, so the former hangars and other large sheds on wartime aerodromes were obvious locations; this example was located at Ashby Road, Kegworth, roughly midway between Derby and Loughborough.

A major customer was the Midland Red concern, and Nudd Bros & Lockyer rebuilt many of the bodies on that company's standard single-decker buses based on its own-make (BMMO) chassis, of SON and related types dating from the late 1930s. This work, which was not far short of building new bodies, understood to be largely metal-framed, though retaining the outline, shaped panels and some fittings of the originals, had been carried out from 1949 to 1951 but then ceased. Much the same was happening with work of this kind farmed out to similar concerns by other major operators as the shortage of new vehicles eased.

Duple acquired the Nudd Bros & Lockyer business in 1952, and at about the same time there was a promising-seeming upturn in the link with Midland Red in an order for 46 metal-framed bodies to the operator's specification on new BMMO S13-type underfloor-engined chassis. Yet the Nudd concern's future path was to be very different. The first

sign of a change must have seemed rather depressing to those employed there when much of the premises were used to provide cheap covered storage for stock vehicles from Hendon, where space for them had long been a problem, but Duple had more constructive plans.

That part of the East Midlands had a history of involvement in bus bodybuilding. At Loughborough, seven miles away, Brush Coachworks Ltd had been one of the leading firms in the country, with its history linked to the Brush electrical engineering business and tramcar manufacture, and a major supplier of bus bodies to companies in the BET group, with which there had been links in earlier years. It was closing down – among its last products was the balance of 50 bodies on S13 chassis for Midland Red. Willowbrook Ltd, also based in Loughborough, had grown in importance in post-war years, not least in business for BET concerns, and was the natural successor to Brush in this sense as well as being a neighbour. However, some of the displaced staff from Brush moved to Nudd.

Duple's efforts at getting into the double-deck bus business had made no real progress since the 1949-50 period but in 1952 an order was secured from Edinburgh Corporation for 60 such bodies on reconditioned wartime Guy Arab II chassis acquired from London Transport and dating from between 1943 and early 1946. Many wartime utility buses were being withdrawn at that time, often mainly because their bodies were in poor condition due to the quality of timber available when they were built. Edinburgh was engaged in a major tram-replacement programme and this purchase provided a means of helping to augment the fleet at low cost.

The utility origins of the chassis were completely disguised in the bodywork, which had a front-end layout intended to give the impression of a full front, with smooth profile and concealed radiator, yet leaving the nearside of the bonnet exposed – indeed what at first glance appeared to be the nearside of the windscreen was an unglazed aperture. The FS26/1 body structure was basically similar to that of the Red & White group highbridge Guy buses of type FS26 built in 1949-50, though the side windows were fixed – ventilation depending on forward-facing vents and louvres. Reduction of weight had quite suddenly returned to prominence at that time after some years when sturdy construction for long life had seemed more important. A combination of steel and aluminium framing gave a body weight of 2 tons 6½ cwt on the prototype despite 8ft body width, which doubtless helped a little in giving adequate performance despite the retention of the Gardner 5LW engine – hitherto Edinburgh had favoured the 6LW for most of its double-deckers. The interiors had Birmingham-style straight staircases, influenced by some

The order for 60 bodies for wartime Guy Arab chassis from Edinburgh Corporation was mainly executed by Nudd Bros & Lockyer Ltd at Kegworth in 1953 as an early step in moving work out of Hendon. The structure was based on that of the double-deck bodies built by Duple in 1949-50 but the appearance was radically different. It gave something of the illusion of a full-width front, though the absence of glazing in the aperture alongside the windscreen was apt to be all too obvious – behind it, there was a lift-up bonnet top accessible through a large opening on the nearside. No.344 (JWS 624), with body number 130/31, is seen here in service during the Edinburgh Festival of 1956.

Metro-Cammell bodies to Birmingham design on post-war Edinburgh Daimlers. Seating on the prototype was for 56 passengers, split 31/25, but later 31/24 was adopted to allow provision of luggage space. The bodies were given serial numbers in the normal manner for Duple products at that time, 130/1 to 130/60, but of these only 130/1 (completed in November 1952) and 130/3 were built at Hendon, the remainder by Nudd, during 1953.

Rugged designs for export were a speciality, and a significant stage in the integration of the business with Duple was the allocation of the FS48 body design number for five Dennis Lancet III J10C chassis built for the Corporation Electricity Board, Port of Spain, Trinidad, in 1953 by Nudd Bros – in the press announcements the latter was described as 'the Kegworth subsidiary factory of Duple Motor Bodies Ltd'.

An obvious step was to use Nudd Bros capabilities to produce metal-framed bus bodies as part of the Duple standard range. A particular case in point was the Bedford SB, in regard to which the market circumstances had changed as a result of the acquisition of Mulliners Ltd by Marshall of Cambridge. Duple re-entered the field with a body built at Kegworth, and for a time both types were offered via the Bedford sales organisation, the Mulliner version still recognisably based on earlier Duple designs. On the other hand, there was a hint of Midland Red practice in the use of recessed windscreen glass and an upright frontal profile in the Kegworth-built product, which achieved modest success with some independent bus operators.

A new generation of coaches

The bus and coach industry had become more conscious of operating costs as the first signs of an end to the post-war boom in numbers of passengers carried. Private motoring began to grow as petrol rationing, which had continued long after the war, ended, and television was beginning to reduce cinema attendance hence evening bus usage was beginning to fall. At the 1952 Show, Leyland had introduced the Tiger Cub PSUC1/1 lightweight underfloor-engined bus chassis, allowing a 44-seat bus to weigh about 2 tons less than an equivalent Royal Tiger and hence offering sizeable savings in fuel and other costs. Although no coach version was offered at first, it was a clear indication of a new trend, as was an upsurge of lightweight bus body designs of which the Edinburgh double-deckers were early examples.

Duple's output was not greatly affected at first, but a significant pointer was the production of a coach body on one of the prototype AEC Reliance chassis in 1953. This model was AEC's answer to the Tiger Cub and, with the AH470 engine of 7.7 litre capacity fitted to most examples, offered better scope

A radically different approach to the styling of the Vega body for Bedford SB chassis was evident in the new FS56 version introduced towards the end of 1953. The overall look was more in the earlier Duple tradition of flowing lines and graceful curves and at the front the bulbous look of the early SB disappeared completely. The main windscreen glasses were now curved and this enabled them to be merged into the contours of the body. The lower windscreen sill line also improved vision from the driver's seat. The new oval grille was perhaps more controversial and only remained in production for the 1954 season, though it may well have inspired ERF's adoption of a similar shape for its goods vehicle cab a couple of years later. This Vauxhall Motors demonstrator registered in November 1953 was a high-specification Super Vega and seated 38, the front-end redesign having made it possible to fit a seat just ahead of the entrance door. The style of side 'flash' was one widely favoured by Duple for the 1954 season. The coach was on a petrol-engined chassis, now officially designated SBG as a result of the introduction of a production SBO diesel option.

The Elizabethan, type FS57, represented a new generation of coach in two senses. The AEC Reliance chassis was a new medium-weight model that caught the mood of the coach industry very effectively, with lighter construction and useful savings in running costs compared to the first-generation heavyweight models such as the AEC Regal Mark IV or Leyland Royal Tiger but yet had a large enough engine to give quite lively performance. For it and equivalent models, Duple introduced the Elizabethan with relatively simple yet neatly executed styling. An initial run of 40 was soon followed by another dozen prefixed 211, including MWP 623 for Marsh of Harvington, with body number 211/8, delivered in July 1954.

as a coach model than the Leyland's O.350 engine of 5.7 litres.

At Duple, another major rethink of policy on manufacturing methods and design philosophy was well under way by mid-1953, by which time Colin Bailey had left Duple. His time there had not been a very happy experience, difficulties in labour relations had frustrated the development of a full range of metal-framed bodies using volume production techniques at Hendon as visualised when he joined the firm five years earlier.

Bailey wrote a letter commenting on an operator association's report on bus body design in the April 1953 issue of 'Bus & Coach' quoting merely 'London, N.W.9' as his address, with no reference to Duple, which looked odd alongside others from senior management of other bodybuilders, all quoting their company's names. It was followed up in the August 1953 issue by an article by him entitled 'What of composite construction?', describing himself simply as 'Technical Consulting Engineer', again making no mention of any individual bodybuilding concern.

Even so, it is revealing as an indication of his views shortly after his time at Duple, as well as of the situation there. Although continuing to favour metal-framed bodies for use where long life and low maintenance cost were paramount, by that date he was taking a pragmatic view on the choice of composite construction for coaches intended to be sold off after a relatively short life where matters of up-to-date appearance and amenities were paramount. There was a revealing comment on the more flexible nature of a timber-framed structure's merit in coping with the weaving stresses

to which the body of a road vehicle is subject, "particularly those associated with the lighter types of chassis." He went into ways in which troubles with composite body designs could be avoided, demonstrating an open-minded approach.

The composite coach body was indeed firmly back in favour at Hendon and with it a revival of the blend of smooth lines and graceful curves that had been so much associated with the marque in earlier years. The rather brash 'American' look of the early SB Vega of 1950 had gone out of favour in Duple's design office. In its place came the FS56 design for the 1954 season, advertised from October 1953, with a smoothly curving profile using a deeper two-panel windscreen with quite strong curvature from side to side and a slight curve in profile. The heavy-looking pillar in front of the entrance door gave way to a slimmer design. The overall effect had a distinct echo of the gently curved outlines of pre-1950 Duple coaches although there was a new oval-shaped front grille. It was described as being of composite lightweight construction and the seating capacity was usually either 36 or 38, available in 7ft 6in or 8ft width.

By that date the SB chassis was available as either petrol, now called SBG, or diesel form, the latter being type SBO and having a Perkins R6 engine, apart from the special case of Eastern Counties Omnibus Co which specified the Gardner 4LK. Sales, which had faltered somewhat since about 1952, revived although the 1051/1 series of numbers running to over 300 also included a few cases of rebodying of AEC Regal III or Daimler CVD6 chassis.

Maybe it was the Coronation in 1953 that encouraged a revival of what was seen as a 'British' look. Duple was very conscious of royal events – at some time around this period, a photograph of the Queen looking out of the window of a Duple coach was put on display in the entrance to the Duple offices at Hendon, remaining there until they closed.

The introduction of a new body for underfloor-engined chassis, type FS57, appropriately christened the Elizabethan, was revealed in advertising in September 1953, this being intended primarily for the new generation of lighter models of this layout. The styling followed the same trend towards smoother, more flowing outlines with a somewhat similar style of windscreen, although in this case there was a prominent reverse-rake pillar behind the foremost side window. The body was of what is generally described as centre-entrance layout, though the doorway was positioned only a little way behind the front axle, as widely favoured at that time.

The Seddon Pennine with Perkins R6 engine mounted vertically under the floor was another new chassis model in this group, with a few examples among early Elizabethan deliveries, at least one dating from late 1953. The Leyland Tiger Cub was now available in PSUC1/2 form for coach bodywork, Scout receiving the first five examples, 199/1-5, early in 1954, from the initial batch of 20 or so to have Elizabethan bodies. Another 20 were produced for the 1955 season.

However it was the AEC Reliance that almost immediately became the most popular choice of chassis for this body, with 40 in the first production batch of the type (201/1 upwards) built in 1954, of which Sheffield United Tours took twelve, with others going to several traditional customers such as

There was some spill-over from the previous generation of coach designs in 1954. Southdown had begun its collection of Duple-bodied Leyland Royal Tiger coaches with batches of the original Ambassador design in 1951 and 1952, followed by the Coronation Ambassador in 1953, No.1649 (MCD 49) with Duple body number 125/5 dating from May of that year being seen (above left) at Bexhill on the South Coast Express Service in August 1956. Clearly the applied decoration of this style was not thought to be in keeping with the company's dignified image, so for 1954 a special design, reverting to the style of external trim on the 1951-52 coaches, with cab side windows to match, though otherwise of the 'Coronation' outline, was introduced.

One of this batch, NUF 79, with body 197/11, new in April 1954, is seen just after winning the Concours d'Elegance at the British Coach Rally at Brighton two years later, soon after conversion to 26-seat capacity for use on extended tours – it was later renumbered 1839.

Wallace Arnold (4), Lewis of Greenwich (2), and Venture of Hendon. Further smaller batches covering design variations followed and, in 1955, the 213/1 batch covered 50 more examples.

Another model in this field, although built only in small numbers as a coach, was the Atkinson PL745H with horizontal Gardner 5HLW engine, on one of which an Elizabethan body was built in 1954 and a similar vehicles was present at the Scottish Show in November 1955.

Some similar bodies were built on heavier-duty chassis including twelve (200/1-12) on Daimler Freeline (including two for Cronshaw) and one on a Leyland Royal Tiger for York Bros of Northampton which was numbered 202/10 in the same series as some bodies on Seddon chassis. There were also a few on the Sentinel SLC/6/30.

At Nudd Bros & Lockyer, beginning to be described as

Duple's Midland factory, metal-framed bus body production continued, at that stage still run independently from Hendon in most respects. A noteworthy order was for 20 Tiger Cub PSUC1/1 for Southdown, in those days a very high-prestige operator, delivered in February-April 1954. They were 39-seaters with front-entrance layout and among early instances of 'full-sized' buses equipped for use without conductors on quieter rural routes as had become permissible for suitable buses of this size by then. Although of simple outline, they were neat-looking vehicles, adding to the general impression of Duple getting its act together again in terms of appearance.

For the 1955 season, the final year of the 17ft 2in wheelbase SB, the Vega – increasingly sold in Super Vega form with better trim – was given what generally became called the butterfly grille in place of the oval 'fishface' style applied to the

East Kent Road Car Co Ltd, liking the Dennis Lancet III as a coach, ordered 30 of the mechanically similar Lancet UF with engine under the floor for delivery in 1954. Dennis had lost momentum in changing over to the underfloor-engined layout with another model that had failed to sell, and East Kent's proved to be the largest order for the Lancet UF. Duple got the body contract and produced another derivative of the Coronation Ambassador style, the main modification being to suit the low driving position of this chassis, though East Kent also sought a toning-down of the applied decoration. The vehicle shown, HJG 9, was the first of the batch to be completed, with body 190/1.

This vehicle might well be taken for a 1954 Bedford SB Vega, but the wheels give a clue that the chassis was an AEC – a 1949 Regal III, type 9621A, with 9.6-litre engine and crash gearbox, to be precise; it had begun life with a Burlingham 33-seat coach body. It received the body shown in 1954 and when its owner, Robin Hood Coaches, of Nottingham, sold out to Barton Transport in 1961, it became No.921 in that fleet, receiving a 7.7-litre engine in 1962.

first year of production of this outline. There was also a revision to the rear dome shape, giving the rear window more of a wrap-round effect. These changes were indicated by type numbers FS56/2 and /3 for 7ft 6in and 8ft versions. Body numbers in the 1055/ series ran to over 400, although again there was at least one instance of a body in this series being used to rebody a Daimler CVD6.

Similar-looking body styles (FS56/4 and /5) were built for the forward-control Leyland Comet ECPO2/1R, originally an export model but by then offered on the home market – numbers suggest that up to 16 may have been built.

More significant were the FS56/6 and /7 on Commer Avenger, a model in the Bedford SB class introduced in 1948 but not hitherto offered with Duple bodywork. As introduced, the model had a six-cylinder petrol engine mounted at the front though inclined so as to lie below the cab floor on the goods

model from which the type was derived but in 1954 a remarkable two-stoke diesel option was introduced, with only three cylinders each having two opposed pistons – it too fitted below the floor. The chassis length was also increased that year, permitting body length to be 30ft and the Duple examples, delivered to operators from July 1954, mostly seated 41. The butterfly grille was mounted lower than on the SB version so as to line up with the Avenger's radiator position, giving a touch of individuality.

The initial 1057/1-up batch of bodies for this chassis comprised 54, the majority on the diesel model, and this increased to 115 for the 1062/1-up series, all diesel, mostly delivered in 1956. There were never as many again but batches of 50 or so continued to be built through the remainder of the 1950s, making this model the main challenger to Bedford among the lighter types bodied by Duple over most of that period. The Vega body name was associated with Bedford and no body name was quoted for early Avenger-based versions but Corinthian was later adopted for them, this having been a name that had been used for a pre-war Commer coach chassis. A further variant of the same basic body was offered on Albion Victor FT39 chassis but only two are thought to have been built, in 1956.

By the mid-1950s, buses barely figured in the output of the Hendon factory, but one more double-deck order was included in its body numbering system, even though the majority were built at Kegworth. This was for 50 bodies on Leyland PD2/20 chassis for Liverpool Corporation, numbered 216/1-50, of which 1, 3 and 4 are known to have been built at Hendon, and from 6 onwards at Kegworth. Liverpool was carrying out a major tramway replacement programme and ordering buses in large batches. It took a detailed interest in body design, and these bodies were built to the operator's drawings, some almost identical bodies also being produced by Alexander. Elements of Weymann and Crossley influence could be detected, although the bow-fronted style was dictated by the design of the full-width bonnet assembly which formed part of the PD2/20 chassis specification and had been first produced for an order using Leyland's own bodywork built for Midland Red. The end-result was among the most harmonious designs used with this design of bonnet. The buses were

Black & White Motorways Ltd, no longer permitted to obtain Bristol chassis as a mainly private-enterprise concern (despite being part-owned by Bristol Tramways & Carriage Co Ltd) turned to Leyland Royal Tiger chassis with Willowbrook bodies in 1951/3 but then purchased sixteen Guy Arab LUF chassis with Duple Elizabethan 37-seat bodies (numbers 191/1-16) in 1954, the last of the batch, No.175 (NDG 175) being seen here in Nottingham in June of that year. The LUF was a lightened version of the underfloor-engined Arab but retained the Gardner engine, six-cylinder in this case and thus reverting to a Black & White tradition. The body was basically standard but the side trim was based on that of the operator's previous Willowbrook batches.

The era of the 'butterfly grille' Vega body style began in the 1955 season – at last, there was a sense of harmony in the whole design and a return to traditional Duple smooth outlines. This example, PCG 100 of Liss & District Omnibus Co Ltd, of Bordon, Hants, dated from 1956 and is seen on the road section of the British Coach Rally in April of that year. Note the large tilting roof vents, opened at the rear – they had largely supplanted the traditional sliding roof. By that time, the SB chassis had the 216in wheelbase and the body, basically of type FS56/10, was of 30ft overall length allowing a 41-seat capacity, though this example had a more spacious 35-seat layout – the extra length in the body was added just behind the front axle. It was a petrol-engined SBG model and had body number 1060/369 in that season's main Vega series.

The Vega-type body was also built on (above) Leyland Comet ECPO2/1R chassis, this one being TBP 250 with body 1056/12 for Mitcham, Warnham of June 1955, and (below) Commer Avenger II, in this case XRB 33 with body 1057/29 built for Lindley, Long Eaton in April 1955, but seen as Barton 752. Note the different grille levels.

Duple's success in gaining an order for 50 double-deck bodies on Leyland Titan PD2/20 chassis for Liverpool Corporation came as quite a surprise at a time of strong competition for such work. The appearance was as specified by the operator, Alexander also building to the same outline, the result being among Liverpool's best-proportioned buses of the period. L116 (RKC 217) with body 216/26 dating from July 1955 was one those built at Kegworth, though the first had been produced at Hendon. This was to prove Duple's last direct involvement with double-deckers.

A winged emblem similar to that forming part of the butterfly grille on the Vega also appeared on the front of standard Elizabethan bodies from 1955. This AEC Reliance MU3RV model, 881 CHK, supplied to Harris's Coaches of Grays, Essex early in that year was representative of the standard 41-seat design with centre entrance – it had body number 213/41. The Harris family took great pride in the appearance of its vehicles, painted in a smart combination of dark green and light grey. The unladen weight, 6 tons 2 cwt 2 qr, was much the same as a typical late pre-war AEC Regal or similar coach despite increased dimensions.

delivered between March and August 1955. By then, further premises had been acquired in Swingbridge Lane, Loughborough, both this and Kegworth being described in Duple advertising as 'Midland factories' with the 'Midland service depot' at Kegworth – production was gradually transferred to Loughborough.

It was decided that, beginning from the new season in the autumn of 1955, the use of separate number series for bodies on 'full-size' and Bedford or other lightweight chassis would cease, the last of the former being 225/1-14, used for coach bodies on Reliance chassis built that year. The 1000-up series hitherto used for bodies on Bedfords etc began to include bodies on all types of passenger chassis from 1063/1, which was the beginning of another small run of AEC Reliance coaches. This system was to continue until the end of bodybuilding at Hendon in 1970, by which date the series number sequence had reached 1227.

There was growing interest in using the same entrance layout as had become usual on underfloor-engined buses for coaches on similar chassis, and by the summer of 1955 the Elizabethan was being offered in this form as an option to the centre entrance layout, an inward-swinging door being cut into the foremost side panel. It also suited a maximum seating capacity layout and Creamline of Bordon, Hants, engaged in leave services for national servicemen from the various Army

bases in that area adopted a 43-seat front-entrance layout for some AEC Reliance coaches, including 1063/1 to 5, mentioned in the previous paragraph. They can hardly have been comfortable for long trips but provided transport at low cost.

The main news of interest to the major part of Duple's clientele that autumn was the introduction of the Bedford SB in 216in (18ft) wheelbase form, enabling the bodywork to be increased to the then maximum legal length of 30ft. This meant that the Super Vega could now seat 41 passengers, and the FS56/10 and 11 designs (the latter 8ft wide) went into production with numbers running from 1060/1 to 450 from late 1955 – most entered service in 1956 though there was the odd straggler from dealers' stock not registered until 1957 or even 1958. Even so, this gives some indication of the scale of demand justifying 450 coaches of a standard design being programmed for a year's output.

The overwhelming majority of them were SBG petrol models as built, the SBO option with Perkins R6 diesel not having proved popular. The Super Vega body design was still of the butterfly grille style, the additional length being barely detectable at a glance, having been added into the body structure just ahead of the entrance door. There was still a 'plain' Vega, with minor trim differences and costing £130 less than the £3,010 quoted for the complete Super Vega on SBG chassis in December 1955 – the diesel Super Vega cost £3,583,

Creamline Motor Services (Bordon) Ltd ran leave services taking national servicemen from Army bases in Hampshire to their home areas in the North and Midlands, for which a maximum-capacity 43-seat front-entrance version of the Elizabethan was developed. The frontal profile was more upright than on the standard model and a full-length roof luggage carrier was an unusual feature, doubtless intended to cope with bulky kit bags. One of an initial fleet of four on AEC Reliance chassis dating from early 1955 is seen here soon after sale to Barton Transport Ltd as its No.772 in 1957 – NOR 511 had an early Reliance chassis, number MU3RV014, and body number 212/5. Other operators proved to like the concept, leading to further developments. Note the Wolseley 4/50 car.

The Britannia body in centre-entrance form was closely related to the standard Elizabethan in much of its structure but, most obviously, did not have the reverse-rake pillars over the front axle and was subtly changed in several respects. The overall effect was a little closer to the contemporary Vega with the unbroken curve of the waistline and at the rear. It was built largely on AEC Reliance chassis but a minority of operators chose the Leyland Tiger Cub in its PSUC1/2 coach-chassis form. Among them was York Bros (Northampton) Ltd, this early example seating 43.

"including sound proofing of engine and 24-volt lighting". The sound proofing amounted to extra-thick trim on the engine cover, but on this and later models it was never very effective.

At about that period, Duple's FS-series type designation system became somewhat confused in the manner which sometimes happens when another generation of staff take over a system whose intended principles they did not properly understand. Up to about 1955, FS56 implied the Vega family of bodies with the smooth-fronted shape and FS57 was the Elizabethan family. Then FS58 was used for a series of what were described as 'Vega FS56 type' body designs intended for rebodying a wide variety of front-engined heavy duty chassis of the period from 1946-50 or so, few of which seem to have been used. A further complication arose when the FS56 series was used from the 1955/56 and later seasons for designs not in the Vega family, as described below, as well as further Vega variants.

The Britannia

A new name was added to the growing list of Duple coach styles when the Britannia was announced late in 1955 – in essentials, it was the Elizabethan without the reverse-rake pillar over the front axle. Vertical pillars were used throughout except at the extreme front and rear, with the waistline and cantrail running in smooth unbroken curves, in what might be called the 'classic' Duple tradition. When first introduced, the more usual entrance position continued to be behind the front wheels, and there was a slightly 'fussy' effect with two unevenly-spaced intermediate pillars between the windscreen and the door. With front entrance, there was a rather tidier effect, though with a very short window behind the entrance.

As indicated above, the Britannia was illogically included in the FS56 series, the earliest entry in a list which has quite a number of blanks (presumably for projects not put into production) being FS56/21 for a centre-entrance 41-seat version on AEC Reliance chassis for the 1955/56 season, with FS56/29 for the Tiger Cub equivalent, and FS56/39 and 40 were for the respective front-entrance versions in which alternative 41 or 43-seat layouts were offered.

The initial production batch comprised 50 centre-entrance bodies on AEC Reliance numbered 1066/1 upwards, most of them entering service with various independent operators in the spring of 1956. The Leyland Tiger Cub was a minority choice for the Britannia, built in smaller numbers. As usual, actual seating capacities varied, some operators choosing more spacious layouts.

The Vega and Britannia ranges continued with minor changes for the 1956-57 season, with much the same pattern of production. Again, both Vega and Britannia designs were included in the FS56 design series, that year's production types

This further instance of a Barton purchase of an ex-Creamline AEC Reliance, RHO 905, had the Britannia body in front-entrance form, allowing comparisons to be made. The front-end had a smoother look than on the Elizabethan front-entrance body and indeed the windscreen and window outlines are more flowing than on the centre-entrance version shown above. This was a 1957 example with body 1079/8, the design introducing 'Britannia' lettering in the moulding above the destination panel though the fussier-looking grille and bumper seem a little retrograde in hindsight. It is seen in September 1958 soon after purchase by Barton, still in Creamline livery.

occupying FS56/43 to 45 covering Bedford (in two widths) and Commer, with /46 to 49 for AEC and Leyland chassis with centre and front entrances. In similar fashion, FS56/50 to 56 covered the similar range of types for 1957/58.

However, a new body type introduced in autumn 1956 not in this list was the Donington, a metal-framed coach for the AEC Reliance and Leyland Tiger Cub from what had become Duple Motor Bodies (Midland) Ltd, the new title for the Kegworth and Loughborough factories. The Donington was more in the dual-purpose mould, with straight waist and, on each side, six small windows having sliding top lights for ventilation – seating could be up to 43. Its production and sales were handled independently from Hendon production. Another noteworthy Duple (Midland) body was fitted in 1956 to the prototype Dennis Pelican, a lightweight underfloor-engined model, which had been exhibited in chassis form at the 1954 Show – as completed it was a 44-seat front-entrance bus.

Bedford introduced its own diesel engine early in 1957, and at the same time adopted a numbered engine identification system, so that the Bedford diesel version was SB1, the petrol equivalent becoming SB3, and another new option was SB8 with Leyland O.350 engine as used in Comet models. However most of the chassis used for that year's Duple Vega production had already been built, so the bodies with number 1074/1-360 built for that season were largely on SBG or occasionally SBO with a minority built late enough to be SB1, SB3 or SB8.

The other makes of new chassis were mostly much as before and there were still occasional rebodying exercises, in this case six Vega-style bodies on Maudslay Marathon III for Royal Arsenal Co-op, late in 1956. A mystery vehicle was Daimler Freeline D650H chassis 25697 with Duple body 1084/1, understood to be a coach, for "USSR trade delegation" and dating from 1957 – it is quoted in both Daimler and Duple records but it is not known if it was actually built or what happened to it.

Much more significant as a portent for the future was body 1085/1, which was a 41-seat Vega-style body on a chassis supplied and retained by the Ford Motor Co Ltd in 1957. Despite its place as one of the world's leading vehicle makers and its strong position in the market for the lighter classes of goods vehicles as well as cars on the British market, Ford's showing in the bus and coach business in Britain had been very

limited since the days of the model T in the 1920s. British-built Ford commercial vehicles were then being marketed under the Thames name and in 1957 the Thames Trader range was introduced in direct competition with the Bedford S and C ranges.

A passenger version competing with the SB was an obvious step and this vehicle was a prototype of type 570E – though built in 1957 it seems not to have been registered until late 1959, when it become 5689 TW, possibly to allow demonstration use carrying members of the public – deliveries of production vehicles began early that year. Even then output was on a small scale and barely publicised, but by 1960 the 570E began to emerge as the most serious challenge to Bedford's dominance in the lighter coach classes since that marque first appeared in 1931.

A further venture in reviving the concept of a Bedford-Duple 29-seat coach was announced at the end of 1957. This was again based on what was basically a goods chassis with passenger modifications, this time the C4-series 4-ton forward-control model which normally carried a cab similar to the heavier S range. As with the SB, the front-end of the completed vehicle was entirely styled by Duple, and the overall effect was of a shorter and slightly simplified Vega – this was body design FS59.

An initial run of 55 bodies, advertised as the New Vista but also called the Super Vista, was built with numbers 1089/1 upwards, sold in ones and twos to independent operators of various types (save for one example sold to Borneo) and mostly delivered during 1958. The petrol-engined C4Z2 was slightly in the majority; the diesels were split between C4Z1 and C5Z1 chassis the latter being slightly heavier-duty 5-ton models. One of that batch on a C4Z2 went to MacBrayne, and in the following year's series of a further 40 numbered 1111/1 up delivered from August 1958 there was a repeat MacBrayne order for six, this time on C5Z1, with others in later years. There were also some further bodies of bus outline for MacBrayne on the C5Z1 chassis.

Another Bedford variant of that period, perhaps intended to liven up demand for a body design that was almost unchanged since 1955 was the Alpine coach on the SB (FS56/59 and 60), basically a Vega with virtually the entire roof panelled in Perspex to give almost unobstructed vision of mountainous scenery. It was advertised in March 1958 as a 36-seater; a few

The quest for a successor to the OB Vista continued. The Bedford A-series bonneted range had succeeded the O-series in the spring of 1953 and although at least one Duple coach body had been built on such a chassis c1953, as seen here, its relatively long bonnet may have made it seem less appealing as a handy coach. Its body design had faint echoes of the Coronation Ambassador. This may have been body number 1041/1, recorded as a 26-seat coach on a Bedford A4LZ6, which indicates a 4-ton long-wheelbase chassis (13ft 11in, looking about right) – the final '6' is slightly mysterious but might be an error for G, indicating 'gasolene', in other words petrol. That body was on a chassis registered in Lancashire as STC 999 in 1954 and operated by Mayers, of Orrell.

More successful was the Super Vista 29-seat coach body built on the forward-control Bedford C4-series model, announced at the end of 1957. The first batch of 55 had sold sufficiently well for this one on a C4Z2 petrol-engined chassis to be exhibited at the 1958 Commercial Motor Show. The body design could be described as more of a mini-Vega, though the front profile was different. The choice of side mouldings offered to purchasers had progressed to a stage where they were identified by letter, this version being described as 'standard J-type mouldings'. The glass roof quarters, top-sliding windows and rear wheel discs were other options.

examples of this capacity or with 37 seats were included in that year's run of Vega-series bodies beginning at 1090/1, though most, with numbers up to 380, had the usual 41. The petrol SB3 was still the majority choice with diesels split between SB1 and SB8.

Willowbrook joins the fold

Although there were a set of revised body styles, Duple was in the news at the time of the 1958 Commercial Motor Show at Earls Court mainly because of the announcement of the takeover of Willowbrook Ltd, of Derby Road, Loughborough, revealed in September. Despite the growth of Duple (Midland) with its premises in the same town as well as nearby at Kegworth, this was a bigger-scale development. The firm had been registered in January 1927, taking over a business based in Leicester, but expansion at the Loughborough address had been rapid.

By the mid-1930s Willowbrook had become well-known for its well-appointed single-deck bodies, often of a character suitable for coach as well as bus use, most then for independent operators though there were some major company and municipal customers. After the war, the proportion of business done with the British Electric Traction group increased and, at the time of takeover, there were 150 bodies on order for that

group. Municipal business had also grown but there were still numbers of independent customers. Double-deckers and coaches were also built.

The acquisition of Willowbrook gave Duple a much firmer foothold in the bus side of the industry. This Leyland Titan PD3 for Potteries Motor Traction Co Ltd was typical of double-deckers being built for various BET group operators and of which output continued undisturbed.

The business was to continue under its own name and Duple's Chairman, H. W. Sydenham, well-known as a city accountant, joined the Willowbrook board, as did Gerald White, Duple's Managing Director, and H. J. (Harry) Bigg, Duple's Works Manager. Two of Willowbrook's Directors continued in place – William Sutton, who had been on the Board since the 1930s and was responsible for a long succession of attractive body designs, and E. J. Foster, Works Director.

An important active addition to the Willowbrook board was R. Beechey Newman, Duple's Sales Manager, who became Sales Director. He had achieved much success at Hendon, but seemed to blossom with Willowbrook, blessed by genuine interest in and knowledge of the key personalities in the industry. I recall him taking the trouble to introduce me to what seemed an immense number of people when I attended my first bus industry trade conference soon after I became a full-time journalist in 1961.

It was significant that at the same time it was announced that another new company was being set up – Duple Motor Bodies (Northern) Ltd. At the time, it was stated that the objective was the strengthening of the sales organisation in the North of England and the establishment of service facilities in the Manchester area – E. S. Walker, formerly of the Duple sales staff, rejoined as a director of this subsidiary. It was stated that the policies of Duple, Willowbrook and Duple (Midland) were unaffected by the changes. While this may have been so in the short term, within a few years there was to be much more to record arising from these announcements.

Several of the Duple models exhibited at the 1958 Show were significantly altered in appearance by a new windscreen design. Techniques for the production of curved glass had developed and the new Duple design as adopted for the 1959-model Super Vega incorporated more of a wrap-around effect, the screen corner pillars being set back and the whole front-end becoming more rounded. There was a new radiator grille design, the surround sweeping outwards to incorporate the headlamps. The rest of the body was not greatly altered, save that at the rear the corners reverted to more conventional curves but with a three-piece rear screen. The new 1959 Vega style was quoted as FS60 (7ft 6in) and FS60/1 (8ft) – FS60/2 was the Commer version but the confusion was again compounded by the use of FS60/3 to 6 for Britannia bodies. The new Super Vega bodies were numbered in a series from 1105/1 to 514, mostly delivered between late 1958 and July 1959 and on SB3, SB1 and SB8 chassis. This was the first of three years when the year's programme of Super Vega bodies for SB chassis exceeded the 500 mark.

Understandably, Ford preferred to avoid the Vega name even though it appears as 'Vega/Ford' in an internal Duple list for what was quoted as the 212in (17ft 8in) wheelbase chassis as FS56/57 (7ft 7in wide) and FS56/58 (8ft wide) for the 1958/59 season – the use of FS59 series numbers suggests it was developed before the FS60 Bedford version. For sales purposes, the Ford version of this style was christened 'Yeoman', the design having basically the same new Vega outline complete with the more rounded windscreen shape as the version mentioned above. The Yeoman body also differed in having a different grille style, almost rectangular and mounted lower than on the Bedford and the rear pillars were of the reversed-rake style, with wrap-round rear window, as used on previous-generation Vega bodies.

The first small production batch of Yeoman bodies was numbered 1112/1 to 35, delivered in 1959. The first of these, supplied to the Ford Motor Co Ltd, was registered 268 RNO and used for a pioneering trip to Moscow – quite an adventure in those days of the cold war. The rest went to various users, among which the last body, /35, was noteworthy as being for Barton Transport, in whose fleet it was numbered 815. At that stage, Commer still held second place in numbers of Vega-style bodies, with 52 in the 1106 series on what had become the Avenger IV chassis, mostly delivered in 1959. The 570E chassis, officially marketed simply as the Thames Trader coach chassis, had the 6D 5.42-litre diesel engine as standard and a general specification much like the SB. There was a 4.9-litre petrol option but this was extremely rare, unlike the Bedford equivalent at that stage.

The new more rounded windscreen was applied to the Britannia body when built in centre-entrance form – it was

Commer was in second place to Bedford in numbers having Vega style bodies, though at only a tenth of the quantity and about to be overtaken by Ford. This Avenger IV for Greatrex Motor Coaches Ltd of Stafford was exhibited at the 1958 Commercial Motor Show, being the first of the type to have the new-style body, number 1106/1. It was numbered 107 in that fleet and registered 8424 E, entering service in March 1959. This model was a little higher built than either Bedford or Thames equivalents.

The first production example of the Yeoman body, 1112/1, to be mounted on the new Thames Trader coach chassis was retained by the Ford Motor Co Ltd, registered 268 YNO and sent on a trip to Moscow, being seen here at Hendon suitably lettered – it was quite a practical and political challenge in those days but produced valuable publicity for the new model. The Yeoman body was almost identical to the Vega but had a different grille and, at first, reverse-rake rear pillars.

introduced on the batch of 20 on AEC Reliance chassis, numbered 1107/1 upwards and delivered in 1959 – Global Tours received six and Samuelson four, and there were also a few in an 1108 series on Tiger Cub chassis. However, the balance of preference had swung to the front-entrance version of the Britanwnia, as was also the case for competitive coach bodies of other makes, and on this the need for compact design ahead of the front axle made it necessary to use a more upright screen glass with less 'wrap-round' effect. There were 49 such bodies in the 1109 series on Reliance chassis also delivered in 1959, including five for Wallace Arnold and four for LeRoy of Torquay, and ten more in the 1110 series on Tiger Cub, largely for Spencer Holidays of Manchester. With a couple of rebodyings of Maudslay Marathon III models for MacBrayne, the total Hendon 1958/59 home-market output was over 700.

Duple (Midland) was expanding its range of bodies suitable for Bedford chassis. A new development arose from the TJ range of bonneted goods models that had been introduced at the time of the 1958 Show. The J2 was the three-ton version and in short-wheelbase tipper form particularly rugged. Its potential as the basis for a tough small bus for use in countries with poor

roads was realised, though in bonneted form the body space was too short to be practicable. Accordingly a forward-control conversion was carried out and a metal-framed body seating up to 21 fitted. It was of simple design yet up-to-date, with curved-glass windscreen. Early applications were for export to Africa, but wider applications gradually arose.

For a time the Donington body for Reliance and Tiger Cub was promoted quite strongly, featuring in Duple advertising frequently in the 1959-60 period, and being rewarded with a fair degree of success notably among BET companies, but the acquisition of Willowbrook made some rationalisation almost inevitable.

The 1959/60 season was largely a repeat exercise, but with a further increase in output of about 200 bodies from Hendon, quite apart from the results of the group's expansion in the Midlands. The designs as established at the 1958 Show were continued for a further season without significant change. Although the bus side of the industry was beginning to decline as numbers of passengers carried started to fall, the coach side continued to prosper – there were still sufficient people without cars to provide customers for the traditional excursions or express services to seaside resorts. In addition, as

Smith's Luxury Coaches (Reading) Ltd was another operator whose Director, A. E. Smith, set great emphasis on smartness – the livery was a distinctive orange and blue. This 41-seat front-entrance Brittania on AEC Reliance 2MU3RV chassis was another 1958 Show exhibit, being later registered as RRD 892. It had body number 1109/1 in a series running to /49. The windscreen was more upright and had less wrap-round effect than that used with entrance behind the front wheel. Note the decorative 'portholes', an idea that very soon went out of fashion.

living standards improved, the idea of coach holidays was gaining wider favour, increasingly to continental Europe.

The 1120 series of body numbers for the 1960 model Super Vega reached 563, mostly delivered between late 1959 and August 1960. This time the balance between petrol and diesel was more – rising costs, notably of wages, were making operators more cost conscious and on the whole the larger firms with diesel buses tended to choose the SB1 or in some cases the SB8 with Leyland engine. Adding to the Bedford total were 27 Vista bodies with 1127-series numbers on C4 and C5 series chassis, including a further seven C5Z1 for MacBrayne.

The Commer Avenger numbers began to drop, with 26 Corinthian bodies in the 1126 series of numbers, though the export of four of them to the Canary Islands was noteworthy. More than compensating from Duple's viewpoint was Ford, for the 1126 series of Yeoman bodies on the Thames 570E mostly delivered in 1960 ran to 205, noteworthy in including several well-known names, notably Wallace Arnold with thirteen examples, Trimdon Motor Services Ltd with twelve and Timpson of London S.E. and Allenways of Birmingham with five each. Ford had gained a real presence in the coach business.

The Britannia was built in the 1960 season in much the same numbers as in 1959, with 23 centre-entrance (including eight for Black & White Motorways) and 50 front-entrance Reliances plus three front-entrance Tiger Cubs, these having body numbers in the 1122, 1124 and 1125 series. However, the Leyland contingent was strengthened by five bodies forming the 1130 series, built on the first chassis to arrive at Duple of a new name soon to become familiar in the British coach industry, the Leopard. These were of the initial L1 type – in effect a Tiger Cub chassis with the larger O.600 engine, much as had been used in the Royal Tiger. These were centre-entrance Britannia coaches built for Cronshaw (2), Harris Greys (10 and Banfield (2).

Yet there were exceptions to general trends as well as new developments. Salopia Saloon Coaches Ltd, of Whitchurch, Shropshire (also known as Salop) had begun applying a policy of buying batches of SB-Vega coaches more or less annually in 1951, at first at about two at a time, and then gradually more,

selling many of them off after quite short lives, sometimes of only a couple of years or so. By 1955 it was official policy to standardise on Vegas for coaching work, the petrol versions continued to be chosen quite deliberately, despite the general trend to diesel, in the interests of quieter running. In April 1960, a new level was reached when ten SB3 were added, four seating 37 and the rest 41, all but three being sold towards the end of 1961. A broadly similar pattern of regular fleet renewal and large-scale early sell-off was continued with later models into the 1970s.

There were several major and quite a few minor operators following a similar buy-new-and-sell-early policy (though more were switching to diesels). The modest new cost and firm market for used coaches of so widely favoured a type as the SB Vega series made such a policy economic and having the appeal, important to firms with limited overhaul facilities, that little more than servicing was needed before the vehicles were sold on. An important element in such a system was the dealer, not only in providing the means of selling and where needed overhauling the numbers of used coaches being 'cascaded' to lower-grade duties by such means, but also in carrying out overhauls where needed.

It was also still at least as true as at any time since the 1930s that the dealers through whom most new coaches were sold played a major part in allowing Duple and its competitors to plan production – much skill went into offering numerous often small firms choice in such matters as livery and seating moquette while allowing standardisation in the more major aspects of production. Bedford and its direct competitors sold all vehicles through dealers, and this was also true of most AEC or Leyland coaches for smaller operators, so relationships with the specialist coach dealers were vitally important.

The beginning of the 1960s was a time of transition, with continuity in the way in which most Duple coaches were recognisably related to those of five years and indeed over ten years earlier, more so than some of the designs of the early 1950s. On the other hand, the acquisitions in the Midlands were already in course of being rationalised and even more far-reaching developments further north were soon to be revealed.

The centre-entrance version of the Britannia body of the 1959 and 1960 seasons had the more strongly curved windscreen, as used on the Vega. Seen here is Black & White A209 (4209 AD) with body number 1122/16, the first of a batch of eight 37-seat AEC Reliance 2MU3RV models dating from 1960.

The Yeoman body for the Thames 570E chassis had a quite different front grille from that of the Vega, no doubt resulting from pressure from Ford to avoid resemblances to a style associated with the rival Bedford SB. This 1960 example was operated by British Overseas Airways Corporation.

The Vega body on Bedford SB chassis continued to be Duple's main product, the vehicle shown having body number 1133/479, that series running to 535. There had been a further face-lift for the 1961 season, the main change being the adoption of what was called the three-panel windscreen. For SB-based chassis, there was also a new grille design, not quite so 'heavy' as the previous type. Most such coaches were built for independent operators, often small, but the State-owned Tilling group had begun slightly to ease what had been very strong standardisation on Bristol-ECW vehicles. At that date, Tillings Transport (BTC) Ltd ran what had been Thomas Tilling Ltd's modest London-based coach fleet, by then the only vehicles to carry the historic name – 8 BXB was one of three Bedford SB8 models having Leyland O.350 engines, much as used in the Leyland Comet. Unladen weight had crept up a little, but at 5 tons 1 cwt 3 qr, this was still a true lightweight – note how top-sliding windows were now accepted for coach use.

In August 1960, Duple announced the purchase of the share capital of H. V. Burlingham Ltd for £550,000. It had been an important rival, having two factories in Blackpool, at Vicarage Lane and Preston New Road. Even if never approaching Duple's massive output on Bedford or similar lightweight chassis, Burlingham, for a time during the earlier 1950s, had become the leading producer of coaches for underfloor-engined chassis during the heyday of its curvaceous Seagull design. Yet, as sometimes happens, it proved difficult to find a worthy successor when that classic type lost the sense of novelty sought by fashion-conscious coach operators. Bus bodywork had also been produced, and this side had been expanded in the late 1950s, when contracts had been obtained from several municipalities, most notably Manchester Corporation which took Burlingham double-deck bodies for 62 trolleybuses and 80 buses in 1955-58.

Metal framing had been adopted in the 1950s, but the works were well equipped for a wide variety of bodybuilding; the possibilities were not lost on Duple's directors. Harry Bigg, who had been Works Manager and a Duple director since 1955, was sent to reorganise the two Blackpool factories with a view to them playing a major part in Duple's future plans.

It was too near the 1960 Show or 1961 season production to make any immediate changes to Burlingham's range and so the Seagull 61 on Bedford SB or Ford 570E and Seagull 70 for Reliance, Tiger Cub or Leopard were built as planned before the takeover, inheriting the type name of their distinctive predecessor but lacking its styling flair. Production under the Burlingham name continued for a couple of seasons, and indeed another type, the Gannet, for Ford 570E chassis and having a revised front-end, was added to the range for the 1962 season.

Duple made modest changes to its own range at the 1960 Show, the main one being a further alteration in windscreen design for the Super Vega and Yeoman, eliminating the centre pillar but with very slender curved strips separating the corner glasses from the main screen panel – the first variants with what was called the three-panel screen listed in the FS series were FS60/18 and 19 for the 7ft 6in and 8ft wide Vega. It was to be the final face-lift for a body style of which the roots dated back to 1953, soon becoming a familiar sight.

The body numbers reached in the various series for this general style in the 1961 and 1962 seasons give an indication of its continuing popularity, even allowing for occasional cancellations reducing some of the numbers actually built. The

Burlingham continued production of its own designs for a time after the take-over. This Seagull 70 body, numbered 7434 in that company's series, was one of a pair on Leyland Tiger Cub for Sunderland District Omnibus Co Ltd built in 1961.

The Britannia also received the three-panel windscreen for the 1961 and 1962 seasons when a centre entrance was specified. This example was a 1960 Earls Court Show exhibit and had body number 1135/1, the first of the 1961 season batch of this type. It had a spacious 32-seat layout and was on an AEC Reliance 2MU3RA air-braked chassis for Worthington Motor Tours Ltd of Birmingham, a concern which specialised in high-grade tours then about to celebrate the 40th anniversary of its foundation in 1921. Bearing in mind how, almost four decades further on, car design has readopted more curvaceous shapes, one wonders whether future coaches might again have such an outline, shorn of the over-fussy-seeming details, instead of today's boxes on wheels.

Super Vega 1133 series used for the 1961 season ran from 1 to 535, followed for 1962 by the 1145 series running to 321. The corresponding Ford Yeoman series numbers were 1139 (running to 360) and 1151 (129), while the Commer Avenger IV series numbers for these two years were 1134 (25) and 1146, the latter covering only five bodies, four of which went to Tenerife – after that, Commer chassis ceased to figure in Duple's output.

Another coach operator increasingly operating a short-life policy was the Whittle concern of Highley, near Kidderminster, which had tended to favour Burlingham in the 1950s, though some orders went to Duple. In 1961, a purchase of 21 Burlingham and nine Duple 41-seat bodies on Bedford SB1 and Ford 570E chassis was made, and in 1962, there were 27 Burlingham and only one Duple, all sold off within not much over a year – in subsequent years Bedford and Duple took almost all the Whittle orders and

Ford was building up a major share of the light coach market with the Thames 570E model, including some orders from major groups. Hebble Motor Services Ltd, based in Halifax, one of the smaller BET group companies, had a fleet largely composed of AEC models in 1961 but took delivery of three Thames Yeoman 41-seat coaches, including No.49 (OCP 87) seen here, followed by two more the following year. The 1961 season Yeoman body continued with the grille as on the previous version but had the three-panel screen.

the blue and red livery became a familiar sight all over the country as they in turn were sold off, quite often operating for a time in the still-smart original colours.

The three-panel screen was also adopted for the centre-entrance Britannia in FS60/21 form for the AEC Reliance and related types, the 1961-season 1135-series examples on Reliance running to 28, including six apiece for Black & White, Samuelson and Essex County Coaches, but the front-entrance version (FS60/23 etc) retained the previous screen for this type, and again these proved more numerous, the 1137 series running to 44. This was more marked for 1962 production at Hendon, with only two centre-entrance Reliance Britannia coaches in the 1147 series and nineteen front-entrance in the 1148 series. The Leyland Leopard was still little-known, with five in 1961 and four in 1962, of which the solitary centre-entrance example was noteworthy, having air suspension, at the time very rare on British coaches, and being sold to St Helens Corporation – at that date, few municipal operators ran coaches.

Duple (Midland) introduced an improved version of the Donington metal-framed coach body having larger side windows and Britannia-style trim, customers including Scout Motor Services Ltd with five on Leopard L2 chassis in 1961 and David Macbrayne Ltd with a batch on AEC Reliance.

Overall, 1961 proved to be the most successful season in terms of numbers of bodies ordered for manufacture at Hendon since the heady early post-war years, the total going over 1,000. Yet the strong demand also revealed a growing challenge from Plaxton, which had been building 200 coach bodies or less in the mid-1950s but whose output in the 1961 season amounted to 501, still only half Duple's total but a sign of things to come. In 1962, conditions worsened for both firms because of a worsening economic climate and Government restrictions on credit.

Duple's main fresh developments for the 1962 season were at opposite ends of the length scale. Bedford, encouraged by the

The Bella Vista body marked the beginning of a fresh era in Duple body styles, quite apart from being associated with a new model of chassis, the Bedford VAS. This example seen on a Highland tour was from the first production batch, having body number 1154/35. Numbered MW284 (TWG 599) it was one of three VAS1 models with Bedford 300 cu in diesel engines and basically standard 29-seat bodywork for W. Alexander & Sons (Midland) Ltd, placed in service in May 1962. The huge Alexander fleet had been split into three area companies the previous year and the Midland company, based at the existing headquarters in Falkirk, continued the blue and cream livery and, on coaches, the Bluebird emblem. An M prefix was added to the previous fleet numbering system and hence this coach was effectively added to Alexander's W series of Bedfords begun in 1933.

level of interest shown in coaches sold on C-series goods chassis, introduced a new smaller passenger chassis aimed at the 29-seat market. This was the VAS, announced towards the end of 1961, a forward-control model which had similar front-end layout to the SB but was shorter and used smaller wheels, as by then adopted for Bedford's medium-sized goods models.

The Bella range

For it, Duple produced a completely new style of body, type FS61 and FS61/1 in 7ft 6in and 8ft forms, called the Bella Vista, continuing the name link with the OB-based 29-seater. Its design was of squarer-cut outline than the Super Vega as being offered on the SB, but with a large single-panel curved-glass windscreen. Most pillars were vertical but those above the rear axle were quite sharply raked, giving a distinctive side elevation.

This combination of features was continued for subsequent designs for longer chassis also in the FS61 series, which became very extensive, with fresh sets of suffix numbers from FS61/20 for the 1964 season, FS61/31 up for 1965 and FS61/41 up for 1966, most types having the Bella prefix to their names. The style was to remain in volume production until the autumn of 1966, with a minor intermediate face-lift in the form of a revised grille, shallower than the original and with chromium-plated surround, introduced in the autumn of 1964 for the 1965 model versions.

An initial body, number 1154/1, on one of the prototype VAS chassis was the first of a batch of 100 Bella Vista coaches, largely delivered during 1962 though some of the later ones reached operators in the earlier months of 1963, being followed

The previous generation body styles on larger chassis continued alongside the Bella Vista for the 1962 season, and indeed greatly outnumbered the new design for that season, the last for the older styles. As air travel grew in importance, there was a growing fondness for publicity photographs to be taken at London Airport. This one shows one of three Bedford SB5 coaches with 41-seat Super Vega bodies placed in service in the summer of 1962 by Charles W. Banfield Ltd in the livery of Cunard Eagle Airways Ltd – another of the batch had body 1145/83. The SB5 had Bedford's new 330 cu in diesel engine, matching the capacity of the Ford 6D used in the Thames 570E. The Banfield business had been established in 1928 and was running 98 vehicles in 1962, although the fleet had been considerably larger when transport for workers building the Isle of Grain in Kent was being provided.

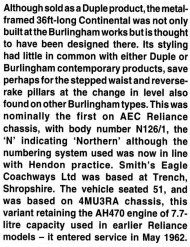

Although sold as a Duple product, the metal-framed 36ft-long Continental was not only built at the Burlingham works but is thought to have been designed there. Its styling had little in common with either Duple or Burlingham contemporary products, save perhaps for the stepped waist and reverse-rake pillars at the change in level also found on other Burlingham types. This was nominally the first on AEC Reliance chassis, with body number N126/1, the 'N' indicating 'Northern' although the numbering system used was now in line with Hendon practice. Smith's Eagle Coachways Ltd was based at Trench, Shropshire. The vehicle seated 51, and was based on 4MU3RA chassis, this variant retaining the AH470 engine of 7.7-litre capacity used in earlier Reliance models – it entered service in May 1962.

Among the best-known Duple Continental bodies were six on Leyland Leopard PSU3/3RT chassis ordered by Scout of Preston but delivered to Ribble in November 1962. They had seats for 40, with a toilet compartment, and were meant for the London service but 702 (SCK 867) with body N127/11, is seen here in Llandudno, evidently in a private hire outing, in July 1966. A feature new at the time but soon to become widely used was the forced-air ventilation system copied from aircraft practice. Air was drawn in from roof-mounted intakes and fed via fans to adjustable nozzles for each passenger in the overhead racks, the main side windows being fixed.

that year by the 1155 series which ran to 30 by that summer. Subsequent yearly batches were of between 50 and 75 similar coaches, mostly with 29 seats and on the VAS1 chassis with Bedford diesel engine, though a minority were VAS2 petrol models with what amounted to the same engine as had been used in the OB. It was thus nowhere near as popular a type as the 'old' Vista of 1946-

The Gannet body was introduced for the 1962 season and sold as a Burlingham product, though included in Duple's N-prefix body numbering system. The windscreen appears to follow the Duple three-panel unit's contours though trimmed to a different outline. This example was on Bedford SB chassis but the N121 production series was on Ford Thames 570E.

50, but catered for a demand not covered by any other true passenger chassis on the British market, remaining in production until the early 1970s.

At the opposite end of the size range, the maximum permitted length for public service vehicles was increased to 36ft, and width to 8ft 2½in (these dimensions approximating to the 11metre and 2.5-metre figures widely accepted in Europe), with effect from July 1961. In practice, delivery of such vehicles did not begin until 1962, the first chassis generally available being new versions of the AEC Reliance and Leyland Leopard. For Duple, the output of such coaches was both an opportunity and a challenge, for space at Hendon was very limited and the decision was taken that the first 36ft types would be built at Blackpool, as well as some overflow of production of other types from Hendon.

Thus the true function of Duple Motor Bodies (Northern) Ltd became apparent, its initial 36ft design seating up to 51 passengers being called the Continental. It followed Burlingham practice in being metal-framed though its styling, with a stepped waistline, was unlike anything previous in either Blackpool or Hendon output. It did not figure in the FS lists and is understood have been designed at Blackpool.

New body number series with an N prefix were used

The appearance of the twin-steering Bedford VAL with Vega Major body, using the same basic body features as the Bella Vista, was quite dramatically different as well as having that elusive quality of 'style'. The 11-metre length was in itself still uncommon and the use of a twin-steering three-axle layout with small-diameter wheels added to the impression of great length, as conveyed in this view of 361 KNM of Costin of Dunstable. It had body 1158/66 and was placed in service in June 1963, being one of about 90 with this body which entered service with British operators from the first season's output. The chassis design pursued Bedford's 'small-wheel' concept, partly to allow parts common to other models to be used. In one respect, it was outstandingly successful, for despite use of conventional leaf springs and beam axles, the VAL was exceptionally steady-riding. On the other hand, the brakes needed frequent attention to maintain efficiency and the front-mounted Leyland O.400 engine, fairly hard-worked, made the internal noise level quite high.

for 'Northern' products, the series including N121/1 to 44 for Burlingham Gannet bodies on Ford 570E chassis, and a batch of Duple Yeoman also on the 570E, with numbers N123/1 to 69, adding to the 1962 season Hendon output of this type. The first of the Continental series was N126/1 to 27, used for those on AEC Reliance 36ft chassis, these including both AH470- and AH590-engined examples. Those on Leyland chassis, mainly Leopard of the PSU3/3 type, though including one diverted export Worldmaster model for Happiways of Manchester, were numbered N127/1 to 13 – they included six ordered by Scout Motor Services Ltd of Preston for its London services but, following that firm's take-over by Ribble, diverted to the latter's fleet – they seated only 40 and had toilet compartments.

The Continental achieved only modest success, though further batches (N135, N136, N152, N153, N157, N158) and in a variant called the Alpine Continental with wider pillar spacing (N137 and N138) were built on Reliance or Leopard chassis for the 1963 to 1965 seasons. The numbers in none of these got beyond seventeen and there were only two further orders for BET concerns – four Alpine Continentals on Leopard for Western Welsh and six on Reliance for Timpson's, all in 1963.

During the early 1960s, Plaxton greatly expanded its output of coaches on underfloor-engined chassis, its Panorama designs with wide side windows being built in substantial numbers and going to quite a high proportion of BET fleets; Harrington also

regained a significant share of this market with its stylish Cavalier design. However, in the larger market for lighter coaches, Duple was as yet still dominant, mainly on the basis of the association with Bedford, although care had been taken not to exclude other chassis makers, among which Ford had by then emerged as by far the strongest challenger since pre-war days. Very largely, this output was respectively based on the SB and the directly comparable 570E.

In September 1962, Bedford created a sensation with the announcement of its VAL coach aimed at capturing a major share of the 36ft coach market. It was of three-axle type, with twin steering axles, this permitting the use of small wheels. It retained a front-engined layout but, with the front axles set back, the entrance was at the extreme front, access to the interior being alongside the engine. It was powered in original VAL14 production form by a vertical version of the Leyland O.400 engine by then used for the Tiger Cub. Early production examples came out around 6½ tons unladen so performance was adequate.

Duple had built the body for the first VAL prototype to type FS61/3 during the previous winter and its styling was basically the same as the Bella Vista used on the VAS, although the effect was quite different because of the extra length. It was christened Vega Major, seating 52 in standard form. Production was at Hendon, initially in a series running from 1158/1 to 92, entering service with independent operators, mostly between March and September 1963. The Vega Major body number series in

Despite the advent of new smaller and larger models, the midrange Bedford SB continued to be the basis for Duple's bestselling product. For the 1963 season, it too was brought into the 'Bella' mould, becoming the Bella Vega. Comparison with the previous three-panel-screen Super Vega underlines the squarer-cut look, in keeping with automobile design trends generally in the 1960s. Yet even if less eye-catching than the VAL with Vega Major body, it looked a tidy 'professional' job. With its angled pillars over the rear axle, the design gave scope for variations of livery style, as on this example on an SB5 for Buckmaster of Leighton Buzzard – registered 21 JBM, it had body 1159/181, being one of a pair placed in service in January 1963.

the succeeding years' programmes for the 1964, 1965 and 1966 seasons ran to 111, 128 and 140 respectively, well ahead of Duple output on heavy-duty chassis but modest by comparison with bodies for the SB.

Indeed, with far less publicity, the corresponding Bella Vega design of 41-seat capacity coach for the SB chassis, initially FS61/4 and FS61/5 (this latter being 8ft 2½in wide), continued the previous Vega tradition of outselling all other Duple products. The first series of body numbers for the type produced foe the 1963 season ran from 1159/1 to 411, largely on the SB5 chassis which had become the standard model with Bedford 330 cu in diesel engine, the petrol SB3 having become a minority choice, though there were also a few SB8 (Leyland O.350 engine) and one SB13 (O.370). The Bella Vega body numbers for the 1964 and 1965 seasons ran to 420 and 450 on a similar mix of chassis, showing that the traditional concept of a low-cost medium-sized Bedford-Duple coach still had strong appeal.

The corresponding 41-seat body with 'Bella' styling for Ford 570E chassis (FS61/7) also introduced in late 1962 was called the Trooper, but this was built in rather smaller numbers, 110 being scheduled for both the 1963 and 1964 seasons and 105 for 1965. In 1963, Ford introduced its 36ft model, type 676E though simply known as the 'Thames 36', more orthodox than the VAL in having two axles but also having the entrance in the front overhang – it had a Ford 330 cu in diesel engine. Duple produced a FS61/18 design and bodied a prototype, body

Only one Astrocoach was built, and it too took part in the rally at Brighton in 1964, failing to pick up any major awards, an outcome which might have been influenced by bad weather that day. As can be seen in this view, the glass roof quarter lights were made almost continuous with the side windows by the use of slim framing, an attractive idea for touring in mountainous terrain. This 51-seat 11-metre body, 1168/1, on AEC Reliance 2U3RA chassis with 9.6-litre engine, was entered by Smith's Tours (Wigan) Ltd, though the Cheshire registration number BTU 200B had been issued when acting a demonstrator for a dealer in that county.

The 'Bella' style was extended to the shorter underfloor-engined models by the Commodore design, retaining the sloping pillars over the rear axle. Few were built but this 45-seat example on AEC Reliance 2MU4RA chassis for Creamline of Bordon is seen being judged in the Concours d'Elegance at the British Coach Rally at Brighton in April 1964 soon after completion. Registered 900 KOT, it had body number 1175/1.

Ford's answer to the VAL was the Thames 36, model 676E, also 11metre and with set-back front wheels but on two axles. Duple's body for it, basically equivalent to the Vega Major, was at first called the Marauder. Ronsway Coaches Ltd of Hemel Hempstead, took the last three of the first production batch of 60 bodies for this model in July 1964, ADY 232B christened 'Miss Switzerland' shown here having body 1174/58.

At Blackpool, the Duple (Northern) Firefly body for lightweight front-engined chassis was introduced from the 1963 season, though the resemblances to the Burlingham Gannet made its origins obvious. A later example is seen here, one of the 49 built in the N160 series on Bedford SB for the 1965 season – GAR 113C with body N160/30 was one of a pair on SB5 chassis for Parkinson's of Hemel Hempstead dating from February of that year.

Meanwhile the 11-metre Continental had progressed to the Alpine Continental with larger side windows. Western Welsh Omnibus Co Ltd put four 49-seat examples into service on Leyland Leopard PSU3/3RT chassis in May 1963, this being the first, No.141 (141 DBO) with body N137/1.

This 1963 Alpine Continental for service in Greece was on a left-hand-drive 11-metre AEC Reliance chassis. It seated 42, had an extra passenger door near the rear and a large baggage rack on the roof. English lettering on the side badge read 'Hellenic Mediterranean Lines' with an anchor emblem, implying that it was for use in connection with shore excursions from cruise liners.

number 1168/1, followed by 1174/1 to 60 for the 1964 season, the body type, by then FS61/27 and basically much the same as a Vega Major, initially called Marauder but later Mariner – 82 followed for 1965 and 100 for 1966.

A replacement for the Britannia for the shorter underfloor-engined chassis was added to the range in 1962, having 'Bella' styling and similar composite construction, complete with sharply-angled pillar just ahead of the rear axle. Although an FS61 variant (the initial AEC version was FS61/9) it was called the Commodore, and available on the '30ft' versions of the Reliance and Leopard, though the actual length was 31ft 10in – the relaxation of the legal length limit made this possible, though overhang became the governing factor in such cases. Seating could be for up to 45 passengers. As it turned out, few were built, mainly because it was soon superseded – there were two series in 1963, 1161, comprising eight on Reliance chassis delivered in 1962-63, and 1163, made up of three on Leopard L2.

What proved to be a one-off product of the same period was body number 1168/1, type FS62/1, again with 'Bella' front-end but given the name Astrocoach by virtue

of its almost completely glazed roof panels, there being no more than a thin strip dividing the side windows from the curved-glass roof panels. It was on a 36ft AEC Reliance 590 chassis, initially a demonstrator though sold to Smith's Tours (Wigan) Ltd just in time to appear at the 1964 British Coach Rally. There had been plans for a range of such bodies but no more were built.

Production at Blackpool went through quite a complex phase in the early 1960s. As well as continuing coach output under the Burlingham name to the 1962 season, a pair of new Duple (Northern) coach designs of composite construction were introduced in 1962 for the 1963 season – the Firefly (with some resemblances to the Gannet) for light front-engined chassis and the similar Dragonfly for underfloor-engined chassis. These were Blackpool designs and not given FS numbers.

The initial runs of the Firefly were the N129 series on Ford 570E, of which there were 33, including four for Hanson's of Huddersfield; the N130 on SB, of which there were 25 and N143 on Albion Victor VT21L, with 30. A similar pattern was repeated for 1964 and 1965, the Firefly total reaching over 250, of which the 71 on VT21L

Another Brighton rally appearance was that of an early Commander body, one of a batch on AEC Reliance chassis for Potteries Motor Traction, at the April 1964 event – it gained the Coach of the Year award, being commended for both external and internal design. Number 489, with body number 1179/5, is seen undergoing judging.

maker, except that Duple (Midland) was kept as a 'badge' name when on Bedford chassis. There were four Burlingham-design bus bodies on AEC Reliance chassis for Reading Corporation in 1962, forming the N128 series; the N132 series were Duple-design buses on Bedford VAS chassis, nine for MacBraynes and eighteen for the Metropolitan Police, and the N140 series comprised two on SB.

The Commander

Yet another new Duple coach design for underfloor-engined chassis was the Commander, initiating the FS63 series, introduced for the 1964 season and with similar front-end to the Commodore. It had large fixed side windows with slim metal pillars set vertically, the Commodore's sloping pillar above the rear axle being eliminated. With simple, clean lines, it was perhaps the firm's best-looking large coach for some time. It was Duple's answer to the Plaxton Panorama, a clear case of flattery by imitation in terms of side window treatment, and responding to the inroads into Duple business, often among major operators, that design was making. Although sales were at first modest, they later built up, restoring Duple's stature in that sector of the market considerably.

Commander output began at Hendon in batches 1175 (three on 'short' Reliance); 1179 (seven on 'long' Reliance, including six for PMT, one of which was 'Coach of the Year' at the April 1964 Brighton rally, helping to draw attention to the new body design); 1180 (a Leopard PSU3 for Cronshaw); 1181 (short Reliance, including twelve for East Kent) and 1182 (a Leopard L2). Three more 36ft examples were built at Hendon towards the end of 1964 – 1190/1 on Reliance, 1191/1 on Leopard and 1195/1 on the new

represented a large proportion of the home-market sales of this model, which had a Leyland O.370 engine. The Bedford examples included some for the Eastern National and Tilling fleets. On the other hand, only six Dragonfly bodies were built, comprising the N133 and N134 series: two demonstrators for Leyland on Leopard PSU3/3RT chassis in 1962 and four Reliance for Samuelson in 1963.

There was also limited bus body construction at Blackpool up to 1963, though in general this was being phased out, Willowbrook becoming the group's bus body

The Daimler Roadliner coach demonstrator, CWK 641C, posed at an idyllic setting at Bourton-on-the-Water; it had been completed in 1964. The Commander body, 1195/1, seated 49 and the author recalls finding it a very agreeable vehicle to drive and to ride in during a road test, but unfortunately the rear-mounted Cummins V6 engine proved to be troublesome in service.

Midland Red returned to Duple for the first time since 1950 with an order for 49 Commander 49-seat bodies on Leyland Leopard PSU3/4R chassis. The tradition of that operator building its own BMMO vehicles was beginning to wind down under the force of economics, although this was the first time bought-out chassis had been purchased for coaches since the early 1920s. The PSU3/4R, increasingly favoured by BET companies, had Leyland's Pneumocylic transmission – the so-called semi-automatic type based on an Wilson-type epicyclic gearbox with a miniature gear lever giving direct selection of the ratio desired via an air-pressure system – they also had air brakes, increasingly common on heavier-duty models. While the LC7 coaches, as they were designated by BMMO, were no match in technology for their predecessors the CM6 and CM5 motorway coaches, they proved reliable for general coaching duties. Commander body production had moved to Blackpool but the design was not visibly changed and this batch were virtually standard, though looking well in Midland Red's livery of red with black roofs, as indicated by this view of No.5800 (CHA 100) with body N163/27 at Victoria Coach Station in September 1965 it was new that same month.

Daimler Roadliner SRC6. This last-mentioned was a prototype/demonstrator, body design FS63/11, and the author recalls being most impressed with it when road testing it for 'Bus & Coach' – the problems with the rear-mounted Cummins V6 engine were yet to become apparent. Interestingly, an FS63/12 design for a coach on rear-engined AEC Swift was planned but not built.

After that, output of Commander bodies was switched to Blackpool and numbers built up, the type becoming the main product of that works on underfloor-engined chassis. It was significant that no further such vehicles were bodied at Hendon, a further indication of the trend of events. The N162 series comprised seventeen 'short' Reliances delivered in the spring and summer

of 1965, including four for Timpson's and two for Greenslades, a Duple customer from the 1930s and now part of BET – there were also two for Wallace Arnold. However the N163 series of 62 on Leopard PSU3 delivered in June-October 1965 was more significant, as 49 coaches were supplied to Midland Red, the first Duple bodies for this fleet since 1950 and its first coaches on non-BMMO chassis since the early 1920s. The N164 series consisted of ten bodies on 36ft Reliance. Further sets of Commander

The hand-over of one of a fleet of Bedford SB Bella Vega coaches to Grey-Green in June 1965 was treated as a major event, it having been calculated that it was the 25,000th Duple body. For the occasion, the preserved 1930 Green Line AEC Regal coach, T219, one of those of that batch with Duple-built bodywork, was sent to Hendon – it had been restored in 1961 under the care of the then British Transport Commission Museum. The Bedford was an SB13 with Leyland O.370 engine and appears to have been DLU 488C, which had body number 1183/321. Posed in front were some of the stalwarts who had served the company well over long periods.

body batches on Reliance or Leopard chassis followed – N168-N171 in 1966, and N175/6/8 in 1967 – the numbers in these were not very great, though N176, on Leopard PSU3/3 ran to 30, of which 25 were for Southdown.

A noteworthy event celebrated in June 1965 was the delivery of what was described as the 25,000th Duple body, a Bella Vega on SB chassis which was also the 100th Duple-bodied Bedford for George Ewer & Co Ltd, better

known as Grey-Green, and its associated companies, notably Orange Luxury Coaches Ltd (formerly Keith & Boyle). In earlier times, Grey-Green had favoured Harrington bodywork, and the event may have been staged to help cement Duple's position as main supplier – later in the year, Harrington's decision to close its coach bodybuilding business came as quite a shock to the industry, even though the firm was smaller than Duple or Plaxton.

The question arises of just how the 25,000-body figure up to that date was calculated, but even if everything from the first car/van body on a Ford model T in 1919, various goods and 1939-45 military bodies was included, it was a remarkable figure, representing an average of about 550 bodies per year over the whole period. In the 1965 season, home market output at Hendon was climbing back towards the 800 mark after dipping below 600 in the 1962 season, but by that date Blackpool had to be included to assess the overall Duple coach picture, and in 1965 and 1966, the combined total was again around the 1,000 mark after three leaner years.

Yet the threat from Plaxton was growing, its output figures for the 1965 and 1966 seasons being

The first production Bella Venture bodies built for Bedford VAM chassis in the 1966 season had a revised style of grille with a chromium-plated surround and the headlamps were set lower, with foglamps alongside them, in nacelles projecting from the corner of the body – these features soon became standard across much of the Duple coach range. Barton Transport 1082 (JNN 128D) was a VAM5 with the Bedford 330 cu in engine placed in service in July 1966 – the cream livery evident in this picture taken the following month suggests it might have been a dealer's stock vehicle acquired at short notice – often painted thus so that a stronger colour could be applied with minimum difficulty where desired, although cream was itself quite fashionable for a time.

uncomfortably close at 804 and 925 respectively. Moreover, all was not happy within Duple – abruptly, Harry Bigg, a director for ten years who had been Works Manager at Hendon and then reorganised production at Blackpool, left the company in 1965 after a policy disagreement.

In 1965, there were developments in the medium-sized lightweight coach category. In June, Bedford introduced the VAM, intended as a replacement for the SB, though with set-back front axle and slightly longer at 32ft 4in as bodied. It incorporated many of the same units as the SB, the initial standard version being the VAM5 with 5.4-litre Bedford 330 diesel engine. In August, Ford followed with its R192 model of similar layout and dimensions, including engine size, and also revised its larger 676E model, this becoming the R226, with 5.9-litre Ford 360 engine – the Thames marque name, never taken all that seriously within the industry, was dropped at this point, the new models being simply known as Ford.

Duple built bodies for the VAM and R192 models to virtually identical 45-seat design, though known respectively as Bella Venture and Empress. A prototype FS61/39 body for the R192, 1196/1, is shown as having been delivered in April 1965, but it seems that one fitted to a VAM prototype, possibly slightly earlier, may not have been recorded as 'delivered'.

The initial production batch of the Empress design for R192 (FS61/45) were numbered 1203/1 to 110, delivered between October 1965 and, for the last few, early 1967. The corresponding Bella Venture on

VAM (FS61/47) were 1205/1 to 330, delivered over much the same period – some 36 went to Ewer and Orange.

The SB continued to be available, and the Bella Vaga run for the 1966 season comprised 1207/1 to 75, of which eight were petrol SB3 models for Salopia, which had also taken eight of the corresponding very rare VAM3. The days of Duple SB coaches being built at the rate of several hundred per year were over, though it was a case of a model that was 'dead' but wouldn't lie down, kept in production because of huge export chassis demand and having enough home-market demand for Duple (and Plaxton) to continue offering bodies for it.

Even so, the range of types being offered for Bedford and Ford was extending – in addition to those already mentioned, Duple's Hendon works body series for the 1966 season (with, in brackets, the numbers they reached) also included 1201, the Bella Vista for VAS (63); 1202, Vega Major for VAL (140), and 1204, the Mariner for R226 (100).

At Blackpool, a further body type had been introduced for the new VAM and R192, called Viscount, reviving a name that had been used briefly by Willowbrook for a coach built in small numbers in the early 1960s and memorable because some of them featured a reverse-rake rear window much as on the contemporary Ford Anglia 105E car. The Duple Viscount was in effect, a scaled-

The Duple Viscount was less well-known than the Bella Venture, being more of a shorter equivalent to the Commander, with three wide windows each side. Crosville Motor Services Ltd had six on Bedford VAM5 chassis. The vehicle shown, fleet number CVT 685, registered NFM 685E, had body N172/90 and dated from February 1967.

By 1966, the former Burlingham premises, bearing the name Duple Motor Bodies (Northern) Ltd, were playing a more important role in overall Duple output, having been made responsible for Commander coach bodies on heavier-duty underfloor-engined chassis, as well as the Viscount of basically similar design for the front-engined Bedford VAM and Ford R192. This scenes shows a VAM Viscount alongside a Leyland Leopard and AEC Reliance both with what by then were being called Commander 36 bodies, seating 51 and 49 respectively, being prepared for demonstration work for the 1976 season.

down version of the Commander, with metal pillars and wide side windows without the sloping pillar over the rear axle. The N166 series of FS63/13 bodies on R192 and the N167 (FS63/14) on VAM ran to 65 and 119 respectively. For the 1967 season, the Viscount continued, unlike most of the Bella range, most being built on VAM chassis, the N172 series running up to 92, together with eleven on R192 in the N173 series – there were also two 52-seat bodies on the R226 chassis in the N174 series for which a type name is not recorded though understood to be a long version of the Viscount – they were supplied to Alpha of Brighton and Bebb of Llantwit Fardre.

Clearly, the question of how best to develop the company continued to engage the Duple board of directors – in 1967 they comprised H. W. Sydenham (Chairman), Gerald R. White (Managing), George A. H. Payze (Sales), R. J. Richards (Secretary), G. J. Lynch, J. G. Rougetel and R. Fripp. Blackpool's importance was clear and it was Hendon's future that was coming into question – in addition to the more difficult labour relations and wage rates in west London, possible expansion there was ruled out by the existence of a roadway round the site.

The Viceroy range

A new FS64 body range replacing the 'Bella' series was announced in August 1966. This used the name Viceroy, applied to all main types of body on Bedford or Ford chassis except those on the VAS (now mildly restyled, slightly lengthened to 25ft and retitled Vista 25, this being type FS65) and the SB, for which the Bella Vega continued in modest-scale production (FS61/51 etc) without publicity. Much of the Viceroy's framing, and in particular the pillars, were of steel although longitudinal framing used both steel and wood, the latter being used as the basis for panel attachment. A new feature was the use of fluorescent interior lighting.

The Viceroy introduced new, rather aggressive and somewhat angular styling, although the forward-inclined pillars at each side of the windscreen had echoes of a mid- to late-1950s generation of General Motors cars, including Vauxhall, by then superseded by a smoother look. There was another forward-raked pillar, at a sharper angle and reminiscent of the Continental body, just behind the front axle. Aft of this point, the side pillars were cranked inwards at the top, the sliding vent windows being in this top portion and thus above conventional cantrail level. Externally, only the front grille carried over from the previous designs, and a rather inconsistent note was the mounting in bulbous housings of the paired headlamps.

Viceroy and other series built at Hendon for the 1967 season (with highest body numbers in brackets) were:- 1208, VAM (326); 1209, VAL (29); 1210, R192 (83); 1211, VAS Vista 25 (73); 1213, SB Bella Vaga (30), and 1214, R226 (55). The small number of VAL models quoted was

The Viceroy range of bodies marked a sharp change from previous generations of Duple body styling, with the adoption of angular outlines and deliberate breaks in the continuity of window and trim lines. The effect was perhaps at its most dramatic on the Bedford VAL, as indicated in this photograph of an example built for Cumberland Motor Services Ltd. It was one of a pair on VAL14 chassis built soon after production of this combination had been transferred to Blackpool and having body numbers N179/25 and 26. Although the lettering had not been completed in this picture, they were numbered 302-3 (LAO 580E and 581E) and were placed in service in May 1967.

By the 1967 season, the Hendon factory was concentrating on the output of standard bodywork for Bedford and Ford chassis, mainly the medium-sized and smaller types. The Bedford VAM was the most numerous single model associated with the Viceroy body style and the Trent Motor Traction Co Ltd's No.78 (MRC 578E) was one of a pair of VAM5 41-seat coaches which dated from April and May 1967. Seen in Nottingham in July 1969 with destination blind set for Cleethorpes, it had body number 1208/105 in a series which ran to 326. Such numbers were not quite as high as the 500-odd reached by the SB Vega combination a few years earlier but for a time such coaches were a familiar sight. Trent was a BET group company when this coach was new but from January 1969 was part of the State-owned National Bus Company.

In general, group policy in the 1960s was that bus bodywork was built in the Midlands either under the Willowbrook or Duple (Midland) names but an order for 70 45-seat bodies of bus outline on Bedford VAM14 chassis built in 1967 was allocated to Blackpool. It was for Ulsterbus Ltd, a new organisation placed under the dynamic management of Mr W. Heubeck and which took over from the previous Ulster Transport Authority in April of that year. This official picture of the first of 9240 (1240 TZ) with body number N180/40 was taken before application of the fleetname – deliveries had begun in March. The external design generally conformed

to the standard style as built by Duple (Midland) for the VAM, with windscreen to a style by then widely standardised by BET and front panel having a touch of the Bella range about it, but the seating was to a more comfortable style than the rather basic bus standard for this model.

because Viceroy production on this chassis was transferred to Blackpool during that season, continuing in the N179 series, where it ran up to 90 more of the same type, giving a combined total of 119. There were also 70 dual-purpose 45-seat bodies on Bedford VAM14 chassis built at Blackpool for Ulsterbus and forming the N180 series.

Bristol bus and coach chassis were re-emerging on the open market in 1966-67 after a period of being restricted to the State-owned sector to which they belonged, although

There had been unnumbered variations on the Commander body when the Commander II body design appeared on four coaches built in June-July 1967. It was something of a hybrid, with windscreen style and three wide main side windows as on the previous Commander, but using Viceroy-type pillars, complete with shallow sliding windows above the normal cantrail level and inclined inwards a little more than the main side windows. These high-level windows were rather obviously an addition to a design not intended to have them and the idea was not repeated in this form. This view shows the first of the batch of four coaches on Bristol RESH6G chassis built for Hants & Dorset Motor Services Ltd, No.912 (JEL 423E) with body number N181/1.

For the 1968 season, the Commander III became the standard Duple coach body style for underfloor-engined chassis. The windscreen and rear window were brought into line with the Viceroy types, requiring the adoption of reverse-rake screen pillars, but the side window layout reverted to the original Commander type. A completely new style of grille was adopted and, for that season, this feature was no longer common to the Viceroy – it had a rectangular outline extending almost to the full width of the coach and horizontal bars, with a neat installation of quadruple headlamps beneath. This coach on AEC Reliance 6U3ZR chassis for York Bros of Northampton was numerically the first of the style, with body number N184/1 and among the first completed, being delivered in March 1968. It was number 89 in the fleet and registered NRP 89F.

as it turned out early orders for Duple-bodied examples went to State-owned fleets. What was designated as the Commander II body (FS63/31) was produced to suit the Bristol RE rear-engined coach chassis in its RESH6G form and of 32ft 7in overall length. Four were built at Blackpool as the N181 series for Hants & Dorset Motor Services Ltd and delivered in June-July 1967.

In August 1967, the Commander III range (FS63/32 to 40) was announced, this combining a Viceroy-style front and rear profile and a shallower roof line, though having a new grille style, with the existing basic concept of wide windows and slender upright pillars – construction was described as basically steel-framed though with some use of wood. Models could be of full 11-metre (36ft 1in) or approximately 32ft 6in length. In the 1968 season, the N184 to 189 series comprised Commander III bodies on, respectively, 20 'long' Reliance; about 29 Leopard PSU3; two 'short' Reliance; 17 Leopard PSU4 (this being the short version current by then); and four Daimler Roadliner (three for PMT). There were also the N190 series of nine Bristol

RELH6G (five for Hants & Dorset and four for Thames Valley) and the N191 of five RESH6G (four Eastern National and one Southern Vectis). A new development was the building of four 41-seat bodies to Commander III specification on Bristol LH6L chassis for South Midland, delivered in May 1968 – the LH was a lightweight underfloor-engined model with the Leyland O.400 engine.

Also built at Blackpool in the period from late 1967 to the following summer were the N182 and N183 series of Viceroy bodies on Bedford VAL (mostly VAL70 with the then new 7.6-litre Bedford 466 engine) of which there were about 87, plus 40 on R226.

By then, output from Hendon was confined to coach bodies on the medium and smaller types of Bedford and Ford. The 1968 season production there consisted of the 1215 series of VAM coaches, mainly VAM70, including some 25 for Whittle but also ten petrol VAM3 for Salopia – the body numbers ran to 248. The 1216 series on R192 went up to 77 and the 1217 programme of Vista 25 on VAS to 75, while the 1219 series of SB Bella Vega numbers ran to 25.

The Daimler Roadliner was still in production, though only limited numbers had been sold, especially as a coach, but was chosen by Woburn Garage, London W.C.1 as the basis for an executive coach, a concept then quite fashionable, with seats for only 30 passengers and lavish refreshment facilities. This view shows the deeper rear window adopted for the Commander III body as well as the additional grilles which indicated the rear location of the Cummins V6 engine. Registered ULR 963F, it had body number N188/4, the first three numbers having been occupied by more conventional 49-seat coaches on the same chassis for PMT.

The Bristol LH, originally intended mainly as a light country bus, had also been made available as a light mid-underfloor-engined coach chassis, generally with Leyland O.400 engine. The mid-length example shown was one of four 41-seat for South Midland dating from May 1968 – at that date, that fleet, originally based in Oxford, was being operated as part of the Thames Valley Traction Co Ltd. Number 430 (RJB 430F) had body number N193/3. The exercise was repeated a year later with a further four forming the N208 body series.

The restyled version of the Viceroy introduced at the time of the 1968 Commercial Motor Show was remarkably effective in giving a fresh look without fundamental structural redesign. The 'jagged' effect which seemed to have been deliberately fostered two years previously was very largely swept away by the use of a new grille and polished trim emphasising continuity of line. Neat detailing of items such as headlamps added to the 'professional' look. Seen here is body N201/1, the first of the 1969 season batch of 70 Viceroy 37 bodies on Ford R226 chassis. R. W. J. Lees of Aston, Birmingham, trading as Claribel Coaches, entered newly-delivered POF 281G in the 1969 National Coach Rally at Blackpool and its driver, Sydney Rose, took the Driver of the Year award.

A plan for Hendon's closure

In June 1968, as that season's deliveries were nearing completion, the official announcement was made of the plan to close the Hendon works and concentrate all Duple coach production at Blackpool. Duple Motor Bodies (Northern) Ltd was to be renamed Duple Coachbuilders Ltd, but Willowbrook Ltd and bus body production at its Loughborough premises were to be unaffected. The intention as then announced was that Hendon production of bodywork would end in August 1968, though production of components was to continue until the spring of 1969 and the service, sales and administrative activities would remain at Hendon.

The Chairman explained that the drop in demand for coach bodies was such as to make it wasteful to continue with the duplication of activities, the Blackpool works being able to meet the demand with a small extension. This comment doubtless reflected Mr Sydenham's accountancy background in its reasoning – there had been a decline in the combined Hendon and Blackpool output of almost a third between the 1966 and 1968 seasons. This was partly a reflection of a general drop in demand – Plaxton production slipped back by about a quarter in the same period – but, taken at face value, it also seemed to imply a rather pessimistic view of Duple's prospects for renewed growth.

By the time of the 1968 Commercial Motor Show held three months later, it began to become clear that implementation of the move was to be delayed. All three of the Duple companies as well as Willowbrook had nominally separate stands, although together forming an 'island' site, and the old company titles remained. The focus was on the revised range, the Viceroy being extensively restyled for 1969 after only two years – itself an indication that its reception on the market had not been enthusiastic. The importance of an effort for Duple to recover the initiative was underlined by the fact that, at that point, the output of Plaxton had caught up with that of Duple's Hendon and Blackpool works combined.

It was revealed that the Viceroy restyling was done by a design consultant, Ken Olsen and there was an obvious resemblance to the previous year's Commander III in regard to the front grille. Yet the Viceroy revamp was about as far-reaching as possible while not making any significant change to the framing. It seemed that his intention was to erase as many of the jagged angular elements of the 1967-8 Viceroy as possible and emphasize continuity of line. There was extensive use of ribbed stainless steel trim, and although too much applied decoration can easily become vulgar, here the theme of horizontal lines and particularly neat detail design gave quite a 'clean' look to a rather uninspired basic shape.

The interior was similarly tidied up and attention paid to noise reduction by the redesign of the engine cover over the vertical Bedford or Ford engines. Although still apt to be strident when working hard, the sound level when cruising was usefully reduced. The maximum overall length limit had been increased to 12 metres (39ft 4in) from September 1967. Although at first very few vehicles took full advantage of this (none being offered in Duple's range until the 1970 season), it was possible to add another foot or so to some models built to the 11-metre limit. Thus the Viceroy 36 bodies for the VAL and R226 became the Viceroy 37, standard seating capacity going from 52 to 53. The Commander III required less drastic change, but was brought into line in regard to the polished trim and tidied-up detail, becoming Commander IV.

Meanwhile, a sequence of events involving Plaxton was beginning to have further effects on Duple – eventually, to be profound. Mr Frank B. Ford had been Plaxton's Sales Director since 1960, a period during which the firm had expanded considerably, including such shrewd if minor moves as acquiring the remnants of the Harrington business in 1966 and taking over Thurgood of Ware, a small but respected coachbuilder, in 1967. Frank Ford had resigned from Plaxton following the collapse in May 1968 of a venture to build buses to the design of the American

The Commander IV incorporated the tidied-up trim and detail-work of the 1969-model Viceroy applied to a design which was basically that of the Commander III. The result was quite a stylish vehicle even if the reverse-rake windscreen pillars looked increasingly outdated a decade or so after those American-influenced parts of the car industry that had taken up the idea dropped it. This example was the last of three on Leyland Leopard PSU3/3RT for Samuelson New Transport Ltd, of London S.W.1. dating from March 1969, XVB 468G having body number N204/7. Samuelson was then using a smart dark blue livery but its position as part of NBC meant that it and indeed the firm's separate existence would be in the melting pot within a couple of years or so.

The Bedford VAS with what had begun as the Bella Vista body had developed into type FS65, called the Vista 25, in the autumn of 1965, the title reflecting its slightly increased length of 25ft – at the same time the inclined pillar over the rear axle had been replaced by a more orthodox arrangement. The grille had altered the following year in line with other models. The type continued to be built at Hendon to the end of production there. This mildly retouched photograph was used for publicity at the time of the 1968 Commercial Motor Show.

Flxible firm at the Scarborough works. No doubt that caused some concern at Plaxton and perhaps even some celebration at Duple, but the momentum of business he had built up was still strong.

However a further element came in the appearance of a new Plaxton body design, largely the work of John Ruddy, also introduced at the 1968 Show. This was the Panorama Elite, which was to set the pattern for the bulk of British coach styling through the 1970s by the introduction of curved-glass side windows, then becoming usual on cars but giving a completely fresh look to a coach. Its impact took a little time to develop, thanks to Plaxton's inept complete lack of pre-Show publicity – by contrast, George Payze had made sure that the new Viceroy got plenty of coverage. Even so, it was the Panorama Elite that was widely judged to be the star coach of the Show.

Under the combined influence of these factors, perhaps more especially the impending move, Duple output remained in the doldrums while Plaxton recovered strongly, going into the lead in the 1969 season. At Hendon, rather a complex pattern of body numbers emerged. The series for Viceroy on VAM delivered from October 1968 began in the usual way at 1221/1 and ran to 170 (mostly delivered by the following summer), but 'jumped' to 1226/171 and continued to 228, deliveries of these extending over a period from March 1969, with a dozen or so in the earlier part of 1970. It is noteworthy that body number 1226/228, the final one in this series and among the last built at Hendon was mounted on a

pre-production mid-engined Bedford YRQ chassis for Vauxhall Motors, registered YXE 844H.

The corresponding Hendon-built Viceroy series on R192 chassis ran from 1222/1 to 20 and 23, mostly delivered in the earlier part of 1969, before jumping to 1227/21, 22 and 24 and continuing to 1227/84, over half of these latter delivered in 1970. The Vista 25 on VAS was more straightforward, the 1223 series reaching 67, most delivered in the earlier part of 1969, though ten ran over into 1970. The venerable Bella Vega lived on in the 1224 series, which reached 25, almost all delivered in 1969.

The picture at Blackpool for the 1969 season was more straightforward, with the Viceroy 37 doing a little better than the previous year's Viceroy 36, the N200 series on VAL70 running to 110 and the N201 on R226 to 70. There were also seventeen Commander IV on Reliance (largely for ex-BET companies by then part of the National Bus Company) in the N202 series and fifteen on Leopard in N203, with two more Bristol RELH for Hants & Dorset forming the N206 series.

With the end of production at Hendon in 1970, all that remained there were the offices of what had become Duple Group Sales Ltd and the drawing office, but that continued only for a few months. Duple's hitherto commanding position among British coach bodybuilders had been seriously undermined by a combination of factors as the decade drew to an end but at least the disruption of the move north was over and a new era could begin.

9 RECOVERY BY THE SEA

The closure of the works in Hendon in 1970 made it possible to concentrate effort on Duple's Blackpool premises but this proved not to be the only major development as a fresh decade began. Frank B. Ford, a name associated with 'the opposition' until 1968, but ever the lively entrepreneur, saw an opportunity arising from the firm's weak sales position and consequent depressed value.

He had been out of the limelight for a couple of years after the collapse of the project to build Flxible buses at Scarborough in which he had been involved, causing his departure from a hitherto successful spell with Plaxton. In September 1970 he bounced back strongly as the leading light in a takeover of Duple Coachbuilders Ltd, his partner in this being George Hughes, previously of IBM, the finance needed having been raised by a private investment company in which Hughes was involved.

Frank Ford was a more flamboyant character than previous generations of Duple top management and brought major changes among the people running the business. Harry Bigg rejoined the company as Managing Director and Alex Gibbins was appointed Marketing Director and Managing Director Designate. On the engineering side, John McHugh, who had also been involved in the Flxible (UK) Ltd project, having resigned from his previous position as Director and General Manager of the Leyland group's bus division, now joined the Duple board; he had been responsible for the Ergonomic tilt cab by then standard on most of Leyland's goods range. Another very significant appointment was that of John Ruddy, who came from Plaxton to become Director responsible for design, with the success of the Panorama Elite as a powerful recommendation. These were clear pointers to future plans.

Meanwhile, there was a more direct task of rebuilding output and sales lost, especially in the period from the announcement of the Hendon closure made in 1968 to its completion two years later. In the 1970 season, Duple's output amounted to 448 bodies whereas Plaxton's was 1,003, a near-catastrophic and almost exact reversal of the situation that had applied nine years earlier.

Coach operators generally want their new vehicles by Easter or, at the latest, Whitsun, so the season's deliveries generally began around the previous September, with sizeable numbers out by the turn of the year. Only three of the 1970 season output were delivered in 1969. There was almost always some spill-over effect into following years as vehicles remained unsold for a time in dealers' stocks, and indeed there were still some Hendon-bodied coaches at dealers at the beginning of 1970, but a slow start was almost impossible to make up and business was lost.

The types produced were basically straightforward, divided into series according to type – the season's series numbers used running from 211 to 216, 219 to 221, 223 and 224. There were 300 bodies on Bedford chassis, the largest group being the 97 Viceroy on VAM70 (series 211), including fifteen for the Whittle group; 90 Vega 31 on SB5 diesel or, in eight for Salopia and three for Jersey operators, SB3 petrol chassis (216); 60 Vista 25 on VAS5 diesel or, in one case, VAS2 petrol chassis (215), and 53 Viceroy 37 on VAL70 (213). Ford chassis were used for 78, made up of 66 Viceroy 37 on R226 (214), including nine for Bebb of Llantwit Fardre, and twelve Viceroy on R192 (212).

The remainder, of which all but ten were for subsidiaries of the recently-formed National Bus Company, were all Commander IV bodies – 22 on AEC Reliance 11-metre chassis (series 219), including eight for East Kent, six for Whyte of Colnbrook and five for Aldershot & District; a single 10-metre Reliance (series 220); 27 on Leyland Leopard PSU3 (series 221), including 20 for Southdown and six for Maidstone & District; four on Bristol RELH (series 223), with two each for Isle of Man Road Services and Eastern National, and sixteen on Bristol LH (series 224), of which twelve were for Western National and four for Thames Valley. Only three vehicles, all VAS, were exported, two for Bermuda Aviation Services and one to Gambia.

Duple managed to make quite a strong recovery in the 1971 and 1972 seasons, despite the Viceroy becoming increasingly outmoded. The introduction at the 1970 Show of

The Vista 25 and Vega 31 bodies came into line with larger types in regard to grille style for 1970 season production. What had been the N-prefix body number series continued, though now the prefix was dropped and so this Vista 25 had body number 215/43. It was one of 25 on Bedford VAS5 chassis built for that year's Commonwealth Expedition, also known as Comex IV – similar fleets had been used in previous years. As built, they seated 20, with extra storage space, but 20 were rebuilt by the Arlington Motor Co to standard 29-seat layout and sold off, mostly in 1971 – they were re-registered with J-suffix numbers for their new owners.

Visually, the later-type Viceroy body suited the Bedford VAL quite well, the small wheel arches allowing the main band of colour on the body side panels to run unbroken over the full length of the coach. This standard 53-seat example was N200/8, placed in service with Wrigley's Coaches of Irlam, Manchester as PTB 869G in March 1969. That series ran to 110 numbers but the totals of corresponding VAL Viceroy coaches built in the 213, 229 and 241 series of the 1970, 1971 and 1972 series were, respectively, 53, 54 and 38 – the appeal of the type was diminishing as the problems of the VAL chassis in regard to need for frequent attention to brakes and excessive tyre wear proved intractable.

Traditionally, Maidstone & District Motor Services Ltd had not been associated with Duple bodywork, having standardised on Harrington for coaches from the early 1930s until that bodybuilder ceased production in the mid-1960s. Twelve Leyland Leopard coaches with Duple Commander III bodies had been added to the fleet in 1968 and six Commander IV 48-seat bodies (221/2227) on Leopard PSU3A/4R chassis were built as part of the 1970 programme although none entered service before August of that year, thus receiving J-suffix registrations. Two did not enter service until May 1971, one of these being 4626 (VKN 626J) with body 221/26, seen here before delivery.

the Bedford YRQ model helped; it was that concern's first venture into the mid-engined class, the 466 cu in (7.6-litre) engine being shallow enough to go under the floor in vertical form. Outwardly, the completed model with Viceroy body looked almost identical to the previous year's VAM70. It still seated 45 as standard but the intrusive engine cover had gone from the front of the gangway and, far more important, the internal noise level was much reduced.

Bedford had chosen a Viceroy-bodied YRQ for its press road tests, and the body numbers for this first production run ran from 227/1 to 247 (of which six were not built), which almost exactly paralleled the 1968 season output at Hendon on the VAM before the worst of the dip in output associated with the move north. Salopia and the Whittle group were among the first customers to order batches, with five and eighteen respectively – the buyers were almost all independent operators, though Edinburgh City Transport had five for its tours fleet, Wilts & Dorset had two and Tyneside PTE had three. The last-mentioned was one of the Passenger Transport Executives set up by the Government to take over responsibility for transport in major urban areas.

There was also a healthy rise in bodies on Ford chassis, which although retaining the front-mounted Ford 360 engine, were offered in turbocharged form from 1970, this option proving to have some benefits in terms of noise reduction as well as increased power. For the 1971 season, the 228 series of Viceroy on R192 chassis ran to 101 and the 230 series of Viceroy 37 on R226 reaching 182 (six not built). This latter greatly outnumbered the 229 series of similar bodies on Bedford VAL70 which only ran to 55 (one not built), this model beginning to seem outdated by the new smaller YRQ, as well as still suffering from a reputation for needing frequent attention to its brakes.

Apart from the Viceroy on YRQ, the best selling Duple body on Bedford chassis in the 1971 season proved to be the Vega 31 on the venerable SB (232 series) running to some 137, mostly standard 41-seaters on SB5 chassis but including four SB3 for Salopia, still happier with petrol coaches for some duties, and four for the Metropolitan Police (these latter being dual-purpose 37-seaters). There were 45 Vista 25 bodies on VAS5 chassis (231 series). Also among the 1971 season output was a single body in series 234, described as an 'all-metal prototype' on a chassis quoted as Bedford VAM Y, in hand in 1970 but understood to have been scrapped when work on the Dominant described later in this chapter was begun.

On the other hand, orders from NBC, which would have been planned in the summer of 1970, were very small – there were two YRQ and two VAL for Wilts & Dorset, three VAL for Shamrock & Rambler and two VAL for Hants & Dorset.

Outwardly unchanged from a 1969-70 Bedford VAM with Viceroy body, the YRQ-based version introduced for the 1971 season was transformed in terms of internal refinement by the underfloor engine position. Edinburgh City Transport, which had used Bedford-Duple coaches for sightseeing tours since the days of the OB Vista (and indeed had five wartime OWB chassis fitted with new Vista bodies in 1952) took delivery of five YRQ-Viceroy 45-seat coaches in May-June 1971. Seen near Arthur's Seat is 241 (VSC 241J) with body 227/201. Just over a year later, Edinburgh, keen to put into service five examples of the similar but longer YRT model by then added to Bedford's range, accepted Viceroy bodies for them too, rather than wait for the new Dominant body.

As a result, output of Duple coach bodies on heavier-duty chassis in the 1971 season was the smallest in any peacetime year since the earliest days, with only six, all for independent operators, on Leopard PSU3 in the 236 series and one Reliance, numbered 238/1, the latter delivered to Osborne of Tollesbury in November 1970. These had the Viceroy 37 body, the Commander series having been dropped. However, the business on Bedford and Ford chassis was good enough to lift output to 761, an impressive increase of 70% on the move-disrupted previous season. Yet Plaxton output also grew, even if less steeply, reaching 1,250 and thus the gap between them was only slightly reduced.

Deliveries of coaches for the 1971 season was still incomplete when there was another organisational upheaval for the group. It stemmed from the incompatibility of the two strong personalities who had taken over the business only the previous autumn. So it was decided that Willowbrook would be split off as a separate business once more, this being purchased by George Hughes, while Frank Ford continued as Duple's Chairman until shortly before his death in 1976. A consequence was that, for three years, Duple was not in a position to offer bus bodywork.

The 1972 season got off to an encouraging start. It had been agreed that the Government's new bus grant, introduced in 1968 to encourage the purchase of new buses of types suitable for one-man operation, would henceforth also be applicable to coaches used on bus services – traditionally, common practice for many rural operators – provided they met the specification laid down. This was particularly attractive as the grant had just been increased to 50%, meaning that successful applicants got a new coach at half price. In practice, the main structural difference from a standard coach was the provision of a wider entrance, and for the 1971 season, Duple introduced a variant called the Viceroy Express to meet this need. It was necessary to use a windscreen of more conventional outline, eliminating the reverse-rake pillars.

The 1972 season run of 250 bodies of standard YRQ Viceroy models (244 series) was augmented by 97 of the Express version (257 series), and in a similar way, the total of equivalent bodies on Ford R192 ran to 98 and 49 respectively. However, the runner-up to the YRQ in terms of quantity was the Viceroy 37 on Ford R226 (240 series) of which 203 were built, including 9 for the Seamarks fleet – the VAL equivalent (241 series) reached a mere 38, this being that model's final year.

Bedford's new 11-metre chassis, the YRT, was announced in the summer of 1972, predictably of similar mid-engined two-axle layout to the YRQ, though including heavier-duty axles. It seems that Edinburgh City Transport was keen to take delivery of a batch for its sightseeing coach fleet to catch the main summer holiday season and five YRT with Viceroy bodies forming the 260 series of body numbers were delivered in July, proving to be the only examples of the combination. The Vega 31 and Vista 25 on Bedford SB and VAS were still

Rather surprisingly, the Commander body was dropped for the 1971 and 1972 seasons and Duple customers with chassis such as the Leyland Leopard had to accept the Viceroy body style hitherto associated with Bedford or Ford models. This PSU3B/4R, SELNEC PTE's No.255 (TXJ 542K) with body 242/22, was the last of a batch of four dating from July 1972.

Duple had offered 12-metre Commander IV bodywork on Leyland and AEC chassis for the 1970 season but none was built and thus this first Duple body of this length was built three years after Plaxton's equivalent, which had been at the 1968 Show. Body 255/1 for Carnell Tours Ltd of Sheffield, was the first of a batch of Viceroy bodies on Seddon Pennine 6 chassis, which had Perkins 5.8-litre turbocharged engine mounted at the front (though below floor level). It seated 57 and was completed in time for display at the Scottish Show of November 1971 and was registered MWB 2K. The extra length made it an impressive-looking vehicle – the paint style, with 'striped' sides, was evidently influenced by Caetano bodywork by then selling in Britain at a modest level. It was used by Seddon for press road tests before delivery to the operator. The author recalls driving it over The Snake Pass on the Glossop to Sheffield road and then down the M1 to the MIRA test track on a murky day with fog at times to write his report for 'Motor Transport'. It handled well, though the synchromesh gear change was hard work and noise level was at times fairly high.

forming a significant proportion of the total output, with 100 and 85 built respectively in the 246 and 248 series.

The Reliance and Leopard did better than in the 1971 season, Viceroy-bodied versions totalling 35 and 25, mostly sold to independent operators, the 22 bodies in the 242 series on Leopard PSU3B/4R (by then with O.680 engine and Pneumocyclic semiautomatic five-speed gearbox as standard) including six for Wallace Arnold and four for SELNEC PTE, this latter being another of the publicly-owned bodies which had taken over former municipal bus operation in and around major cities, in this case Manchester. Another was sold to the Chinese Embassy in London, remaining in use until 1985. The 31 on Reliance 11-metre (seventeen on the heavier-duty 6U3ZR chassis with AH691 engine and six-speed ZF gearbox and the rest on 6MU4R with AH505 engine and AEC constant-mesh gearbox) were all sold to independent operators, notably six more for Whyte of Colnbrook and four for Park of Hamilton. The balance of 10-metre bodies on these models were in the 252 and 253 series, three on Leopard PSU4B/4R and four on Reliance 6MU4R.

Seddon had made a significant return to the coach chassis scene with the Pennine 6, a front-engined model using a turbocharged Perkins 6.354 engine, and Viceroy bodies were built for 49, of which 19 in the 255 series were of 12-metre length, seating 57, Duple's first standardised design built to this length. Bebb, of Llantwit Fardre, had four, plus another four of 11-metre length from the 254 series of 23 such vehicles and seven of a shorter 45-seat version forming Duple's 260 series.

Overall, the 1972 season had been a surprisingly good one, and taking the output from the Blackpool premises to 1,034, the best yet and a figure reminiscent of Hendon in its more productive days, as well as a triumph of salesmanship bearing in mind that the range being offered was widely seen as outdated. Actual deliveries to British operators within the calendar year were still well below the 1,000 mark due to the restoration of the usual spread over a period from August 1971 to well into 1973, the latter applying to a significant number of the smaller models. Exports, other than to the Channel Islands, where the smaller Bedford-Duple coaches continued to sell partly because of their size, or the occasional vehicle for Ireland, were very small – in the 1972 season there were only four more Vista 25 coaches for Bermuda and the Bahamas. Overall, Plaxton was still well ahead with an output total of 1,285 that season but the lead, at 251, had closed considerably.

The Dominant

Duple's big news at the 1972 Show was of a completely new coach range, called the Dominant. It was metal-framed, much being made of the strength of its construction, with what were described as hoop frames at each bay, based on research carried out as part of a study by John McHugh.

However, John Ruddy's contribution was far more obvious to the casual observer, for the Dominant's main new external feature was the adoption of curved glass for the side windows. It was decided to use the same radius of curvature for the glass, and hence the pillars, as had been adopted by Plaxton for the Panorama Elite, partly because this saved considerably on costs, though in any case the scope for a different form within the practical needs of coach design was not considered enough to be visually significant. Similar standardisation of

The appearance, in both senses, of the Dominant marked another turning point in Duple's history. Curves were again in favour, even though the waist and roof lines were straight – this time, it was the side windows that gave the coach a much-changed look. Although curved glass had been in use for the side windows of some cars for a decade or so, the relative height of a coach to bystanders made the effect of reflections much more strongly evident. The vehicle seen here was the 11-metre 53-seat body on Ford R1114 chassis exhibited at the 1972 Commercial Motor Show.

Yet the basic theme of the Dominant's appearance was very obviously not new. Plaxton's Panorama Elite body had appeared at the 1968 Show and by 1972 was already very well established. This example of an Elite body on a Bristol RELH6G had been built for the Tilling section of Eastern National's fleet in 1972, an early example of NBC's white National corporate coach livery. The radius of curvature of the side window glazing was common to Plaxton and Duple, partly for glass manufacturing reasons; although a change in this dimension would have given some difference in look, the practical scope for such variation was limited. Plaxton had continued the 'big window' theme that had served it so well on previous Panorama designs and here Duple chose not to follow so slavishly, the window bays lengths were shorter, generally implying an extra window each side in a typical coach. Trim details, most notably the ribbed polished waistline strip used on most Dominant coaches but not favoured by Plaxton, also provided useful distinguishing features.

glass for the divided windscreen, more likely to need replacement, had obvious practical benefit from an operating viewpoint. The spacing of the side pillars was closer than had become traditional for Plaxton, though perhaps the most obvious identity feature of the Dominant was the ribbed stainless-steel waistband moulding fitted to almost all coaches of the type, contrasting with the single slender strip on the Elite.

Even so, the Dominant's overall appearance, especially when viewed on the road as an oncoming vehicle, was such as to cause many people to have difficulty in distinguishing it from the Elite. In one sense, the two designs, coming onto the road at a combined rate of something like 2,000 examples per year, rapidly transformed the British coach scene, making almost everything else look outdated.

As it happened, the National Bus Company, created by the Transport Act 1968 to take over the former Tilling and BET

bus company groups as a single State-owned concern, had just decided to adopt a new standardised coach livery of all-over white, with only the National fleetname in blue and red lettering as relief. The sense of a fresh corporate identity was heightened by the similarity of the two designs adopted for the bulk of new NBC group coach deliveries and the rapid growth of their numbers on the network of main-road express routes on which most were used.

Admittedly, Duple lost out in the sense that the Dominant's identity was so obviously a near-duplication of the existing market-leading brand and those operators looking for something 'different' were less likely to be attracted. In practice, this attitude did not prove significant for at least five years and indeed the 'flattery by imitation' bandwagon was joined by ECW and, towards the end of the decade, Willowbrook, in both cases to suit NBC preferences.

Clearly, the switch to metal-framing for the new range meant a major reorganisation of the factory, even though there had been earlier experience in Burlingham's day and with such models as the Continental. Trade union power was still strong, but it must have been particularly galling for Duple, hopeful that it had left the more extreme types of militancy behind in leaving London, to find the construction of 1972 Show exhibits badly disrupted. Only one, an 11-metre 53-seater on what was by then called the Ford R1114 chassis (hitherto the R226) was on display. Even so, plenty of orders rolled in.

With its new YRT 11-metre model following the pattern of the well-received YRQ, Bedford was in a strong position, with a strong revival of the traditional combination of this make with Duple bodywork, now also of a new style, save for the Vista 25 and Vega 31 which continued for a final year for the VAS and SB.

A revised body numbering system made tracing quantities for individual types less simple – the three-figure series or contract number prefix for each major variant continued but using a common serial number series, though there were still blocks of numbers for each type. The series of numbers for Dominant bodies began with the initial batch on Bedford YRQ chassis at 266/1, running to 266/271 in much the same way as before, but, if the continuity of the individual serial numbers is followed, the prefix numbers became out of sequence for a time, so the series for bodies on Ford 11-metre chassis began at 270/301, followed by 268/601 up for Ford 10-metre, and so on.

The highest recorded serial number noted for a 1973 season body is 3462, but the true output was much less because of the large gaps left between each series – the total quantity delivered to British operators that year was nearer 1100. Even so, this was not only the highest since the move to Blackpool, but exceeded the best Hendon or 'Hendon plus Blackpool' totals reached during the 1960s. Plaxton was still in front, with a total output of 1,317 for that season, but the gap had narrowed further.

Although output was becoming more standardised in terms of basic body design, the range of chassis types and variants, with 'express' as well as standard coach versions of several, was becoming more complex, The 1973 season output included some 26 types sufficiently different to be given separate series, though the total of well over 600 confirmed Bedford-based deliveries in Britain still outnumbered all other products put together and put the Bedford-Duple combination back into a strong position reminiscent of the SB heyday. Ford slipped a little with a total under half that of Bedford but were still in second place.

A fresh trend was indicated by a significant rise in the numbers of bodies on heavier-duty chassis, with over 100 on Leyland Leopard, mainly the contemporary 11-metre PSU3B but also including five 12-metre coaches on PSU5 variants. There were also nearly 50 AEC Reliance of varying lengths, again including four 12-metre, 22 Seddon Pennine VI, two Bristol LHL (the 11-metre version of the lightweight LH mid-engined model) and, most significant in long-term implications, the first examples of Volvo coach chassis, of the B58 type, with sixteen examples noted. Volvo had first begun to import this model with its smooth and powerful turbocharged 9.6-litre underfloor engine into Britain in 1972, and although the numbers were limited at first it attracted a steadily growing number of buyers, at first all independent operators.

Most of Duple's customers continued to be independent operators, almost all purchasing via dealers, Bedford and Ford insisting on this method and it was normal practice for such customers where makes such as Leyland or AEC were concerned. NBC had evolved a central purchasing system for its subsidiaries, which were again increasingly figuring in the order books. There were 75 Leopard PSU3B/4R and 36 Reliance for various NBC fleets in the 1973 season, the largest individual deliveries being 28 Leopards for Ribble and Standerwick, fifteen for Southdown, ten for Black & White, plus eighteen Reliance for East Kent and ten for Sheffield United Tours. There were also smaller batches for NBC on Bedford and Ford chassis.

There were changes in the management team around this time. During 1973, Alex Gibbins became Managing Director, following the retirement of Harry Bigg, and saw a need to expand the Duple range to re-establish its links with bus as well as coach travel. Harry Bigg's organisational skills had been effectively employed in the raising of output at Blackpool beyond 1,000 bodies per year.

The two factories inherited from Burlingham were not ideal in this regard as chassis, stored in a field near the Preston New Road premises, were first driven to the main factory nearer the town centre at Vicarage Lane where the plywood floor was fitted and the sides, front and rear and roof assemblies were fitted and panelled. The vehicle was then driven to the Preston New Road premises, painted and partially trimmed and then taken back to Vicarage Lane for finishing, the complete process taking about six weeks.

It should also be recorded that Herbert White, the founder of the company, had died in 1972, at the age of 94. He had remained President since 1954 and although no longer directly involved in its management had remained fit enough to drive and play golf until near the end. A nice touch was the naming of a subsidiary company making minor components, by then located in premises adjoining the Preston New Road works, Bifort Engineering Ltd, picking up the name given to Mr White's original dual-purpose car design.

The 1974 season was overshadowed by world events and their aftermath, as an Arab-Israeli war the previous year created shortages and then a big increase in oil prices, tending to reduce demand as well as disrupting production. Duple coped with the problems well, with only a slight drop in output thanks largely to strong demand from NBC subsidiaries counterbalancing a dip in demand from independents – some of the dealers' stocks did not find buyers until well into 1975.

Plaxton output was cut back more severely at that stage, causing Duple to catch up and the two great rivals producing roughly equal quantities, even if only briefly.

A new feature of the body numbering system for the 1974 season was that the series or contract numbers all began with '4', ranging between 411 and 475, though again not all were used, and this pattern of the first digit indicating the year was to continue in following years. The individual serial numbers were again in blocks for each type, beginning at 1000 and ranging up to 6800, normally in sequence with the series numbers grouped by chassis make and type as well as body variants.

The pattern of demand among the types built at Duple was not greatly changed, although there was a tendency for larger coaches to grow in favour – among Bedfords, the emphasis swung more strongly to the YRT, with a total only a little short of 400, while the YRQ fell back to a little over 150. The Dominant body had now also been adapted to the smaller models and over 70 of the VAS were built, though the SB was down to single figures. Ford was well behind, though again the 11-metre R1114 (or the equivalent R226, of which some chassis were still going through) at about 150 built, was about twice as popular as the R1014 or R192.

Demand for heavier-duty models remained very steady, with over 110 Leyland Leopards and 38 AEC Reliance, although the Volvo B58 was not far behind with 29, accounting for almost half the total number of that model sold in Britain that year – still a very modest-seeming presence on the British coach market, though beginning to grow. The 12-metre coach was still a minority choice, although also just beginning to grow – there were fourteen of the PSU5 version of the Leopard, including six for Maidstone & District, five Reliance of this length, and five B58, including two for Park of Hamilton, who also took six of the 11-metre version.

Coaches built for independent operators on Bedford chassis continued to form the major part of Duple's output. In the 1974 season, it was the 11-metre YRT model that became the most numerous type, and Premier Coaches (Watford) Ltd was representative in choosing this model with Dominant 53-seat bodywork for a delivery of five coaches in April of that year, including WUR 83M with body 417/3105 seen on the left of this garage view. The vehicle on the right, BRO 77K, was a YRQ with Viceroy 45-seat body number 246/96, one of four dating from May 1972. The Hewitt family, proprietors of Premier, had by then gained control of Albanian Coaches Ltd of St Albans, hence the use of Premier-Albanian fleetnames, though the two firms continued to be run separately.

The Leyland Leopard was the principal choice of coach chassis for NBC subsidiaries during the 1970s. Although this example in the fleet of East Midland Motor Services Ltd was one of a small group of four 53-seat coaches dating from March 1974, they formed part of a sequence of orders amounting to 65 Dominant coach bodies numbered 433/5103-67, all on PSU3B/4R chassis, for companies in that group, placed in service between January and August that year. In addition, there were nine Dominant Express on the same type of chassis, two of the shorter PSU4 type and six of the 12-metre PSU5, making 82 Leopard coaches for this group, accounting for three-quarters of Duple's output on this model. The white livery was difficult to keep fresh-looking, but C2 (NNN 2M) was in smart condition when seen at Mansfield in July 1975.

Buses added to the range once more

The main new development for the 1975 range was the reintroduction of Duple bus bodywork. The splitting-off of Willowbrook had left Duple without access to the bus market, but at the 1974 Show, a bus body was exhibited on a Bedford YRQ chassis alongside coaches on Leopard and Bedford VAS chassis (the latter by then sometimes quoted as PJK under Bedford's computer-compatible designation system). Another bus body was to be found on Ford's stand. The use of the Dominant name for the new bus design as well as the by-then well-established coach body was rather misleading, for they had little in common, apart from using metal framing. Quite angular styling was adopted for the bus, in contrast to the rounded form of the coach – the adjective that comes to mind is 'chunky' – but the overall effect was both distinctive and well-proportioned.

The British single-deck bus market was still reeling from the shock of the advent of the Leyland National which, as a partnership between Leyland and NBC, was automatically adopted for the bulk of the latter's needs for this class of vehicle, beginning in 1972. It thereby virtually cut off the largest group of customers for single-deck buses in the country from other suppliers – Willowbrook was among the worst hit, incidentally, causing it to build up its coach business and thus again become a direct competitor to Duple. However, independent and municipal operators, especially the smaller undertakings, were rarely attracted to the National, and over 40 Dominant buses were built on Bedford YRQ, YRT, Ford R-series and Leyland Leopard chassis in the 1975 season – modest by comparison with the coach output but an encouraging first showing in a depressed market.

Newton's of Dingwall ordered eleven Ford R-series 53-seat buses to carry workers to and from an oil rig construction site at Nigg. Another early Dominant bus user was Cleveland Transit (the name from 1974 for what had been Teesside Municipal Transport) which took four Bedford YRQ with 47-seat bodies and five Leyland Leopard 53-seaters in late 1974 and 1975.

The coach business was also somewhat depressed, and even with bus bodies, Duple's output in the 1975 season was down, reflecting a drop in demand, with indications that unsold stock at dealers was a factor – Plaxton, however, began to recover and never looked back. NBC ordered far fewer coaches for 1975, and Duple's share of them was even less, amounting to five 12-metre AEC Reliances for East Kent plus a few YRT coaches for Wessex National (the former Wessex concern, now taken into the group) and National Travel, a name with area suffix titles by then adopted for some of the group's coach operating companies.

Easily the largest orders for Leyland Leopards with coach-outline bodies came from Nottingham City Transport, following up a single coach delivered earlier in 1974, painted in a special lilac livery for use on a park and ride scheme and intended to be unique. However, it was so well received that seventeen more built in Duple's 1975 programme were painted similarly, becoming famous as the Lilac Leopards. A further ten vehicles for Nottingham that year had bus seats for 53 passengers in the Dominant coach outline, the combination being known as the Dominant E type, not to be confused with the Dominant Express coach, which continued in favour where bus grant could be obtained.

Overall sales to British operators from 1975 season production was down to not much over 700, with Bedford again accounting for well over half, and the proportions of most makes much the same. The Leopard total was down to 90, though that would have been regarded as very good a few years earlier. Volvo, with 30, was ahead of AEC and there were ten Bristol, all LH variants, with the short LHS, on which a 35-seat Dominant coach had become available, accounting for six.

A fresh development was the appearance of Mercedes-Benz with its small 608 model, offering a challenge to the Bedford VAS as a basis for a 29-seat Dominant coach, with a couple of examples. Another new name for Duple was DAF, the Dutch manufacturer, with an example of its MB200DKL mid-engined model using a DAF 11.1-litre engine to a design

The Dominant bus was so different in visual character to the coach that the use of the same name seemed a surprise, even though some parts of the structure were similar and minor items such as grille and lamp fittings were common. The growth of the North Sea oil industry created a need for better transport and S. M. Newton of Dingwall, based at the landward end of the Cromarty Firth, was in a strong position to transport workers to a remote site at Nigg at the seaward end. The vehicle shown, HAS 953N, with body 525/4765 was the last of a batch of eight Ford R1014 buses delivered in May 1975 – like three vehicles that had been delivered in February, they had seating for 53, achieved on these 10-metre buses by a three-and-two seating layout.

The Dominant coach body was also offered in a form suited to part- or full-time bus work. Burnley & Pendle Joint Transport was the new name, effective from April 1974, for what had been the Burnley, Colne & Nelson Joint Transport Committee and, like many municipal operators, it added coaches to its fleet to broaden the range of work that could be done. The Dominant Express model conformed to new bus grant requirements, with its wider entrance and glider doors – No.4 (YHG 4N) with body 434/5319 was one of a pair of Leyland Leopard PSU3B/4R 49-seat coaches dating from November 1974.

Nottingham City Transport's fleet of Leyland Leopard coaches was intended mainly for use on a park-and-ride scheme. Some were to Dominant Express specification, with 53 coach seats, becoming famous as the 'Lilac Leopards' because of their special livery. However, ten built in Duple's 1975 programme and then a further fourteen in the 1976 programme were to what became known as the Dominant E type, with bus seats, also for 53, these being in a cream, green and black livery. No.758 (MTV 758P) with body 634/5177 was one of these latter, dating from March 1976 and is seen in Maid Marion Way on the 301 Park & Ride service.

originally derived from the Leyland O.680, the first with right-hand drive to be imported to Britain receiving a 12-metre Dominant body, number 585/9050 at the end of the 1975 season series and going to T. Robinson, of Appleby in May of that year.

Helping to counterbalance depressed demand in Britain to some degree was a revival of exports – during the period of the association with Willowbrook, Duple's export business had been handled almost entirely by the Loughborough factory, the call being almost always for buses. There were occasional

Hong Kong was a fast-developing market for British vehicles and this Bedford YRQ with Dominant coach body was sent as a demonstrator to the Kowloon Motor Bus Co in 1974 (left). It had special windows to give extra ventilation and a luggage pen reduced the seating capacity to 41. It was purchased by KMB in 1975 and used on an airport service.

KMB preferred front-engined chassis and, although the Dominant body was favoured, chose the Albion Viking in an export EVK55CL form for a batch of 50, later expanded to 70 and then 100, which entered service between January 1975 and August 1976. They were lettered as Leyland though KMB issued CA fleet numbers, signifying 'Coach, Albion' – two are seen (above right) leaving Duple's works. Most were used on express services paralleling the normal bus services and seated 42.

The China Motor Bus Co Ltd also took delivery of one basically similar but shorter vehicle on a Viking EVK55CY chassis with 26-seat capacity, but in that case no more were ordered. The poor quality of some these official photgraphs may be an early sign of a tightening of the official belt, reflecting the changing state of the company – money for publicity and photography was obviously being cut back as, presumably, economies were having to be made.

instances of coach bodies finding overseas buyers in places such as Cyprus or Australia, although many markets were beginning to resist imports of complete vehicles as an effort to encourage local industry.

Hong Kong, fast growing, was a special case, though much of the demand there was for double-deck buses. However, a Bedford YRQ with Dominant coach body was sent to the Kowloon Motor Bus Co in May 1974 and later purchased. In place of the curved-glass side windows, it had an arrangement of plain glass split horizontally into three sections, of which the centre was composed of deep sliders, giving the additional ventilation needed for that climate. A front-engined chassis was preferred and 50 Albion Viking EVK55CL with Leyland EO.401 engines (based on the O.400) and generally similar Dominant bodies were delivered between December 1974 and the earlier part of 1975 for use on special express services – standard seating was for 42. A further 50 were added, delivery continuing into 1976. At about the same time a single shorter 26-seat EVK55CY version of the same model was supplied to the China Motor Bus Co Ltd for operation on Hong Kong island. These vehicles were badged as Leyland, as increasingly usual for group products sent to export markets.

The 1976 trading season followed much the same general pattern in terms of the types built but the British market picked up appreciably, notably with quite a strong revival of orders from NBC, taking the season's total home market output above 900. However, an order for 30 Ford R1014 left-hand-drive models with Dominant bus bodies for Nigeria built in 1975 was followed by a repeat order for 70 more in 1976.

The introduction of the Volvo B58 in Britain led to interest in the reverse direction, and a left-hand-drive B58-60 12-metre example was fitted with a special coach body based on the Dominant structure but with double-glazed side windows using flat glass, which removed the model's key feature although the pillars retained the usual curved shape. It was equipped with heated laminated windscreen glasses and external mirrors. It had body number 680/7311 and was delivered in December 1975 for exhibition at a Motor Show in Sweden. The body was given the name Goldliner, and although not then taken up, that name was to be revived for a different project in 1981.

NBC subsidiaries, largely National Travel area companies, took coaches on 70 Leyland Leopard, 26 Bedford YMT and ten AEC Reliance but a new development was the ordering of 50 Ford R1014 with Dominant bus bodies, the largest batches

Goldliner was a name that seemed to appeal to Duple, being applied to two unrelated projects of 1975-6, even though its main application was to relate to a different design of about five years later. The vehicle shown above in Victoria coach station, having a Dominant coach body outwardly to typical NBC specification and in corporate white livery was built in the 1975 programme as a demonstrator on the newly-introduced Bedford YMT chassis, with more powerful 500 engine of 8.2-litre capacity, for Vauxhall Motors Ltd. Its registration number JKX 742N indicated issue in about May of that year, the body number 527/3011 a 'one-off'. It was described in publicity issued in April 1976 as a 'Dominant Goldliner prototype'. By then orders had been placed on behalf of three of the National Travel companies formed as amalgamations of existing NBC coach operators for a total of 26 similar coaches for the 1976 season.

The other Goldliner of that period was a left-hand-drive Volvo B58 12-metre coach (above right), with body 680/7311 delivered to Sweden in December 1975 – it had double-glazed side windows, using flat glass and thus did not have the characteristic look of standard Dominant coaches. Moseley was at that time much engaged in importing bodywork from Continental makers to Britain as well as being an agent for Volvo coaches, but this was a venture in an opposite direction.

being fifteen for South Wales and ten for United Counties. Ten R1114 with a special version of the Dominant bus body having wide doors on both sides was used as airside buses at London Airport, conveying passengers to or from air liners not directly accessible from the terminal buildings – they were operated by Whyte's Airport Services Ltd.

These helped to boost the total of Ford chassis bodied by Duple for British operators to well over 300, not far short of the Bedford total that year, which had dropped somewhat, as had Bedford's coach sales nationally. The arrival of a new Bedford engine, the 500, of 8.1-litre capacity, caused the Y-series passenger models to change from YRQ to YLQ for the 10-metre type and YRT to YMT for the 11-metre. This change

was announced in mid-1975, but chassis in stock meant that the earlier types were still entering service in some numbers up to the summer of 1976.

The share of Duple output on Leyland Leopard chassis was well up, reaching over 160, due not only to the NBC coaches and a further fourteen of the Dominant E type for Nottingham but also to orders for buses for the municipal fleets at Rhymney Valley, Chester and Darlington, amounting together to sixteen. There were also more AEC Reliance, the total reaching 50, including seventeen for Smith's Tours (Wigan) Ltd, which, with its subsidiaries, was becoming known as the Blundell group, using a 'Smiths Happiway-Spencers' fleetname on the sides of its vehicles.

Volvo was quietly growing in importance in Britain. The B58 was first introduced to this market in 1972 and by 1975-6, around 70 were being registered annually. Trathen, of Yelverton, Devon, itself also a concern growing in importance, had eleven with Dominant bodies to various specifications in the 1975 programme and there were three 12-metre examples in that for 1976, including LUT 773P with body number 675/7106 placed in service in June and seen here. It had spacious seating for 42 passengers with a roof-mounted air-conditioning unit and a toilet compartment.

The Dominant II was a restyling exercise, the deeper windscreen giving a fresh look. Michelotti was given the credit though otherwise there was little more than a tidying-up of grille and lamps. This was the first example, with body 643/5676, built in the 1976 programme to appear at the Commercial Motor Show in September of that year. It was an 11-metre AEC Reliance of the 6U3ZR type which from 1973 had the AH760 12.4-litre engine as standard. It was built for Smith's Tours (Wigan) Ltd, which was another example of the mergers that were producing bigger groups. In this case, the fleetname also acknowledged the goodwill value still attached to the Happiway and Spencer's names.

Dominant II

A serious accident involving a Viceroy-bodied Bedford VAM which occurred in 1975, followed by other incidents built up into a media campaign, had focused public attention on the roof strength of coaches, even though that initial crash, involving overturning and a fall from an embankment of about 20ft, would have been catastrophic to the occupants even if the vehicle had been of tank-like build. International interest in coach safety was also rising, and these factors led to a Department of Environment proposal for a static test in which the roof was to be able to support a 10-tonne load. In response, from September 1976, Duple adopted a revised structure using welded square-section tube for all Dominant coaches, although not in itself altering appearance – a similar form of construction was already in use for the Dominant bus.

At the same time, the Dominant II was introduced, this having a deeper windscreen, the waistline being stepped down locally to suit, and the rear window waist level was raised. The layout of lamps and bumpers was revised, the quadruple headlamps now being of squared outline. The restyling work, doubtless intended at least in part as an answer to Plaxton's mildly restyled Panorama Supreme, was entrusted to Michelotti of Turin, Italian styling being much in fashion although in fact the basic design of the coach was no more than marginally affected. The previous Dominant continued to be available where preferred, becoming Dominant I.

The first Dominant II was built as part of the 1976 programme, being one of the AEC Reliance coaches for the Smiths Happiway Spencer fleet mentioned above – an 11-metre 47-seater, it had body number 643/5676 and was registered ODJ 53R, dating from August 1976 though completed for display at the Commercial Show the following month. However another early example, body 679/7300, was completed as a 57-seat coach on a Bedford YMT specially lengthened for Tricentrol, of Dunstable, a concern which was soon to be much associated with non-standard length coaches, short as well as long, acting as a dealer as well as operator.

Alongside the Reliance on Duple's stand at the 1976 Show were a Bedford VAS with 29-seat Dominant I coach body for the Corvedale branch of J. T. Whittle & Son, displaying the 'Go Whittle' fleetname by then adopted by that organisation, and a Ford R1014 43-seat bus for the South Wales fleet, this latter unusual in having Allison automatic transmission.

The scene was set for the rest of the decade, with no more than minor changes to the basic Dominant design, and a period of relative stability in terms of production figures, not quite reaching as high as the 1973 peak yet good enough to be looked back on from the much harsher 1980s as something of a golden age, even if the target of recapturing the lead from Plaxton proved out of reach.

The 1977 season production programme was made more complicated by the building of both Dominant I and II bodies, often with Express variants of each, on most of the main types. Total Duple deliveries to British operators dropped to around 800 as Plaxton's climbed, allowing the latter to widen its lead to about 300, although the two firms between them still had 90% of the British coach market. Duple sales to independent operators were down though there was compensation in strong orders not only from NBC but also from the Scottish Bus Group, partly due to a diversion of business from Alexander, SBG's traditional main supplier, afflicted by a trade dispute that year.

In terms of makes and models, Bedford remained steady in numbers, with the YMT accounting for two-thirds of the 330-odd Duple bodies based on this make of chassis. Individual orders included 24 for National Travel companies and 21 for Grey Green. Ford's share of Duple output, on the other hand, dropped to not much over 180, more of a fall for this chassis make than with other bodywork, suggesting that one or more of the dealers in Ford coaches turned elsewhere. The saving grace here was a fleet of 48 R1114 coaches for SBG companies, including 26 for Highland – Duple had gained some such orders before but not on this scale.

Leyland thus took second place among the makes bodied with just over 200 Leopards, mainly due to the 119 for various

Also exhibited at the 1976 Show was this Bedford VAS5 (officially being described as PJK under Bedford's designation system by then in force, though the older code was too familiar to die out) with Dominant I 29-seat body number 712/1051. It was No.42 in the fleet of the Corvedale Travel fleet of Ludlow, which, since 1969, was controlled by the Whittle concern – hence the 'Go Whittle' fleetname. Whittle's policy of large-scale and frequent fleet renewal, using Duple bodywork almost exclusively from 1960, had made the group one of the firm's most important customers. The Dominant body style had taken over from the Vista 25 for the VAS from the 1974 season, creating a unity of coach styling across the range but, to the author at least, seemed to give rather an over-bodied look not evident with the previous styles.

Six NBC subsidiaries took delivery of a combined total of 50 Ford R1014 buses with Dominant 43-seat bus bodies in 1976. Lincolnshire 2405 (OFE 264P) with body 625/4759 was the last of five for that fleet, entering service in August. It is seen in Newark bus station in the following June.

NBC subsidiaries, accounting for over half the group's intake of coaches on that chassis. There were also 25 for Wallace Arnold and nineteen for Alexander subsidiaries. There were 41 AEC Reliance, including fifteen for London Country's Green Line services, a happy revival of a Green Line link with AEC-Duple coaches that went back to 1931, and with five for National Travel these brought the 1977 season NBC share of Duple's output to 163. There was only one Bristol, an LHS 30-seat coach for Greater Manchester PTE and the output on Volvo B58 was down to nine, of which the most interesting were perhaps the three with centre-entrance 38-seat bodies for Glenton Tours.

The 1978 picture can be summed up as more of the same in the sense that overall output rose usefully, with a total destined for British operators of nearly 1,000, with much the same main constituents. The number on Leyland Leopard chassis rose strongly to 274, drawing well ahead of the 200 Ford and even drawing nearer the figure of a little over 350 Bedford. There were just over 50 AEC Reliance and one Bristol LHS (for Park of Hamilton). Absent from the list was Volvo, despite a modest national rise in sales – admittedly an adverse exchange rate had held sales back in 1977 but Alex

Gibbins was endeavouring to streamline production and had decided against quoting for what seemed likely to be an uneconomic quantity when order books were almost filling the factory capacity.

A design change on the Ford R1014 and R1114 chassis introduced an inclined engine position, allowing it to be entirely below floor level, even though still positioned at the front. It did not affect the chassis designation, but Duple separated them from the previous vertical engined type in the blocks of body numbers issued, though most of the 1978 programme build were of the new type. One R1014 chassis had been shortened and fitted with a 'compact' 35-seat Dominant coach body for Swinard, a concept to become increasingly popular in later years.

NBC constituents accounted for 170 of the 1978 programme build, mainly Leopards for the regular fleets but also including 11 Bedford YMT for Eastern National and two apiece for Hants & Dorset and National Travel (East), together with 12 more Reliances for Green Line. The Scottish Bus Group also again figured quite strongly, if a little less so than in the previous year, with 35 Leyland Leopard and ten Ford R1014, all with Dominant Express bodies for Alexander

The Dominant I, as built alongside the Dominant II, retained the previous windscreen but the front grille was of a new simpler style. The NBC favoured the Dominant I in Express form for a substantial part of its 1977 intake of Leyland Leopard coaches. The example shown, West Riding Automobile Co Ltd 5 (RYG 396R) with body 734/5283 entered service in January of that year. The specification and dual-purpose green and white livery with grey wheels (lacking coach trim discs) conveyed that this was a 'working' coach intended to take its turn on bus duties. By that date, West Riding was closely associated with Yorkshire (Woollen District) for operational purposes – dual fleetnames were quite common on NBC group coaches at that time. The collapse of the 'E' at the end of the Duple lettering on the wall was perhaps an omen of troubled times to come, though hardly foreseeable then.

constituent companies. Among independents, Whittle continued to figure regularly, that year taking seven YLQ and seven YMT. Grey Green received seventeen YMT, while Wallace Arnold had 35 Leopards. Bus body orders continued to be modest, adding up to 20 for British operators, of which half were covered by an order from Maidstone Corporation for ten Bedford YMT.

In the 1979 season, there was a slight increase in output, but it was enough to push the total deliveries to British operators over the 1,000 mark again – it was to prove the final time this was achieved. The coach market was buoyant, but the pleasure was doubtless tempered by knowledge that Plaxton was well in front – in fact, that firm's output for the season reached 1,399. A smaller cloud on that horizon though one that had been gently growing in the later 1970s was the growth of competition for orders from British fleets from foreign bodybuilders. Caetano, based in Portugal, had taken some such business through the decade, though its sales had fallen somewhat latterly, but a more serious-seeming challenge was coming from Van Hool, with headquarters in Belgium, which sold 95 coaches in Britain in 1979, putting it into third place among those competing for business from independent operators.

Duple's total on Bedford chassis went over 400, the highest since earlier in the decade, of which there were 276 on the YMT, with the Leyland Leopard slightly down at 248 and the Ford total 216. There were 75 AEC Reliance models, quite a strong showing having regard to the fact that it had been announced towards the end of 1978 that production at the Southall factory was to cease, this occurring in May 1979. With a healthy order book, Alex Gibbins told a high-level delegation from Volvo that he was unwilling to body the B58 unless he had orders for at least 30. He is reported as seeming surprised when promptly given that order, subsequently placed

with various dealers. Other customers then came in, taking the total to 79, a clear indication of demand that was beginning to climb more steeply, helped along by some former AEC users unwilling to switch to Leyland.

There were 219 coaches for NBC, among which 45 more Reliances for Green Line duty were the largest single group although the Leopard remained the main group choice overall, as usual, and there were 39 Bedford YMT, but the Scottish Bus Group orders dropped back to ten. Among independents, Smith of Wigan turned to the Ford R1114 with an order for 21. Wallace Arnold, significantly, took ten Volvo B58 as well as seven Leopards. Grey Green chose Bedford chassis, spread between seven YMT, four YLQ of standard length and two short-chassis variants of the latter, seating 35. In all there were seven short YLQ and some 28 short R1014 with bodies seating around 35, as well as three Bedford YMT extended to 12-metre and seating 57.

Bus body demand remained relatively low, comprising fourteen on Bedford Y-type, eight on Ford R1014 (of which six were for the Isle of Wight County Council), fourteen Leyland Leopard (including ten for Trimdon Motor Services and three for Lancaster Corporation) and six Reliance (four for Hutchison of Wishaw).

As the 1970s came to an end, the repercussions of a major political event had yet to have any significant impact on Duple's business. This was the election of a Conservative Government in June 1979, with Mrs Margaret Thatcher as Prime Minister and having a radical agenda. There had been many changes of the party in power since the Duple business was established, several resulting in major legislation affecting the transport industry, yet with surprisingly little overall impact on the firm's customers, taken as a whole. This time it was to prove different.

10 SLIDING TOWARDS THE ABYSS

In planning for the 1980 season, the omens must have seemed quite encouraging. Many of Duple's independent coach operator customers doubtless welcomed the Thatcher Government and its policies. A Transport Bill to 'deregulate' longer-distance services was soon introduced, opening up the prospect of fresh opportunities for many of them.

In the event, about 821 bodies for British operators were included in the 1980 programme, a drop of about 20% on the previous year and, as it turned out, the beginning of a final slide leading ultimately to extinction. NBC put more of its resources into buying new double-deck buses than for several years, both as a result of a policy change and an effort to obtain benefit of the new bus grant, about to be phased out, so NBC coach purchases were cut back. Those independent operators who tended to leave their purchases of new coaches until nearer the beginning of the spring began to become a little nervous as the first signs of what was to prove the worst recession since the 1930s became evident, and several dealers found themselves with some stock coaches not sold until well into 1981, itself influencing their orders the following year.

The series numbers used as a prefix to body numbers followed the same pattern as previously, though prefixed '0' to signify 1980; thus 011/1000 was a Bedford VAS coach, the individual serial numbers running in blocks and the span of both is indicated by the highest-numbered 1980 series, for bus bodies on Volvo B58, which ran from 052/8000 to 8007. Variants meant that there were 30 'active' series for home market types that season.

The largest single series in the 1980 programme was again the standard Bedford YMT 11-metre coach, usually seating 53 passengers, of which the series beginning at 017/2400 ran to 2641, from which there were 208 confirmed deliveries to British operators. Among these were 20 for the Whittle group and thirteen for National Travel (East). Overall, the YMT continued to be the most popular model, with 249 confirmed home-market coach and twelve bus deliveries.

Bedford was also still the most popular chassis make among Duple-bodied deliveries, though for the last time, with 347 confirmed examples for British fleets. The 10-metre YLQ was being superseded by the similar but slightly uprated YMQ but the combined total was much less than in the type's heyday, at 37 coaches and 2 buses of standard length plus seven short coaches seating 35 or so. There were 26 VAS and fourteen SB coaches for British users, the latter largely 7ft 6in-wide versions for use in Jersey.

Ford recovered second place with 203 confirmed deliveries, though this number was slightly down from the previous season's total. Here too, the 11-metre model remained the most popular, with 173 coach bodies on the R1114 chassis, the remainder being R1014, including four buses for Jersey Motor Transport and 13 of the shortened coach version seating 35 or so.

The Leyland-based share of Duple output was down because of the NBC cut-back on coaches that season, yet there remained a still creditable total of 140 Leopard coaches and eight buses, of which the largest single group was nineteen PSU3E/4R for Grey-Green. There were 35 of the 12-metre PSU5 type, of which ten were for Fox of Hayes and seven for Ebdon of Sidcup. Of the PSU3 series, the Alexander (Midland) and Alexander (Northern) companies had five each, and eight went to PTE fleets, four for South Yorkshire, three for Greater Manchester and one for Merseyside. Trimdon Motor Services took five with bus bodies. Remarkably, despite approaching the

Trimdon Motor Services Ltd, of Trimdon, County Durham, was one of a number of substantial independent operators in that area which had survived through several decades when take-over by a major group or nationalisation had seemed probable. By the end of the 1970s, it had taken on something of a 'big operator' image itself, with regular intakes of Leyland Leopard Duple Dominant 55-seat buses. That shown, TBR 527V with body 939/5630, was one of a batch of three PSU3E/4R dating from September 1979, but there had been seven in February that year, and a further five were built in the 1980 programme, delivered in March.

The long association between AEC chassis and Duple coach bodywork ended about a year after the former's works closed with the completion of final batches of bodies on Reliance chassis in the 1980 programme. This one, with 53-seat Dominant II body number 041/5702, entered service as XSW 678W with John J. Little & Sons of Annan, Dumfriesshire in August 1980, but when photographed passing through Glencoe six years later was owned by Lyall of Blanefield.

Dominant III and IV

In September 1980, Duple announced a revised range for 1981 in the run-up to the combined Car and Commercial Vehicle Show by then being held in alternate years at the National Exhibition Centre, Birmingham, although it was decided not to exhibit there, relying on its own shows held in Blackpool, Wembley and Glasgow. By not appearing, it seemed to some that Plaxton's leading position was being conceded.

Even so, there were two new Dominant coach variants. The Dominant III appeared at first glance to be virtually a copy of Alexander's M-type body introduced in 1968 for the motorway services to London of Scottish Omnibuses (the old SMT fleetname had by then been dropped in favour of the less evocative 'Eastern Scottish') and Western SMT – the Duple version had arisen from Scottish Bus Group's need for replacements and Alexander's problems in meeting delivery requirements due to the high demand for double-deckers. These vehicles were intended largely for travel at night and had a higher waistline, with smaller windows than usual on British coaches. A 'different' look was given by forward-sloping pillars or, more correctly, window-outlines shaped to give that effect – the structural pillars remained vertical.

The Dominant III reproduced this effect, though the front and rear ends and other details used standard Dominant assemblies. Overall, both the M-type and the Dominant III were reminiscent of earlier Australian and, before that, American coaches using similar window outlines. Duple's marketing it as a production option lead to it also being adopted by quite a number of independent operators, mainly in England or Wales, though it is doubtful if any significant overall gain in sales resulted.

The Dominant IV was more obviously related to Dominant I and II, though here too the waistline was raised by 5.5in, and the previous ribbed moulding replaced by a single strip, this latter change applying across their range. However the side windows continued to be in curved glass and of normal Dominant style. Both Dominant III and IV coaches could be fitted with double- or single-glazing in plain or tinted glass. The Dominant I and II continued, the former by then more associated with the lighter chassis such as the Bedford VAS or SB. There were also minor revisions to existing models, such as the detachable lower front panel common to Dominant II, III and IV models.

An effect of this widened choice was that combinations of chassis types and body variants became even more complex in the 1981 season. With the Express variants, there were at least 65 identifiable series produced that season, and although most of these were assembled from largely standardised parts in the manner of a Meccano set, reduced overall demand meant that the average run proved to be about eight vehicles of each type, hardly making for efficient production. Long gone were the days of making annual runs of 500 or so SB coaches rarely differing save for colour and trim fabric.

Another development of this period was the formation of Duple (Metsec) Ltd, in co-operation with Metal Sections Ltd of Oldbury, Staffs, the latter having supplied framing for bodywork, often for export, notably to Hong Kong from the first double-deckers to be operated there in 1949. The new company was described as Duple's export division and was intended to

end of its run, the Leopard had become the largest-selling single-decker model on the British market in 1980, with the YMT in third place behind the Leyland National bus.

However, the Volvo B58 continued to grow in importance, confirmed deliveries amounting to 101. Nearly half of these, 47, were B58-61 with 12-metre bodywork, usually seating up to 57, though Smith of Wigan chose 53-seat capacity for its fleet of ten. There were significant users previously associated with AEC or Leyland – London Country had two B58-56 with 49-seat bodywork for Green Line duty, and Grey-Green also had two similar coaches.

AEC had closed in May 1979, but a final fifteen Reliance for London Country with 49-seat coach bodies were included in Duple's 1980 programme and delivered in November-December 1979. Also included were six coaches on Reliance chassis for other operators, the last delivered in September 1981, and a 53-seat bus for Hutchison of Overtown. Significantly, Hutchison switched to the Volvo B58 for five further Dominant bus bodies, included in the Volvo total quoted above.

On June 1980, the Transport Act of that year became law and so its provision for the deregulation of longer-distance services from 6th October could be taken into account in policy-making by Duple and its customers. Six major independents joined forces in a set-up named 'British Coachways' to compete with NBC. However, an effect that was to prove of great importance was the lifting of restrictions on existing operators' services, notably those designed to limit competition with the railways, and indeed NBC planned a major expansion, meeting the anticipated competition head-on – accordingly a new 'National Express' fleetname was adopted from the end of 1980.

The Dominant III introduced by Duple for 1981 might be thought to have been a 'rip-off' of the Alexander M-type motorway coach first seen in 1968, though in fact introduced in response to a Scottish Bus Group need when Alexander could not help. It was offered generally and what must have seemed rather cheeky early purchases were made by a small firm based in Perth, at the time trading as Gloagtrotter, though soon using the name Stagecoach. They took Dominant III coaches on Volvo B58 12-metre chassis for a new London service established as an early consequence of deregulation – one was delivered in February 1981 and the vehicle shown, HSP 593W, was the second to arrive, with body 149/8070, dating from June of 1981. It is seen here engaged on more local duty in Pitlochry in June 1987, by which time Stagecoach had just begun its rise to fame with purchases of ex-NBC concerns.

respond to the increasing demand for local assembly, although the first body of a batch was sometimes assembled in Britain.

Deliveries of 150 Duple (Metsec) bodies on Dennis Jubilant front-engined chassis to the Kowloon Motor Bus Co fleet began in May 1981, introducing design improvements which gave a more 'professional' product than previous generations of Metsec body. Further large-scale deliveries to both the Kowloon and China Motor Bus concerns are too complex to detail here but continued to enter service up to 1994, long after manufacture of Duple's own bodywork ceased.

The era of deregulation brought a new atmosphere of competition. This applied not only between operators but increased that among manufacturers. There had been some penetration by imported chassis and bodywork in the previous decade or so, but independent operators were becoming less

inhibited in giving up what used to be an almost complete 'buy British' policy across the industry. At that stage, imported bodywork remained in the minority, but there was no room for complacency. Underlying the overall picture was concern at the growing effects of the recession – the fast-rising numbers of unemployed had no spare cash for coach trips or holidays and this was having its effect on operators' new vehicle purchases.

What was particularly alarming for Duple was the undermining of the whole pattern of volume production of coaches on what traditionally had been low-cost lightweight chassis. For several years there had been a growing trend towards heavier-duty models, found to be more reliable when covering high mileages at fast speeds on motorways at home or abroad, but in 1980-81 the market for so-called light coach chassis collapsed in a remarkable way.

The Dominant IV was more subtly 'different', with its raised waist on an otherwise relatively standard body. This one, FCJ 400W with body number 118/2775, was a 53-seat Express version on Bedford YMT chassis dating from February 1981 for Yeoman's of Canon Pyon, Hereford, a Duple customer since the mid-1930s. The old pattern of making several hundred almost identical Bedford-Duple coaches was collapsing at an alarming rate, with only about 160 bodies on Bedford chassis in the 1981 programme and these split into 22 varieties, even though some were quite simple to build as 'Meccano-set' options. There were about a dozen of the 11-metre Dominant IV Express on YMT or YNT chassis, with body numbers beginning at 118/2770.

Many small operators with reduced turnover simply found they lacked the capital, or access to credit, to buy new vehicles, while at the other end of the scale the trend for those wishing to compete in intensive long-distance work was to high-specification 12-metre vehicles for which light chassis were unsuited. Sales of Bedford and Ford passenger chassis in Britain had fluctuated in earlier years but the drop experienced in the 1981 season could only be described as catastrophic and it was little comfort that Plaxton as well as Duple suffered in consequence, both firms having to lay off workers.

Total confirmed home-market deliveries from Duple's 1981 programme amounted to only a little over 500 vehicles, down by over 300, largely among those on Bedford and Ford chassis. Bedford's total of about 160 was under half that of the previous year and, for the first peacetime year since the 1930s, slipped from first place among the chassis makes on which Duple built. Ford suffered even more, dropping to 89 confirmed deliveries.

Against such figures, producing 22 body varieties on Bedford and fifteen on Ford seems disproportionate. Among them, the largest single group was that numbered 117/2625 upwards, including 42 examples of the Dominant IV body on Bedford YMT and the closely-related YNT model (the latter with turbocharged engine). The directly equivalent choice of Dominant IV on Ford R1114 was chosen in 25 cases – there were examples of each of the Dominant I, II, III and IV, plus Dominant Express II, III and IV, among the 70 Ford R1114

With optional waist heights, it was inevitable that someone would think of combining them, and E. J. Bostock & Sons of Congleton, Cheshire had a Dominant "II/IV" 57-seat coach body, numbered 135/5489 among the 1981-season Dominant IV series on Leyland chassis beginning at 135/5460. Dating from April 1981, BCA 126W was a Tiger TRCTL11/3R model, then recently introduced, and was borrowed back by Leyland for use as a press road test vehicle – it had the 245bhp version of the TL11H engine – and was another vehicle the author recalls driving, in this case for a 'Coaching Journal' test published in May 1982. It performed well and returned 11.8mpg over the Pennines on the M62 but the ZF synchromesh gearbox was hard work when using the lower gears.

bodied that season. Some of the old names still recurred, however, with the Whittle group as customers for seven YNT (in one case YMT) and Smith of Wigan for 21 R1114, these latter Dominant II.

Leyland became the most numerous choice of chassis in Duple's 1981 programme for the first time, with 185 examples, although it has to be said that this position was reached by virtue of an unusual order for eighteen Dominant 31-seat bus bodies on Leyland Cub CU435 chassis for Lothian Regional Transport, this being a light bus chassis derived from the Terrier goods model with origins traceable to the BMC goods range.

The Leopard was the main choice among Duple-bodied Leylands, as had been so for 20 years even though the model had been revised considerably over that time, but its intended successor appeared for the first time, having been introduced at the 1980 Show, even though its name was not at first revealed. It was christened Tiger, previously used for Leyland's best-known front-engined single-deck model. The new underfloor-engined Tiger was designated TRCTL11 in the most-widely used form – the TL11 engine was a turbocharged 11.1-litre unit derived from the 680. The chassis specification included air suspension as standard, with a choice of Pneumocyclic or ZF synchromesh gearbox, the latter also available on late versions of the Leopard.

The Tiger went into production in limited numbers at first, there being 20 in the 1981 Duple programme, intermingled among Leopards, the largest Tiger batch being eight 12-metre models for Scottish Omnibuses, fitted with Dominant III 'sloping-pillar' bodies. Others included two 11-metre examples with Dominant II Express bodies for Southend Borough, which was branching into coach operation on quite a large scale, plus examples for various independent operators, possibly the most interesting being one for J. Bostock of Congleton, who chose a combination of Dominant II and IV windows, thereby reviving the idea of a stepped waistline.

The largest group among the 147 bodies on Leopard chassis was that numbered 134/5341-97, comprising some 57 Dominant IV to Express specification, all but one of which were for NBC subsidiaries, mostly on PSU3F/4R chassis, included batches of fifteen each for United Counties and London Country, plus twelve for West Yorkshire Road Car. The Dominant II Express version was chosen for another five apiece for the Alexander Midland and Northern fleets, while 'plain' Dominant IV included three for Yorkshire Traction and two for Eastern National.

Of the 152 coach bodies on Leopard and Tiger, 52 were of 12-metre length – Whittle chose the Dominant III for three 12-metre Leopards, a break with the long-standing tradition of standardising exclusively on Bedford. Others included ten Dominant IV on Leopard for National Travel (West) and five for Grey Green. There were also fifteen Leopard buses, including six more for Trimdon Motor Services and five of the 10-metre PSU4 type for Merthyr Tydfil Corporation.

The Volvo share of the 1981 programme amounted to 74 examples, and here too, there was an important new model with air suspension as standard, the B10M, intended to supersede the B58 and, as with the Tiger, retaining many features of its predecessor – the 9.6-litre engine now developed 262 bhp. It was at first available only in 12-metre B10M-61 form and as with Leyland there was a mix, with the older model remaining in the majority. Of the 20 B10M with Duple bodywork that season, the most important were 12 examples for Western SMT with Dominant III bodywork delivered in May-June 1981, these forming part of the same SBG deal that included the eight similar bodies on Tiger chassis for Scottish Omnibuses. There were also three Dominant IV for York Bros of Northampton.

The major part of Volvo customers opted for 12-metre versions, there being 40 B58 models of this length as well as twelve of 11-metre length with Dominant coach bodies of various types in that season's programme.

Perhaps the most significant in historical terms were three B58-61 with Dominant III bodies from the 1981 programme, plus one from the 1982 programme, supplied in February, June and then two in October 1981 to a small firm then known as Gloagtrotter, based in Perth and already running a well-used third-hand B58 with Dominant body on a new London service. The Gloag referred to Ann Gloag who, with her brother Brian Souter, later switched the fleetname to 'The Stage Coach', and then simply Stagecoach – the rest is history. There were also two B58 chassis with Dominant bus bodies, for Whippet of Hunstanton and A1 Services of Ardrossan.

Although the AEC Reliance was fading into history, two were rebodied in the 1981 programme and another model becoming a rarity was a Bristol LHS with 35-seat Dominant I body for Stokes of Carstairs. DAF came back into the picture with four examples on MB200 chassis including a Dominant IV demonstrator for DAF's British headquarters at Marlow. A significant one-off was a Dennis Falcon 51-seat bus for Leicester Corporation, this model being a rear-engined chassis with Gardner engine and layout reminiscent of the Bristol RE.

An example of Duple (Metsec) activity was an order for bodies on Mercedes-Benz OF1417 front-engined chassis for operation by Oman National Transport Co Ltd, ten being buses and ten coaches, although basically of similar design.

Goldliner

An important if short-lived addition to the range was developed in mid-1981 and introduced in the autumn as the major new development for the 1982 season. It was given the name Goldliner, previously used for a double-glazed version of the Dominant built in 1975 for an export project that did not go into production. This time it was given to a new high-floor design, a concept in which interest had been growing for some time. By raising the floor approximately 1ft (300mm), luggage accommodation could be greatly increased and passengers given an elevated viewpoint for sightseeing – internal noise was also reduced. Plaxton already had such an option called the Viewmaster, built in small numbers from 1977, but it may have been the growing interest in bodywork of such layout imported from European bodybuilders that prompted this rather belated response from Duple.

A prototype Goldliner body, 249/9040, on a B10M-61 chassis was built for Volvo and displayed at trade shows in the autumn of 1981. This could be described as a Dominant II with the main part of the body raised, though leaving a short front portion as far back as the rear of the entrance door at its standard height. There was thus a marked step in the roof line, reminiscent of some American coaches of earlier decades.

Yet again, the system of permutations and combinations gave rise in due course to Goldliner II, III and IV versions, the Roman numerals signifying the style of side windows as on standard-height Dominants.

By late 1981, tight Government financial policy had brought a big slow-down of industry – closures and major lay-offs of staff were widespread. The coach operating industry, stirred up by deregulation, was at that stage a relatively bright spot in the generally depressed economy as reflected by the investment in new coaches, and indeed the number of coaches being put into service nationally in 1982 was a little up on 1981, though still

The prototype Goldliner body, 249/9040, was all too obviously a Dominant II with the main part of the body raised by about 1ft while leaving the front end at its normal level. It was based on a Volvo B10M chassis registered CNS 549X and displayed at trade shows in the autumn of 1981.

The Super Goldliner was developed for the rear-engined Dennis Falcon V, being designed and ten vehicles built in great haste to meet a need foreseen by NBC for suitable high-grade vehicles for new Rapide services for its National Express network. The bodies (243/5730-9), as well as being of high-floor type, had a plug-type entrance door, seen open in this view, and the roof line was extended forward, providing space for a destination box above the windscreen. These features were adopted for Goldliner bodies built on other chassis, including some completed before the Falcon batch were ready. This one was placed in service with West Yorkshire Road Car Co in December 1982 but had been transferred to United Automobile Services Ltd when seen at Victoria coach station, London in April 1984.

below 1980. So far as Duple and Plaxton were concerned, the trend was still slightly downwards because of an upswing of imports. The main threat was coming from three firms, Van Hool, Jonckheere and Bova, with sales of 84, 90 and 92 on the British market in 1982, but other brands showing increases included Setra, MAN and Mercedes-Benz. These, Bova and some Van Hool were of integral construction and rear-engined layout, representing another form of challenge to previous practice.

Duple's production pattern for the 1982 season was slightly down on 1981 in overall numbers, confirmed home-market deliveries dropping below 500, but the Bedford and Ford proportion continued to drop sharply, neither firm reaching 100. Leyland was again the leading make of chassis, though the total of about 160 was slightly down, with Volvo increasingly snapping at its heels with nearly 130.

There were also four more DAF MB200 and another Bristol LHS but the most interesting of the smaller totals was that of Dennis, with thirteen. Ten of these were a new coach version of the Falcon rear-engined model, developed at very short notice at the request of NBC, seeking a suitably advanced design of coach for its high-grade Rapide services intended to give it a competitive edge and due to be introduced in the spring of 1982 – the project had only been agreed in December 1981. The required performance was given by using a Perkins turbocharged V8 engine of 10.5 litres developing 260bhp, and Voith automatic gearbox. Duple also agreed to produce a special high-floor body for it, this being the Super Goldliner, with the main roof line carried forward to the windscreen and using a plug-type door, another Continental feature coming into favour in Britain, claimed to give better sealing and freedom from wind noise at speed. The balance of three Dennis vehicles had another instance of revival of a famous name, being Lancet models with Dominant dual-purpose 31-seat bodies for Leicester, delivered in October-December 1982. The new-generation Lancet was rather more basic than the Falcon V, being a lightweight mid-engined model with Perkins engine.

Meanwhile, Park of Hamilton was one of the independent operators rapidly expanding its services as well as being a

founding partner in the British Coachways project – it had been an early user of the Plaxton Viewmaster. It became the first major customer for the Goldliner with an order announced in November 1981 for 32 on Volvo B10M chassis at a cost of £1.5 million. In the event, this was expanded to 40, all of the Goldliner IV type but with seating varying from 43 to 53 to suit use on express and tours work, some being in the liveries of customers. All were included in the body series begun by the prototype and were delivered in time for entry into service in April 1982.

Remarkably, by the end of that month, Dennis had built the ten Falcon V chassis for NBC and delivered them to Duple, and body construction was carried out as rapidly as possible – the cost of the completed vehicles was £75,000 apiece. The time scale was hopelessly impractical, and although it was quite an achievement to deliver the first coach in September 1982 and complete the order by January 1983, the consequence was a

Goldliner bodies were quite widely favoured in Scotland. The Scottish Bus Group continued with its lozenge-shaped side windows and hence its examples were Goldliner III. The coach shown was one of six on Leyland Tiger TRCTL11/3R chassis supplied to Alexander (Northern) in late 1982 for the Aberdeen-London service but VSS 4X (with body 236/5530) is seen here in July 1986 as Strathtay Scottish ST3 in Scottish Citylink livery while passing through Stratford-on-Avon bound for Birmingham operating on hire on a National Express working.

series of operational problems; no further such vehicles were built – yet, even so, some of the batch had covered 200,000 miles within two years.

Even so, the new Goldliner series of bodies did figure prominently in the 1982 programme, but mainly on more conventional though up-to-date mid-engined chassis. Altogether, there were 68 on Volvo B10M – in addition to the Park orders for 40, these included ten further Super Goldliner on this chassis for National Travel (East) delivered in May-June 1982 and two Goldliner III for Western SMT in July. There were also 36 Goldliner-class bodies on the Leyland Tiger, delivered between June 1982 and April 1983 and including 20 Goldliner III for the Scottish Bus Group, six for Grey-Green and two each for West Yorkshire PTE and Bostock.

The 12-metre coach had become much more widely accepted as the most economic proposition wherever the volume of passengers and operating conditions were suitable. In addition to the Goldliner versions, there were 73 Dominant coach bodies of this length on Leyland and 55 on Volvo chassis – in all, there were over 240 coaches of 12-metre length in Duple's 1982 programme output, easily outnumbering all types of coach on Bedford and Ford chassis. The balance of product had swung decisively towards the big heavy-duty coach. In terms of value, this went some way towards compensating for the drop in numbers of lighter types since 1980.

Laser and Caribbean

In September 1982, a preliminary announcement of two completely new coach body styles, the normal-height Laser and the high-floor Caribbean, was made, just ten years after the Dominant first appeared. Both were offered with a range of internal trim options which gave a range of body prices for 12-metre examples between £32,350 for the most basic Laser (marginally above the equivalent Dominant), to £49,985 for the Caribbean in Executive form, with an overlap between the top Laser and the bottom Caribbean. Complete coach prices could thus run to over £80,000 or even more, about ten times the figure for a top-class coach of 20 years earlier. The problem faced by both Duple and Plaxton was to create a 'fresh' and preferably distinctive look in each case, after a decade of styles linked by the chain of events described in the previous chapter.

By that date, R. G. (Dick) West was Managing Director. He had been trained as an aeronautical engineer and hence favoured a concept of improved aerodynamic efficiency. The Laser reflected this approach, with sharply raked windscreen and greater 'tumble-home' effect (inward taper) above the waistline. The frontal profile, in particular, departed from what had become the accepted coach convention of relatively upright lines and, inevitably, was controversial, in much the same way as the contemporary Ford Sierra car, something perhaps more difficult to understand in hindsight than at the time.

Doug Jack recalls that, soon after he had been appointed as Sales & Marketing Director early in 1982, there was a visit to Duple by Sandy Glennie, in charge of Volvo's increasingly successful activities in Britain since 1978. He was shown the Laser drawings but took against the concept, stating that the market wanted high-deck coaches. His personal status and Volvo's growing importance was such that although Duple was committed to the Laser, the high floor version was hastily redesigned with a much more upright and angular look and called the Caribbean.

The Laser represented a fresh approach to coach design, based on aerodynamic principles and influenced by the early training of Dick West, at that stage Managing Director, as an aeronautical engineer. The resulting appearance was striking if not to everyone's taste, as conveyed in this view of one of a pair of early 57-seat examples on Leyland Tiger TRCTL11/3R chassis supplied to Tyne & Wear Passenger Transport Executive, then operating public transport in the industrial area surrounding parts of those two rivers. Number 11 (TTN 11Y) dating from May 1983, with body number 335/5329 (in a Tiger/Laser series beginning at 335/5300), was painted in that PTE's coach livery using the Armstrong Galley fleetname inherited from two well-known independent coach operators whose businesses had been acquired.

The Caribbean was given a tall, angular look reminiscent of Continental designs of the 1970s, emphasized by its introduction alongside the Laser. The South Wales Transport Co Ltd took delivery of five 46-seat examples with refreshment and toilet facilities on Leyland Tiger TRCTL11/3R chassis, these having the 260bhp engine by then available. They were for the Rapide Swansea-London service, the first one, No.117 (RCY 117Y), being seen here at Victoria. It had body number 335/5352 in the initial Tiger-Caribbean series beginning at 5350 and entered service in May 1983.

As once again a part-time journalist by then, I saw the artist's impressions and then the actual coaches a little later and, highly as I regard Sandy Glennie, remember that my own reactions were almost exactly opposite. The Laser looked interestingly 'fresh' whilst the Caribbean seemed to me to echo the harsh-looking and very angular designs favoured by Van Hool, Jonckheere and others in the 1970s and by then tending to be succeeded by slightly 'softer' outlines.

This difference of opinion reflects a dilemma then facing Duple. The decision to introduce two radically different new designs simultaneously undermined the impact of either, as did the continuation of Dominant production, so there was no single fresh style being built in quantity to catch the eye. Officially, only Dominant III and IV were to be retained, but in fact examples of other versions, including the Goldliner range, were produced in the 1983 season. The two new models did share some features, such as the smoother one-piece side panels in place of the traditional separate panels for each bay, and the front grille, though the latter was not particularly inspired.

As usual, the proof of the pudding was in the eating and, sadly, Duple's decline continued, at a time when overall British demand for coaches was still being buoyed up by the growth of express coach travel that had followed the 1980 deregulation. The number of new coaches registered in Britain in 1983 was slightly up at 1,871 on the 1982 figure of 1,793, according to Paul Heels's survey for 'Omnibus Magazine', and the advance of imported makes was at least temporarily halted.

Yet it was Plaxton which had achieved this with its new Paramount range, with a healthy rise of registrations in the calendar year from 694 to 865, while the corresponding Duple figures were 449 and 340, the latter lower even than the disastrous-seeming 1970 total when the disruption of the move from Hendon could be largely blamed. As usual, these figures do not tie in precisely with actual construction in the production 'season' beginning the previous autumn, being affected by vehicles in dealer stock and such factors as the rebodying of existing vehicles. Duple also tended to pick up small-scale but useful business from such users as local authorities or police authorities, some of whose vehicles were not registered as PSVs. Even with a few exported home-market style bodies the 1983 season total did not quite reach 400.

Once again, Bedford and Ford totals were almost in free-fall, both only struggling above 50 apiece in the 1983 total by inclusion of the above-mentioned borderline cases. What used to be the big 11-metre coach categories had shrunk to 45 Bedford YNT and 50 Ford R-type, the latter including both R1114 and the final R1115 version with the 150bhp 5.9-litre engine introduced as a forlorn effort to revitalise the model. Ford admitted defeat and ceased production of its R-series chassis, though a handful of coaches were to be found in dealers's stocks before finding buyers over the next year or two. Bedford struggled on, and indeed was developing a 12-metre chassis, but such loss of buyers was virtually impossible to reverse.

By contrast, the total on Leyland chassis increased a little, at 176, almost all Tiger, including fourteen of bus outline (one a Leopard) and six replacement coach bodies for existing Leopard chassis. Of these, 121 were for public-sector concerns of one kind or another, a situation which, while helpful in providing a bright spot in a rather gloomy overall picture, had its pitfalls at a time when the Government was making its dislike of either State or local-authority ownership all too obvious.

The confirmed total on Volvo chassis dropped back somewhat to 91, itself out of line with the national upward trend for this make. Six of these were for National Travel (East) and one a replacement body for one of Western SMT's 1981 batch of B10M coaches, but otherwise all were for independent operators.

The split of body styles, with 84 Laser (including 24 on Bedford YNT) and 68 Caribbean together representing together only about 38% of the 1983 season output, was hardly encouraging for the new styles. Setting aside buses and smaller or lighter models for which the new body styles were not available, the Dominant IV or II was chosen for 108 bodies on Tiger or B10M chassis, and Goldliner variants for seventeen. Overall, Dominant variants were still in a majority, and while some of this reflected continuation of existing contracts – several NBC fleets stayed with the Dominant IV and Smith's of Wigan continued to favour it for both Ford and Volvo coaches – the overall picture was hardly a ringing endorsement for change.

The adaptability of the Dominant bus, still in production, enabled it to remain viable when designs intended for volume production were becoming uneconomic. Geoffrey Hilditch was an enthusiastic supporter of the Dennis Falcon chassis design with rear-mounted Gardner 6HLXB engine (now called Falcon H), and it was hardly surprising that Leicester City Transport, of which he was General Manager, ordered some examples. Number 95 (A 95 FRY) was one of the final three 52-seat buses dating from March 1984, with body number 445/3101. Co-operation in this and the very different NBC Falcon V coach project doubtless played its part in Hestair, already owning Dennis, deciding to take over Duple.

Meanwhile, a decision had been taken to offer a Duple integral coach and in March 1983, a preliminary announcement was made of a joint venture with Neoplan for the use of its underframe, which in turn used a Mercedes-Benz engine and other units under a Caribbean-style body. However, this project was superseded before it got off the ground by one with Bova, a small Dutch concern which had achieved creditable success in Britain with its own EL26 integral coach using a rear-mounted DAF engine and running gear, so modestly priced as to capture some sales from Bedford and Ford. The result was the Calypso, which used the EL26 underframe with the Caribbean-style body. This did go into production in 1984, 50 such coaches being produced.

The Hestair era

However, before this happened, in June 1983, Duple had been sold to the Hestair group, which had already acquired the old-established Dennis commercial vehicle business. The new management said later that Duple had been losing something like £5,000 per body produced at the time and the sale received 84% approval among the shareholders.

Just as Dennis became Hestair Dennis Ltd, Duple was renamed Hestair Duple Ltd, though inevitably the prefix was dropped in all but the most formal references. Management changes included the appointment of David Hargreaves as Chairman of Hestair-Duple as well as the parent company, Barrie Mealing, with an engineering background already used elsewhere in the group, became Deputy Chairman, and although Dick West continued for a time as Managing Director, Peter Wragg succeeded him, also taking charge of sales and marketing, Doug Jack having left before the take-over. The production facilities were reorganised to allow more efficient production from a smaller workforce but a major investment was made in a new £1 million paintshop.

The Calypso contract was fulfilled but the idea of an integral Duple coach moved to a third basis as an in-group project. Co-operation between Dennis and Duple was in one sense an obvious step, but it was realised that Duple's business was far too much related to customers committed to other makes of chassis to attempt to restrict their choice.

In practice, however, the boot was apt to be on the other foot, for some dealers were tied to other chassis makers and,

doubtless influenced by them, became less willing to specify Duple in pre-season bulk orders, discouraging operators to ask for Duple bodywork on the chassis makes in question. There seems to be evidence suggesting that Duple may have lost substantial business in this way, possibly helping to tip the balance towards its ultimate demise.

Production of 1984 season bodies began using the existing system of issuing body numbers in classified groups, using three-figure prefixes beginning with '4'. However, during the year, a new system was adopted, with four-figure prefixes beginning '83', '84' etc and evidently signifying the year of ordering, followed by serial numbers which were no longer in classified groups. This made the analysis of trends on a season-to-season basis more difficult, but the overall picture remained gloomy and the numbers built continued to fall.

In fairness, there was an overall drop in the numbers of coaches being placed in service by British operators, down to 1,483 in the calendar year 1984 from 1,871 in 1983, according to Paul Heel's analysis. The Duple total was down to 270, and in fairness this was a relatively modest drop of 70 while Plaxton dipped some 291, though still ending at 574, well over twice Duple's total. Bus bodies amounted to 36, thus bringing Duple's overall home market deliveries in the year to 306 – the full-sized single-deck bus business was virtually 'on the floor' with a total of only 131 from all manufacturers and, remarkably, Duple's figure put them in second place behind the once mighty Leyland National, of which only 39 were delivered that year, compared to 899 in 1978.

Of Duple's 1984 total, nearly half were on Leyland Tiger chassis (many of them for NBC fleets), with the 50 Bova Calypso the second largest group, closely followed by Bedford, whose figure was helped by ten on SB chassis (including three SB3 with petrol engines) for operators based in St Helier, Jersey. Significantly in this first year after Duple's implied link to Dennis via Hestair, the total of Volvo chassis bodied by Duple fell dramatically to below 30 even though total B10M sales in Britain remained steady. However DAF numbers increased and there were seven Dennis – three more Falcon buses for Leicester and four of a new Dorchester coach chassis with Gardner 6HLXC engine. An ominous sign was that, in the independent sector, Van Hool, with almost 200 coach bodies sold in Britain, had moved in front of Duple.

The Laser and Caribbean were mildly restyled for the 1985 season, with a simpler, neater grille and tidier detailing. Both the coaches seen here were part of an NBC bulk order for 62 Duple coach bodies on Leyland Tiger TRCTL11/3RH chassis and having body serial numbers, under the new system then introduced, running from 0441 to 0502, though those for individual companies varied in the body type chosen, the prefix number varying accordingly – other orders took NBC's total that season to 93 Tiger coaches from Duple, the last time so large a figurew was reached. Thus Wessex National Ltd (sharing the Lawrence Hill, Bristol, address of Bristol Omnibus Co Ltd), had Laser 2 body number 8413/0451 on B224 WEU, which was effectively the eighth in a batch of Laser-bodied Tiger coaches for BOC. It dated from December 1984 and is seen at Bradford Interchange on the National Express service to Bristol in August 1985.

Western National Ltd was a new company which, in the restructuring of NBC, had taken over the Cornwall and South Devon operations of the much larger Western National Omnibus Co Ltd from January 1983 – it chose the Caribbean II body for its two coaches from the 1985 season order. Number 2221 (B338 BGL) had body number 8471/0459 and was new in March 1985, being seen here about to leave Truro, by then WN's headquarters, on the Rapide service to London in April 1986 – it carried 'Cornwall Coachways' lettering in yet another layer of confusing local identity.

The first visible signs of the Hestair ownership came in the run up to the 1984 Show, when the Laser 2 and Caribbean II were announced – the use of Arabic numerals for one and Roman for the other was official, incidentally. A restyling exercise by John Worker Design had introduced bonded glazing, a broader and bolder rectangular grille and neater detailing, giving a considerably smoother look.

By then, the industry was bracing itself for another and bigger political upheaval, with the issue of a White Paper outlining the plans to privatise and deregulate the bus industry, with ideas far more radical than those in the Transport Act of 1980. Nicholas Ridley, appointed Secretary of State for Transport in 1983, outlined the plans at a conference in September 1984 and when he suggested that a dip in orders for new vehicles would be followed by an increase, it was David Hargreaves who shouted "Rubbish". Subsequent events were to confirm his pessimism, with catastrophic damage to the whole of the British road transport manufacturing industry.

Exports were a way of keeping manufacturers in work when home demand flagged, but this too was becoming more difficult. However, Duple (Metsec) sought to open up fresh business with a semi-integral 12-metre coach of up-to-date and well-equipped specification with air suspension and air conditioning as options, designed from scratch as a CKD ('completely knocked-down') product. Scania's K112 underframe comprised front and rear sub-frame assemblies which, with the rear-mounted 305bhp engine and other units in place, could be temporarily joined to form a driveable 'chassis' for delivery. With the body structure supplied in CKD form, it was possible for a coach of advanced design to be assembled in suitable workshops. The first order was for 25 vehicles for operation in Egypt, of which one was assembled at Blackpool in 1982 and the rest supplied in parts sent out from Oldbury for assembly in new workshops of Ghabbour Bros, Cairo.

The 425

When the Show opened, the promised integral coach duly appeared, proving to be a completely fresh design rather than of Caribbean outline, as anticipated from earlier sketches, even though the Show exhibit was far from being a fully developed vehicle. It was called the Integral 425, this being derived from the aerodynamic drag factor of 0.425, claimed to be the best among coaches. John Worker was again responsible for the design, although there was little in common with his revamped versions of the Laser and Caribbean. Surprisingly, in the face of the evidence of the drag figure, it had an oddly angular profile, with relatively upright main windscreen and abrupt change of shape to a sharply angled tinted glass panel above it. A key objective was to maximise the potential seating capacity, at up to 63 passengers, or six more than the 57 hitherto regarded as the limit in a conventional 12-metre coach. A special design of seat was partly responsible for this, though the spacing was tight for tall passengers. In practice, most operators settled for 57 or less in the interests of comfort.

The mechanical design developed jointly with Dennis engineers incorporated some features from existing Dennis products, the rear air suspension being derived from the Dorchester chassis, though at the front independent suspension was provided. The standard engine was the 10-litre Cummins LT10, already beginning to build a good reputation since its introduction in 1982. It was mounted vertically at the rear, and there was a ZF six-speed synchromesh gearbox. The price quoted was £66,000, a competitive figure for a vehicle of such specification, and reaction was encouraging, several orders being taken purely on the basis of the Show exhibit, though it was to be almost a year before production examples began to enter service.

Yet none of these efforts could prevent a further drop in Duple's sales, dipping to just over 200 deliveries to British operators in 1985, a level lower than it had achieved in a peacetime year since 1929, although the products of those early days were much less sophisticated. To a large extent, this was due to the atmosphere of uncertainty created by the Government's plans for radical change in the structure of the industry as well as deregulation, but the depression in business was set to continue and indeed Duple did not recover from this low level in subsequent years.

Nationally, output of almost all types of bus or coach continued to fall in 1985, the exception being minibuses, hitherto used only in small numbers but now seen by NBC in particular as a way of coping with the anticipated competition resulting from deregulation. Plaxton not only managed to expand coach deliveries slightly, against the general trend, to just over 600 that year, but by its take-over of Reeve Burgess was poised to secure a major part of the body conversion or construction in this big increase of minibus deliveries.

Duple's largest customer was still the NBC group, and between October 1984 and April 1985, 93 coaches on Leyland Tiger chassis were delivered to fourteen of its subsidiaries, the last time so large or widely spread a group order was fulfilled. Most were Laser 2, including eighteen for Ribble, ten for Wilts & Dorset, eight for Crosville, seven apiece for Bristol Omnibus, Devon General and Midland Red (North), the last-mentioned an instance of the splitting of large companies that had come into favour – Wilts & Dorset and Devon General were also virtually reincarnations of the former operators of those names, which had disappeared when 'big was beautiful'. The Caribbean II body was chosen for a further sixteen Tigers for Ribble, plus four apiece for Southdown and South Wales, three for Midland Red (Express), a pair for Western National and one for Black & White.

The Scottish Bus Group also formed a useful part of the order book and early in 1985; there were fifteen Tiger coaches, comprising six Laser 2 for Highland and three for Midland Scottish, with six Caribbean II for Eastern Scottish – here the trend was to 'geographic' company and fleet names. There were also a few instances of local authority users, Nottingham adding one Laser 2 and one Caribbean II and Cardiff two Caribbean, all on Tiger chassis, in 1985.

The Integral 425 prototype was the talk of the 1984 Motor Show among coach operators, even though it was far from being a developed product ready to go into production. Although such a project had been first announced early the previous year, the completed vehicle had mechanical design developed jointly with Dennis and hence was to some degree a product of the link with that firm as a fellow member of the Hestair group. However, the rear-mounted engine was the Cummins LT10 which was building a good reputation for efficiency and reliability. The unusual outline hardly looked streamlined with the abrupt junction between a near-vertical windscreen and the inclined panel above, yet the 425 was a reference to an aerodynamic drag factor of 0.425, claimed to be the best among coaches of the day.

Among independent customers, Bedford coaches, mainly Laser 2, accounted for a little over 50 deliveries in 1985, largely YNT but including fifteen or so of the new YNV 12-metre model which had been introduced at the 1984 Show, including one for Whittle. This type was given the model name Venturer, being the first and only Bedford coach chassis to have that distinction – it had air suspension but used the same turbocharged 8.2-litre Bedford engine as the YNT and this may have limited its appeal even though its performance with a Laser 2 body was agreeably relaxed. There were about 20 Leyland Tiger coaches for independent operators, but DAF was about equally strong with the MB200 and, near the end of 1985, the similar but uprated MB230 – the numbers

of Duple-bodied Volvo B10M delivered that year were down again to single figures despite the model's growing following nationally. Deliveries of the Integral 425 model, some at least registered as 'Hestair', began in the autumn of 1985, eight being known to have reached operators by the end of the year – Whittle took three and Hutchison two, plus the first of three for Western SMT, one for Southdown and the first of two for Ambassador, which was another case of a revived name for what had been a coaching department of Eastern Counties. A noteworthy 1985 bus contract was for the rebodying of four Leyland Leopard chassis as buses for the East Midlands fleet – there were also four new Tiger for Trimdon Motor Services.

A casualty of the take-over by Hestair was the Calypso, a joint effort with the small but enterprising Bova concern of Valkenswaard, Holland, which had made Britain its main export market with its own integral coach using mainly DAF mechanical units but sought to gain further sales by linking with a British bodybuilder. The Bova EL26 underframes were shipped to Blackpool and fitted with what was effectively Caribbean bodywork above floor level. A total of 50 such coaches were built and given body numbers 458/1200-49. The example shown was one of the first to enter service – it had body 1204 and was supplied to Happy Days, of Woodseaves near Stafford in January 1984, registered A487 JRE. Hestair wished to see an in-house development and the contract was not renewed, though deliveries to operators of those built continued until mid-1985.

A few independent operators with stage carriage (bus) services were expanding their single-deck fleets, contrary to the national trend at the time. Delaine Coaches Ltd, of Bourne, Lincs, added KTL 27Y, this Leyland Tiger TRCTL11/2R with Dominant 62-seat bus body 339/5621 to its fleet in January 1983 and a further similar bus was supplied in August of that year. Delaine was to be the last operator to receive a new vehicle with Dominant bus body, a further Tiger, in August 1988.

11 FIGHTING FOR SURVIVAL

Surprisingly, two new Duple coach body designs were introduced at the Bus and Coach Show held at the old venue of Earls Court, London, in September 1985, replacing the Laser and Caribbean only a year after they had been relaunched after extensive redesign work. Also on display was the Integral 425, by then in production form, looking much as first shown but the subject of an intensive development programme; there was now a choice of engines, with the DAF 11.6-litre DKSB engine of 316bhp as an option to the 290bhp 10-litre Cummins.

The new body types, collectively known as the 300 series, were simply designated 320 and 340, signifying their 3.2 and 3.4 metre height. The modest difference of 20cm (under 8in) meant that it proved possible to use the same glazing for both, the difference in overall height being accommodated by a curve-down of the roof line at the front of the 340, whereas the lower-built 320 had more angular lines at this point. It thereby took on a distinct family resemblance to the angular-looking Caribbean and indeed both types, reverting to flat glass for the side windows and with squared-up rear end, were closer to that model in general looks, the Laser's more adventurous style not being pursued further. The 320 was available in 11-metre or 12-metre form on Bedford or Leyland and as a 12-metre on DAF or Volvo, while the 340 was offered as 12-metre only on DAF, Leyland or Volvo. The Dominant bus body, in 11-metre form and suitable for Bedford YMT or YNT, Tiger or B10M chassis

was the only survivor from the previous range still listed as a standard type.

This was Duple's final throw in terms of fresh coach designs; it was obvious that the production engineer had a major influence and that this time the changeover brought more standardisation. However, the signals for the biggest upheaval in the operating industry since motor bus operation began were set by the passing of the Transport Act 1985 the following month. Hence the management of the nationalised companies knew that the break-up and sale of the NBC and in due course SBG groups was only a matter of time.

In a shrinking market, Duple did well to hang on to an almost identical delivery total to British customers in 1986 of just over 200, although admittedly quite a number of those supplied to independents appear to have been from dealers' stocks. The total of all types of coach sold in Britain fell by 22% to under 1,000 and almost all bodybuilders suffered accordingly, so Duple improved its market share simply by holding firm.

NBC subsidiaries were still the largest single group of customers, accounting for upwards of 50 coach bodies, even if not in the large-scale co-ordinated manner of earlier times – early deliveries of 320-type bodies in March-April 1986 included 20 for London Country and three for Wessex, while the 340 was chosen by Crosville for fifteen, Midland Red Coaches (three) and West Yorkshire (two), all of these being on Tiger chassis.

The 'Meccano-set' production-line approach of using many common parts for the alternative-height 320 and 340 bodies is conveyed by these two views of early examples, delivered in 1986. The upper one shows a 320 body for S. A. Bebb Ltd of Llantwit Fardre, near Pontypridd, thought to be 8894/0712, which was a Bedford YNT registered as C31 JKG – the days of Bedford-Duple coaches, once the leading combination and a familiar sight all over Britain, were almost at an end, the announcement of the phasing-out of production of Bedford truck and coach chassis coming in September of that year.

The higher-built 340 is represented by this coach for Roman City Ltd of Bath, one of a pair of 12-metre coaches on DAF MB230 chassis, probably body number 8591/0702, a 57-seat coach registered D617 SJX. The 340 model's additional height compared to the 320 was given by lifting the main part of the body by 20cm while retaining the same entrance door and windscreen, curving the roof line downwards at the front to suit.

The Scottish Bus Group showing was smaller, with five 320 bodies for what was by then called Central Scottish, though these were of interest in being on Tiger TRCLXC chassis with Gardner 6HLXC engines, an option then freshly available. The sale of Leyland Bus itself to a management buy-out was announced in July 1986.

Even so, it was hardly surprising that Leyland continued to provide more of the chassis for 1986 deliveries of Duple-bodied vehicles to British operators than any other make though with a total a little below 100. Bedford was in second place even though below 50 – deliveries of the YNV Venturer had grown only a little above 20 and with a dozen YNT and the odd YMT, the numbers were made up only by another nine SB coaches, mainly for operators in Jersey. Bedford had been greatly weakened by a combination of circumstances and it was announced in September 1986 that truck and passenger chassis production was to be phased out.

The lower-built but squarer-cut 320 was chosen for five coaches placed in service by Central Scottish Omnibuses Ltd (as the former Central SMT Ltd had become in 1985) in April 1986. They were on Leyland Tiger chassis of the rare Gardner-engined TRCLXC type, C10 (C110 JCS) with body 8588/0731 being seen at Drumochter Summit in August 1986.

Most of the growth was in the DAF contribution, with about 33. Most were on the MB series of mid-engined chassis with 11.6-litre engines, including at least sixteen of the new MB230, but there were also seven of the SB 2300 model, with rear-mounted 8.25-litre engine. The Volvo B10M continued to be under-represented in relation to its overall popularity in Britain, barely managing to get into double figures, and deliveries of the Integral 425 were slow in building up, with not much over half-a-dozen entering operators' fleets within the calendar year, although including one for South Wales which was delivered in National Holidays livery in April 1986.

In October 1986, deregulation of buses services had arrived and the break-up and sale of NBC was under way, the first business to be sold being National Holidays in July 1986, though it had no vehicles of its own. While this sale and a parallel programme aimed at getting local authorities to sell off their bus undertakings were under way, a blight tended to descend on vehicle purchases for the undertakings involved – sellers felt inhibited, especially where management buy-outs were in the offing, while buyers were rarely in a financial position to spend large sums on fleet renewal.

An oasis of stability in all this, temporarily at least, was the Scottish Bus Group, its structure not at that stage disturbed, and in April-May 1987, a run of 25 Tiger coaches mostly with 340-type bodies, this time on standard TRCTL11 chassis, were delivered to six of the group's companies – Eastern, Fife, Highland, Central, Kelvin and Midland Scottish. There were other batch orders but NBC or even former NBC concerns were virtually a spent force, with the strongest showing a batch of five 320-type bodies replacing Dominant I on Leopard PSU3E/4R for Northumbria Motor Services Ltd. This was a concern split off from United Automobile Services Ltd by Government order in 1986 – they were delivered in September 1987 just as a management buy-out went through. Among independent operators, six Tigers with ZF synchromesh gearboxes and 320-type bodies were supplied to Limebourne Coaches

The Integral 425 had taken a little time to get into production but by late 1985 and early 1986 deliveries were beginning to get under way, even though still quite slowly. A significant early buyer was Western Scottish Omnibuses Ltd, the former Western SMT, long regarded as a home of high engineering standards. Three 55-seat examples were added to the fleet between December 1985 and early 1986, initially numbered H205-7 and registered C205-7 HSD, with body numbers 8585/0643-5. Re-organisation of the industry, and a widely-followed wish to disguise the age of vehicles, had led to the coach shown, Western LH106, becoming VLT 206 when seen at Buchannan Street bus station in Glasgow during September 1994. The L-prefix to the fleet number indicated that it was a 'London-pool' vehicle, allocated to long-distance routes, and at that stage such vehicles were being registered as 'Hestair-Duple' or sometimes simply 'Hestair'.

of London SW1, three being in National Express livery – although that name and style was to continue as the sole visible legacy of NBC, the coaches used were now increasingly from the independent sector.

Overall, Duple's 1987 deliveries to British operators dropped to a new low at 176 coach and seven bus bodies. Thanks to the effect of the SBG business, Leyland still held first place among numbers of chassis, representing about a third of the total. Bedford, despite the previous year's announcement, was still in second place, the number of YNV coaches delivered going up to a couple of dozen – when chassis production had ceased, there were considerable stocks yet to find buyers. The proportion of Volvo B10M chassis rose, reaching a similar level to the combined DAF representation, yet each amounted to less than half the Leyland figure, far out of line with the national coach trend, where Volvo now outnumbered Leyland and DAF put together.

Deliveries of the Integral 425 had also stepped up, to 24, and it was significant that the SB2300 represented over half the DAF contingent though, even so, these two rear-engined models still accounted for only just over a fifth of Duple's output – most British coach operators continued to prefer the mid-underfloor engine position. There were two Dennis demonstrators delivered during 1987, a Lancet with Cummins B-series 5.9-litre engine and Dominant 43-seat bus body which had been completed in time for the October 1986 Motor Show and added for comparative trials to the Northumbria fleet.

More significant was one of the first examples of the Dennis Javelin, which had also first appeared, in chassis form, at the 1986 Show. Its introduction had been happily timed, as it could be regarded as a suitable and, as it turned out, far more successful, successor to the Bedford YNV, though more flexible in being available in 11- or 12-metre

The Scottish Bus Group was still able to place an order for 25 Leyland Tigers, this time standard TRCTL11 models, for delivery to six subsidiaries in the spring of 1987, by which time NBC, in the throes of privatisation, was no longer able to act as a co-ordinated organisation in such a way. A new body number series had again begun at 0001 in 1986 and this batch with prefix 8695 ran from 0304 to 0329, the vehicle shown (with body 8695/0327) being Midland Scottish MPT144 (D144 HMS), one of a batch of five dating from May 1987. It is seen in Pitlochry the following year.

The Dennis Javelin took up a concept which paralleled the Bedford Venturer in using a mid-mounted vertical engine and, by contemporary standards, of relatively modest cost, but proved far more successful. The engine in this case was the Cummins 6CTA of 8.3-litre capacity, turbocharged and giving up to 240bhp, mounted sufficiently close to the rear axle to leave two-thirds of the space between the axles clear for luggage, in addition to the rear boot. This illustration showing a vehicle with Duple 320 body was used on a leaflet issued at the model's launch in September 1986 and although no Javelin had then been bodied, this design was used for the demonstrator the following year and many production examples were similar.

forms, to which a short version for 35-seat bodywork and bus versions were added. Common features were relatively light weight with an engine in the 8-litre class mounted vertically under the floor, air suspension as standard and a chassis price of about £25,000. The Javelin also used a Cummins engine, in this case a C-series, mounted close enough to the rear axle to allow a roomy space for luggage ahead of it as well as the traditional rear boot. The demonstrator had a 57-seat 320 body.

By 1988, further upheavals were under way or signalled. Leyland Bus, starved of orders for buses in particular as the operating industry coped with the dual problems of privatisation and deregulation, decided to sell out to Volvo, the deal being announced on 28th March. This seemed to improve Leyland's previously grim prospects, at least in the short term – the major models, including the Tiger, were to continue, even though there were obvious doubts about the implications over a longer time-scale – another result was a plan to build the Volvo B10M in Britain, underlining Volvo's commitment here.

The Government, with the sales of NBC subsidiaries completed that month, announced its intention to sell off the Scottish Bus Group, and hence that too was plunged into the same situation of cutting back on new vehicle orders.

Fortunately the coach side of the industry did regain enough confidence to buy more new vehicles, though the national growth from 1,023 to 1,275 coaches delivered in the year still left a total market for coaches in Britain of less than half the size of 1979. Despite the loss of business from what had been its most important customers, Duple did manage to increase deliveries to operators to 233 coaches and 15 buses. By this time, the Dominant bus was being phased out in favour of a design which fitted more readily into the current range, known as the 300 and suitable for Leyland Tiger, Volvo B10M and similar chassis, but it was built only in small numbers.

The different pattern of demand was reflected in the choice of chassis for Duple's 1988 deliveries, the major development being the almost instantaneous success of the Dennis Javelin, which did much more than fill the vacancy left by Bedford, going into first place among Duple-bodied products with about a third of the coaches on separate chassis. Taken in conjunction with the Integral 425, of which 24 were again

The upheaval in the operating industry caused by privatisation and deregulation meant that many operators were inhibited from buying new vehicles. Duple Services Ltd sought to attract refurbishing work, among the customers being some of the SBG companies. This Leyland Leopard PSU3E/4R with Dominant I 49-seat body 8345263 in the fleet of Fife Scottish had been new to Alexander (Fife) in July 1978 and is seen in June 1987 after refurbishing in this way – alongside is KGS 485Y, a Leyland Tiger with Caribbean body 335/5374, one of a batch of six built for Travellers, Hounslow. A leaflet issued that year invited such work 'on Dominants, Supremes or any other marque' and quoted addresses at Barrhead, Glasgow; The Hyde, Hendon, as well as Burton Road, Blackpool.

The last element of Dominant production ended with the replacement of the bus version – the last example being The Delaine No.100 (E100 AFW) with body 8612/0422 on a Leyland Tiger dating from August 1987. The first new-generation 300-type bus was body number 8721/0543 on a Volvo B10M E107 DJR, for Langley Park Motor Co (G. Cox) of Durham, which used the fleetname Gypsy Queen, seen here – it was new in December 1987. The 300 bus was a relatively plain design with shallow roof, recognisably related to the 300-series coaches by the front grille.

delivered, the all-Hestair element of output was doubtless a cause for some cautious celebration at headquarters even though the overall picture was still worrying.

Overall, imported chassis were in the majority, with the Volvo B10M picking up second place behind the Javelin, with about 40 examples. The Swedish element was also slightly increased by a first appearance among home-market Duple-bodied products of Scania, with five of its K92 rear-engined model with 8.5-litre engine. DAF was represented by over 30 examples and here too attention was mainly on the rear-engined SB series, though the MB230 mid-engined type was chosen for the second year as a basis for five coaches by OK Motor Services of Bishop Auckland, an example, not uncommon at that period, of the old-established type of independent operator expanding its business to take advantage of the new freedoms.

One-time regular market leader Bedford was down to about a dozen Duple-bodied coaches drawn from the supply of stock chassis after production ceased, and Leyland, although still quite a major supplier nationally, was down to a similar number of Tiger chassis arriving at Blackpool for bodying.

At the Motor Show held at the NEC in October 1988, Dennis introduced its new Dart chassis, a 9-metre rear-engined model in what was apt to be described as the midibus class, bridging the gap between the minibus, whose limitations were becoming increasingly obvious, and the full-sized and, all too often, very heavy full-sized single-decker. It was of lightweight but soundly engineered construction, with Cummins B-series 5.9-litre engine and Allison automatic gearbox and used small-diameter wheels to allow a relatively low floor level.

For the Dart, a new Duple 39-seat bus body was produced, stainless steel-framed with aluminium panels bonded to it, constructionally derived from the 300-series but looking very different, with an unusual front profile having a windscreen with single-curvature glass, stepped down at the nearside and the panel below it having a concave curvature. One in plain red livery was on the Duple stand, alongside an Integral 425, the latter noteworthy in having left-hand drive. The Dart aroused

considerable interest and the plan at that date was to offer it initially only with Duple body.

Hestair pulls out

The announcement in November 1988 that Hestair was selling its vehicle engineering division, including both Dennis and Duple and their subsidiaries, to a management buy-out team sent uncertain signals. At the time, it was stated that City investors had 'reservations' about Hestair's involvement in a diversity of markets and that an upturn in profitability in this division, expected to be between £4 and £5 million for the year on a turnover of £75 million, had provided an opportune time to sell. The price subsequently quoted for the buy-out was £25.5 million.

The team of new owners, which adopted the name Trinity Holdings and taking over from January 1989, was led by Geoff Hollyhead, Chairman of the division under Hestair, together with the Managing Directors of Duple and Dennis, Richard Owen and Steve Burton respectively. Financial backing came from city institutions, Bankers Trust Co and Citycorp Venture Capital. There were plans to offer equity to other senior managers and possibly a share ownership scheme for the 1,600 employees within the group.

The Duple concerns involved comprised the main business, Hestair Dennis Ltd; Duple Services Ltd; Duple (Metsec) Ltd and Bifort Engineering Ltd, the last-mentioned by then making plastics mouldings. The business was given the new title of Duple International and the forecast made at the time that Duple's output for 1988/89 would be just under 400 buses and coaches, though seeming wildly optimistic to many observers, may have included sets of body framing produced by Duple (Metsec) for assembly overseas. A £2.5 million order for 35 double-deckers for Hong Kong shared by Dennis and Duple (Metsec) was mentioned, as well as one worth £9 million over three years for Duple (Metsec) involving 600 buses for Sri Lanka.

On the Dennis side, the popularity of the Javelin was put forward as a major factor, it being claimed that 350 chassis were due to be built by January 1989. In fact, the number

In some respects, all seemed quite normal as the 1989 season got under way. What had been Smiths Happiway-Spencer a decade or so earlier had become Smiths Shearings but there were regular intakes of coaches, of which Duple had continued to obtain a share, although significantly Van Hool as well as Plaxton had been major suppliers for several years. No.790 (F790 GNA) was one of a batch of ten Leyland Tiger coaches with Duple 320 53-seat bodies supplied early in 1989, being seen here at Devil's Bridge in August of that year. A further ten, with G...RNC registrations were to follow shortly afterwards....but that was to prove the end, Duple having closed before the next orders for this group were placed.

bodied and in service in British fleets at the end of 1988 proved to be less than half this, but even so it proved to be the most popular British-made coach chassis. The reaction to the Dart from operators large and small was also encouraging and production was planned to start in mid-1989.

There was a fairly upbeat atmosphere in the coach trade as the 1989 season began, and Duple seemed to have reasonable cause for optimism. However, an old problem of the coach bodybuilding trade that was tending to recur was the mid-summer slump in work in progress – dealers and chassis makers had been willing to bridge this with stock orders for summertime build when the overall demand was strong, but dealers were often already carrying more stock than they wished and interest rates had risen sharply, discouraging such commitment.

A way of overcoming this was the building of more bus bodies, and in press briefings, Richard Owen, by then Chief Executive of Duple, said that the Dart was expected to be helpful by 1990 – the first production chassis was due at Duple in July 1989. However, despite a preliminary announcement of another bus project in June 1989, a plan to build a new design of bodywork on Scania N113 low-floor chassis to compete with the Leyland Lynx and the DAF-based Optare Delta, it was being announced at the same time that 45 staff were being laid off, with the expectation of more.

Then the blow fell. In July 1989, it was announced that Trinity Holdings had decided to close down Duple's bodybuilding operation at Blackpool, selling Duple Services Ltd, together with manufacturing rights and jigs for 300-series bodies and the Integral 425, to Plaxton for £4 million. It was stated that Hestair had pumped £14 million into Duple in the five years after its purchase in 1983, of which £10 million was required to cover losses. Overstocking of new coaches, said to extend to 300-400 vehicles over the whole British market, was cited as a major reason for the decision. Cab building for Dennis fire engines and refuse vehicles, also carried out at Blackpool, was to be

transferred to part of a new £10 million Dennis plant at Guildford. About 350 redundancies were anticipated.

As usual, the bulk of 1989 output was already on order, and a survey indicated that 208 Duple-bodied coaches and 32 buses entered service in British fleets during that year, although some of these were from the dealers' stock mentioned in the announcement. This was slightly down on 1988 and not far out of line with the average from 1985 but clearly not a satisfactory output for premises which had built 1,000 bodies annually only a few years earlier. The types built in that final year were generally similar to 1988, with the Javelin as the most popular type, but there was a broad spread of DAF, Leyland Tiger and Volvo B10M as well as the Duple 425 and smaller numbers of Scania. A much smaller number of vehicles was registered in 1990.

In the event, plans for continued manufacture by Plaxton largely collapsed. That concern, perhaps noting the problems in regard to relations with other chassis makers suffered by Hestair, opted not to become involved in 'chassis' manufacture at Scarborough. There were a few stock Integral 425 models to sell and then it was announced that the model was to be built by Carrosserie Lorraine, a French bodybuilder that had been acquired by Plaxton from 1991, but in the event that did not happen.

In October 1989, it was announced that Carlyle Group had acquired the Duple body design rights, demonstration bodies, drawings, fixtures and order books for the Dennis Dart – at that stage 20 orders had been confirmed. Carlyle was the name adopted for the former Midland Red works in Birmingham, known to earlier generations as Carlyle Works, and responsible for many advanced designs of bus when Midland Red made its own vehicles. Latterly it had carried out large-scale conversions of Ford Transit vans to minibuses in the last years of NBC but had been sold off as a separate business. Both shorter and longer versions of the body, later christened Dartline, were to be offered when production began in 1990, and it was at first the only body design to be available on the Dart, though this was soon to alter.

What could be described as the final Duple legacy in terms of coach bodybuilding was the manufacture, beginning in late 1990, of a batch of 25 bodies to a design which was based on the Duple 320, closely resembling its appearance but with various Plaxton-style details and sold as the Plaxton 321. Rather surprisingly, they were on Leyland Tiger chassis with Cummins engines (the TL11 by then no longer being available), the declared aim being the offer of a heavy-duty chassis with 12-metre body having 53 reclining seats and quite a comprehensive level of trim at a lower price than a comparable coach with Paramount body, and competitive in price with say a Javelin or even a recent used coach. It seems probable that there was more than a little of the philosophy of 'using up stocks'.

So ended the Duple story, effectively 70 years after it had all begun with the formation of Duple Bodies and Motors Ltd in 1919 in Hornsey, London. Happily, there are many Duple-bodied vehicles still earning their keep and quite a substantial number of preserved examples, some going back to the 1930s to remind us of some of the huge variety of designs of coach and bus bodywork for which the firm in all its manifestations had been responsible.

Delivered in June 1989, shortly before the closure decision was announced, this Integral 425, registered as F32 KHS, with 53 seat body number 8885/0880, was for Allenways Coaches Ltd of Birmingham, an old-established and, in earlier times, conservative operator, one of thousands for whom Duple had been a name forming part of the fabric of the coach industry for over 60 years.
The Integral 425 may not have been particularly good-looking but the promise of fuel economy given by its low drag figure had been confirmed in practice – Noel Millier reported 13.3mpg from one with Cummins LTA10 engine running at 14 tons gross in a 1987 Commercial Motor test over a 700-mile route over motorways and main roads including hilly stretches, the best achieved in its class. It had been hoped the model would continue in production after Duple closed but this was not to be.

A rather surprising final Duple design was the bus body for the Dennis Dart – its 'curvy' profile was certainly 'different'. Production vehicles retained this style when deliveries began early in 1990. By then, the body designs had been sold to Carlyle though in fact manufacture had begun at Blackpool and a fresh series of body numbers starting at 0001 reached 0061, deliveries beginning in time for entries into service from January 1990 and including the first 27 of the DT class of London Buses. Early Carlyle-built buses were to similar 9-metre design, but by the beginning of 1991 a new 9.8-metre version had appeared, this having an extended destination box. This example in the fleet of Stagecoach Selkent had taken a former Routemaster registration number, VLT 240. So, in more than one sense, the Duple story could be said to have ended where it began, in London.

and finally . . . . .

The production of this volume has, as mentioned, drawn heavily on Duple photographs held in the Senior Transport Archive. There is enough material to produce a follow-on picture album at some stage in the future, but we would like more information on the people concerned in the Duple story, and especially those included in photographs reproduced in this volume who we were unable to identify. Can you help?? If so please contact Venture at 128 Pikes Lane, Glossop.

Similarly we are always on the look out for material – photographs, drawings, records, anecdotes etc. – concerning other manufacturers. We have now covered many of the main bodybuilding companies but whilst any material is always of interest, Burlingham, East Lancs, Harrington, Metro-Cammell, Weymann and Willowbrook material would be of great interest to the Editorial Team for possible inclusion in future projects.

The End

INDEX

163